Creating a Meaningful Life

Creating a Meaningful Life builds on the tenets of mindfulness-based cognitive therapy (MBCT) to answer some of life's basic questions, such as "How do I create a meaningful, purposeful life?" and "Is the life I am living one that brings me fulfillment, purpose, and a sense of inner peace?"

Using a variety of techniques, including journaling, grounding exercises, cognitive self-talk restructuring, and more, chapters invite counseling professionals and students to explore their inner landscape, better understand themselves, and find communion with others.

Shannon Hodges, PhD, is a professor of clinical mental health counseling at Niagara University, USA.

"Dr. Hodges seamlessly intertwines pragmatic, spiritual, existential, and counseling concepts in a way that is applicable to all in the helping professions. This book will help counselors challenge themselves, make meaning in life, and be better clinicians."

Fred Dombrowski, *PhD, LMHC, department chair and assistant professor of clinical mental health counseling, University of Bridgeport*

"More people are questioning the quality of their lives and the meaning of their existence. This book is a much-needed guide to personal growth and a more fulfilling life."

Tim Osberg, *PhD, professor of psychology at Niagara University*

Creating a Meaningful Life

A Practical Guide for Counselors, Therapists, and Other Helping Professionals

Shannon Hodges

Routledge
Taylor & Francis Group
NEW YORK AND LONDON

Cover image: Getty Image

First published 2023
by Routledge
605 Third Avenue, New York, NY 10158

and by Routledge
4 Park Square, Milton Park, Abingdon, Oxon, OX14 4RN

Routledge is an imprint of the Taylor & Francis Group, an informa business

Library of Congress Cataloging-in-Publication Data
Names: Hodges, Shannon, author.
Title: Creating a meaningful life: a practical guide for counselors, therapists, and other helping professionals/ Shannon Hodges.
Description: 1 Edition. | New York, NY : Routledge, 2023. | Includes bibliographical references and index.
Identifiers: LCCN 2022021Z171 (print) | LCCN 2022021Z172 (ebook) | ISBN 9780367764364 (hardback) | ISBN 9780367764357 (paperback) | ISBN 9781003168324 (ebook)
Subjects: LCSH: Counseling—Vocational guidance. | Mindfulness-based cognitive therapy.
Classification: LCC BF636.64 H6273 2023 (print) | LCC BF636.64 (ebook) | DDC 158.1/3—dc23/eng/20220521
LC record available at https://lccn.loc.gov/2022021Z171
LC ebook record available at https://lccn.loc.gov/2022021Z172

ISBN: 978-0-367-76436-4 (hbk)
ISBN: 978-0-367-76435-7 (pbk)
ISBN: 978-1-003-16832-4 (ebk)

DOI: 10.4324/9781003168324

Typeset in Baskerville
by Apex CoVantage, LLC

This text is dedicated to most deserving friends and colleagues, Kristine Augustyniak, department chair and professor of clinical mental health counseling at Niagara University in Lewiston, New York, and Cheryl Edward, senior psychologist and pastoral and well-being officer throughout various remote schools in the Northern Territory of Australia. Through her leadership, teaching, and professional advocacy, Kristine has blazed a trail for the profession and her scores of students. Cheryl has traveled numerous washboard roads throughout the Northern Territory to support the mental health needs of Indigenous children, often accomplishing the seemingly impossible. Both are stalwarts of their profession and the gold standard for the counseling and psychology professions.

May peace and purpose be your companion all the days of your life.

Contents

Foreword by Shoshanna Cogan

Not many people blow out their birthday candles wishing for a more meaningful existence. And yet who among us hasn't wondered at some point, *what am I doing here?* and *does what I do really matter?* Before getting my graduate counseling degree in the 1980s, I had the great privilege of working in home-care for the dying. Between bedpans and bedside listening, what repeatedly struck me was the difference between the people who believed they'd led a decent life, even leaving some small goodness behind, versus others who were riddled with regrets for what they deemed a foolish, wasted life.

If you're fortunate to live long enough, you too may confront the so-called "Deathbed Test." Imagine, if you are willing, you're at the grand finale of your existence. Face-to-face with unvarnished truth and lucid hindsight, you know it's your time to go. Who will be your final companions: Acceptance, Gratitude, Despair, Regret, or another? Some individuals embark on their life-meaning quest younger than others. Until I met Shannon Hodges in 1994, I'd never met anyone as ablaze with purpose and direction. Yet his determination to leave a life legacy wasn't incubated in a privileged early life. Like a phoenix rising, his early struggles, poverty, and trauma became the launching pad propelling a meaning-filled life. But I get ahead of myself . . .

In 1994, it was immediately clear to many of us that Shannon's passions for teaching, counseling, and service would not be impeded by anything or anyone. Therefore, it's unsurprising that Shannon accumulated 32 years of university teaching experience (including 25 years of counseling nationally and globally), has presented on four continents and traveled to seven, and authored nine prior books for the mental health profession.

Written for anyone in the helping profession, as well as anyone who cares deeply about living a meaningful life, Hodges' tenth professional book unravels 13 crucial intertwined themes.

In case you're unsure if this is the book for you, consider the following:

Are you someone who pauses to reflect on the activities and trajectory of your own life? **Chapter 1** explores what is meant by meaning in life and why it matters.

Do you yearn for a greater sense of happiness and fulfillment? **Chapter 2** investigates the intersection of neuroscience and the brain's bent for a purpose-driven mindset.

Have you even asked yourself that iconic defining question, "Who am I?" **Chapter 3** confirms that you're in good company with theologians, philosophers, and psychologists, among others throughout the millennia.

Are you someone who endeavors to learn from your own and others' difficult experiences? **Chapter 4** draws from recent and past history, offering selected examples of existential challenges faced by some of our greatest role models when confronted by demons of anxiety, depression, human suffering, and their own mortality.

What's most precious to you: Fun, family, a 401K, personal fulfillment? Viktor Frankl wrote extensively on the power of meaning to uplift one's life. Have you discovered your "Goldilocks Zone," that habitable zone of your ultimate thriving? In **Chapter 5**, the author offers a diverse array of stories demonstrating how for better or worse, life purpose can infuse us or elude us as we inhabit the material world.

Ever consider how you can emerge from failure, loss, and even trauma with strengthened resilience? **Chapter 6** invites us to journey from the depths of disappointment to transformative growth.

Lest we briefly forget we're part of a larger local and global community, **Chapter 7** widens our lens to the larger spheres of our lives, where societal challenges like inequity, a pandemic, and climate change ultimately leave no one unscathed.

Chapters 8 and 9 lead us on the inward discovery of awakened self-awareness, igniting our power to choose our attitude despite difficult circumstances. While massaging our "mindfulness muscle," we're reminded of the truism that though we do not control all of what happens to us, we do choose how we respond.

Mere desire does not equal meaning. Without action, influence, and impact, our inner gifts are diminished. Whatever our personal and professional roles in life, **Chapter 10** highlights the reciprocal power of mentoring and coaching.

When we fully embrace being the co-creator/co-author of our own life story, we dismiss victimhood and step more fluidly from our comfort zone into our courage zone. As we consciously transition from what was to what could be, **Chapter 11** offers us a scaffold for healthy risk-taking and active self-transformation.

Chapters 12 and 13 usher us into the innermost sanctum of human existence—relationships, love, grief, and joy. As we dismiss the polarity of "good and bad emotions," we more compassionately accept and welcome ourselves, complete with our flaws, foibles, passions, and purpose. As we fully inhabit our own precious presence and life purpose, we finally embrace who we are and maybe even light the path for other seekers.

Written with compassion, depth, and humility, *Creating a Meaningful Life: A Practical Guide for Counselors, Therapists, and Other Helping Professionals* offers readers the author's substantive cross-cultural experiences and stories. Each of the 13 chapters gifts us with sections on lessons learned, provocative self-inquiry questions, and optional explorative activities for finding and living with purpose. Many of us squander valuable energy and irreplaceable time distracting ourselves in search of external focus and fulfillment. Lacking guides or a North Star, freedom can be elusive. Here is a book that offers various routes and roadmaps for the journey ahead; may it be a guide on the side for your path forward. To create a meaningful life is like returning home for the first time.

Shoshanna Cogan, M.S.
CEO, Shoshanna Cogan International
Training and Coaching

About the Author

Shannon Hodges, PhD, is professor of clinical mental health counseling and assistant coordinator of the Center for Mindful Practice at Niagara University. He has 25 years of providing counseling in community mental health clinics, university counseling centers, residential communities, and overseas, and 30 years of teaching experience in the US and Australia. Some of his recent books include *The Professional Counselor: Challenges and Opportunities*, *The Counselor's Practicum and Internship Manual: A Resource for Counseling Programs (3rd. Ed,)* and *101 Careers in counseling (2nd Ed.)*. For three years, he authored a monthly column with *Counseling Today*. Shannon, a longtime member of the American Counseling Association, has provided trainings in South African orphanages and in Indigenous communities throughout remote Australia. He and his wife Shoshanna live in historic Lewiston, New York.

Chapter 1

What Is Meant by Meaning in Life and Why Is It Important?

While the professional psychotherapeutic literature is chock full of various and sundry approaches to treating depression, anxiety, PTSD, schizophrenia, etc., one approach has always stood apart. No, not Psychoanalysis, although Freud's theory certainly differs from most contemporary approaches. The theoretical outlier is Logotherapy, developed by Viennese psychiatrist and Holocaust survivor Viktor Frankl (Frankl, 1946). The term Logotherapy comes from the Latin root logos (discourse) and literally means a therapy of meaning (Frankl, 1946). Readers might raise their eyebrows pondering just what makes a life meaningful. Admittedly, all therapeutic approaches posit some semblance of meaning at their core, albeit in differing ways. Unlike approaches primarily addressing thinking errors (cognitive therapy), behavioral concerns (Behavioral Therapy), or both (Rational Emotional Behavior Therapy or REBT, Cognitive Behavior Therapy or CBT), various existential-humanistic approaches (i.e., Gestalt Therapy, Person-Centered Therapy, etc.), post-modern approaches (Solution-Focused Therapy, Narrative Therapy, Feminist Therapy, etc.), Psychoanalysis, and numerous others, Logotherapy is the sole approach focusing exclusively on the cultivation of meaning. Thus, this springboard chapter will address meaning in life, and offer various strategies whereby one may engage with it. Each chapter will flow from this seminal beginning in various ways and with different foci.

Many years ago, I noticed a thick tome in the university library on the topic of meaning. As I was researching Viktor Frankl for a graduate school assignment, I picked up the hefty volume—no easy task, as it was quite heavy. Titled *Meaning and Void: Inner Experiences and the Incentives in People's Liv*es (Klinger, 1977), the text was a virtual gem with regard to the field of psychology's view of meaning in life. The book's limitation, however, was the text's focus solely on psychological, as opposed to philosophical and theological, underpinnings. Klinger's narrower focus was nevertheless a springboard for my deeper dive into Frankl's Logotherapy (1986), and was further instructive as I was contemplating a life in a religious order while simultaneously completing a doctoral degree in counseling. Klinger's book served in a complimentary fashion to Frankl's, providing solid grounding on previous research on the subject of meaning in life. This text, however, will veer into areas of philosophy, theology, and various other

DOI:10.4324/9781003168324-1

fields. In short, my own hypothesis is that meaning in life is the thread running throughout many professions.

Frankl's profound experience of personal suffering in the Nazi death camps, where virtually all his close family members, including his wife and children, perished, ironically confirmed his hypothesis that the will to meaning was the driving force in life (Frankl, 1946). Although he had much respect for Alfred Adler, he disagreed with Adler's view that the drive for power was the key to understanding human nature (Frankl, 1969). More significantly, he disagreed sharply with Freud's theoretical underpinnings regarding human nature being a complex set of sexual drives and instincts (Frankl, 1986). Frankl's belief was that meaning is something discovered, not a commodity one produces, and is encountered through experiential, creative, or attitudinal values. Values realized in experience are experiential values, examples being fulfilling work or leisure activities. Values realized in creative action represent creative values, such as appreciating the beauty of nature or art. The third group of values lies in one's attitude toward life challenges. Our very response to these foundational challenges provide us what he referred to as attitudinal values. One's attitude in addressing the brunt of life challenges, as in the courage Frankl found manifest among some fellow of his fellow death camp inmates, is the measuring stick of human fulfillment.

Let us consider the creative aspect of encountering meaning. Psychologist Mihaly Csikszentmihalyi recognized and coined the psychological concept of *flow*, a highly focused mental state of productivity (Csikszentmihalyi, 1990). The flow state occurs when the individual engages in some type of fulfilling act of creation. This creation is manifest in a number of ways towards an infinite number of ends: for example, the visual artist working diligently in creating a portrait, the author writing in creative bursts of prose (or more realistically, in long stretches of pages!), the poet painstakingly constructing verses illustrating the human condition, or the architect laboriously designing plans for a building. These creative endeavors require some type of flow or rhythm. No doubt, creativity also requires equally strong doses of patience and resilience to continue the creative process in the face of adversity. Perhaps losing oneself in the creative process, whatever that creation involves, is most illustrative of personally crafted meaning. To this end, I will recount an example from my adolescent days.

During high school, in my small, rural Ozark foothill home, I recall a fellow student two grades ahead of me. During his senior year, one of his relatives towed a junked car to our high school and parked it by the shop building. This student spent the entire academic year rebuilding the engine, and detailing the interior and body of the car. He found new hubcaps, added required fluids and new tires, and before graduation, drove his newly rehabilitated car home. As a lifelong mechanical klutz, to whom motor vehicles remain somewhat mysterious, his ability to rebuild a car from the junkyard to functional vehicle was impressive! I recall asking him about the project and he offered restoring the car was the highlight of his day. "I just lose myself in it," he added. Neither he nor I had heard of Csikszentmihalyi at that point, but no doubt, this budding master mechanic was the embodiment of flow when resurrecting his car.

During high school I had begun long-distance running as a means of staying fit during the summer. I desired to be in peak physical condition, and running was my primary vehicle. Coincidentally, the national running craze had just hit the country. While US Olympian Frank Shorter had won the gold medal in the Olympic marathon in 1972, it was Jim Fixx, author of the *Complete Book of Running* (1977) and George Sheehan, who wrote *Running and Being: The Total Experience* (1978) who popularized the sport. Both books were *New York Times* bestsellers. While both books proved helpful in different ways, I was intrigued with Sheehan's, a Boston cardiologist with a philosophical bent towards running. If Fixx was the running world's guru archetype, Sheehan was the movement's grounded elder statesman. While each spoke of required discipline, Sheehan framed the experience as if running should be more play, as opposed to competition and exertion. More significantly, he suggested we ponder what lessons running might teach us about ourselves and framed running as more a *being* than a *doing*, something akin to existential philosophy (Sheehan, 1978).

I far preferred Sheehan's philosophical books to Fixx's hardcore approach. However, I found the notion of the runner's high puzzling, never seeming to reach that euphoric state. Running in brutal southern heat and humidity likely had something to do with my inability to achieve this aerobic nirvana. Nearing summer's end, however, a friend and I took a ten-mile run at night. This particular evening was cooler than most, and for the first time my body felt light and my energy level seemed inexhaustible. During this long jaunt—my longest at that point—I lost myself in the experience. My leg muscles did not ache and fatigue was nonexistent. My body and the ground seemingly flowed together in some type of joint athletic and artistic endeavor. I recall wanting to keep running when reaching the ten-mile point, though thankfully my friend insisted we stop. After this experience, Sheehan's prose on the runner's high finally made sense. The separation between my effort as a runner and my losing myself during this ten-mile process merged in a time-space continuum, eliminating everything that was extraneous. Decades later, while reading Csikszentmihalyi's book, I identified Sheehan's runner's high as another manifestation of that flow Csikszentmihalyi wrote so astutely about.

What I take from these disparate examples of car rehabbing and distance running is that a flow state involves meaning and purpose merging to create a brief suspended animation, where the person engaged in whatever creative experience loses herself in the act of creativity. As an awkward adolescent apparently lacking any particular skill or talent, running was my first experience of flow. I had finally discovered the fulfillment, purpose, and meaning that had eluded me throughout adolescence. Like Frankl, I developed the hypothesis that everyone needed to develop some creative outlet in order to experience this sense of meaning and purpose. As I was in my late teens, however, I would soon lose sight of this important lesson, grappling with depression and anxiety for more than a decade. What pulled me from darkness and helped alleviate my anxiety was rediscovering the importance of meaning in life. Had I remained stuck in that void of meaning, I would not have become a professor, author, or marathoner, and my life likely would be unimaginable.

The Existential Vacuum

Frankl further distanced himself from Freud in hypothesizing the major neurosis challenging 20th-century people was not sex, aggression, or power, but a definable lack of meaning. He referred to this malady as the *existential vacuum* (Frankl, 1986). The existential vacuum refers to a condition whereby an individual comes to find life meaningless, unfulfilling, and perhaps boring. Frankl developed Logotherapy as the therapy of choice to address this lack of meaning and fulfillment. His approach involved getting to understand the patient well, then utilizing a variety of interventions within and beyond the session. For example, he might inquire of the client, "When was the last time you found your life meaningful?" or "What was different when your life was meaningful?" His process-oriented approach to therapeutic discussions of meaning proved fruitful and provided him anecdotal evidence of Logotherapy's efficacy. Frankl structured Logotherapy on six basic assumptions, outlined below:

Basic Assumptions

Logotherapy consists of six basic assumptions about life and methods of discovering meaning (1986):

1. Body, mind, and spirit:

   As humans, we are entities composed of a body (soma), mind (psyche), and soul (noos). Frankl argued that we have body and mind, but the spirit is our core entity. Frankl's theory was not theological in nature, but his language approximates a spiritual approach.

2. Life has meaning in all circumstances:

   Frankl hypothesized life had meaning regardless of circumstances, even in an existence as miserable as in the death camps. He emphasized that even when life seems unendurable, terrible, and tragic, meaning still remains present.

3. Humans have a will to meaning:

   Logotherapy proposes the primary motivation in life as the will to meaning. Such meaning is transcendent, allowing the individual to endure even great pain and suffering, and far exceeds the desire to achieve power and pleasure.

4. Freedom and meaning:

   Frankl argued that in all circumstances, individuals have the freedom to access that will to discover meaning. He based this theory on his and other's personal experiences of pain, grief, and suffering with the discovery that he could choose his attitude regardless of the circumstances. Furthermore, attitude was something no one, not even the Nazi guards, could take from him.

5. Meaning of the moment:

   The fifth assumption argues that for life to be meaningful, individuals must address the demands and inequities in society. That is, when one encounters injustice, one works to promote justice. This is exemplified in advocating for the oppressed and the most vulnerable in society.

6. Individuals are unique:

   Frankl believed every individual is unique and irreplaceable, regardless of societal standing. He went on to elaborate that attitude, as opposed to occupational title, is a better measure of worth. For example, the custodian who fulfills his role with a healthy attitude of helping his fellow humans may do society a greater service than a Fortune 500 CEO with a massive ego who treats his employees as disposable pawns.

Logotherapy in Practice

Frankl believed it possible to transform physical and emotional suffering into personal achievement and fulfillment. He considered guilt an opportunity to improve oneself, and life transitions as the opportunity to take responsible action. In this manner, Logotherapy focuses on assisting patients to make better use of their spiritual (noos) resources to withstand adversity. In his books, he often cited his own personal examples to explain therapeutic concepts. Frankl kept his approach and his philosophy simple, thereby making it understandable to a broad range of readers. A large part of his approach involved reframing suffering from being devoid of meaning to offering a pathway towards meaning (Frankl, 1986). Without question, one must never lose sight of the fact that suffering and trauma, particularly cultural genocide, apartheid, and other mass atrocities, and individual ones such as sexual assault, are scarcely anyone's preferred means toward achieving a sense of meaning. The *good* news part of the message is that transcendence and meaning are possible even under the direst circumstances.

Regarding Logotherapy's simplicity, Frankl leaned heavily on three techniques. These techniques are de-reflection, paradoxical intention, and the Socratic dialogue. I shall elaborate on these three key techniques below.

1. De-reflection: De-reflection is a process of assisting a patient who feels she will be unable to achieve the goals she set for herself. De-reflection then involves having the patient focus on the present and to accept herself without judgment. De-reflection could also involve asking, "If you were to accept yourself without judgment, how might you feel about yourself? What might close friends notice being different about you? How might you begin this journey to self-acceptance and nonjudgment?"
2. Paradoxical intention: Paradoxical intention is a technique that has the patient confronting what she most fears. For example, a person fearing looking foolish might be encouraged to look foolish on purpose. Paradoxically, when directly challenging the phobia, the fear diminishes over time. In fact, Albert Ellis was famous for using paradoxical intention in therapy and in his writings (Ellis & Doyle, 1988).
3. Socratic dialogue: The Socratic dialogue is a tool to assist a patient through the process of self-discovery through the patient's own words. For example, if a patient says, "I feel like I missed the bus with my career," the Logotherapist might ask, "What's it like to miss the bus with your career?"

Readers who are counselors, psychologists, social workers, or related mental health professionals can see how Logotherapy techniques overlap with more contemporary forms of psychotherapy such as Cognitive-Behavioral Therapy (CBT), Rational Emotional Behavior Therapy (REBT), and Acceptance and Commitment Therapy (ACT), to cite a few. Frankl also emphasized the value of therapeutic presence, much in the way Carl Rogers would (1965). De-reflection, moreover, sounds akin to what John Kabit-Zinn refers to as mindfulness (2017).

The Personal-Professional Nexus

Over the past 35 years, I have had many roles: counselor, professor, clinical director, and author of counseling books and articles. Perhaps more significantly, I have been a client in therapy for extended periods. During childhood, I lived with my parents and younger brother in Kansas City. It was just the four of us, or so I thought, as this was my reality. I attended Head Start just a few blocks from our home in a residential section. Then, one day, my mother left, with my father vague as to her whereabouts. Soon thereafter, my grandfather came north on the train from Arkansas and took my brother and me with him. By train, we journeyed to our grandparents' home in the rural Ozark foothills of Arkansas. To my astonishment, I discovered the two young boys already living there were also my siblings. Furthermore, I had an additional brother living with an aunt and uncle. My grandparents gathered us and explained, "Your mother's going to be in the hospital for a while." They went on to say we would be living with them for the near future.

The term *hospital* held bad memories for me. My father had taken my brother and me to visit my mother in the hospital back in Kansas. The *hospital* was a psychiatric facility with that ubiquitous "early Halloween" style architecture depicted in horror films. I had traumatic memories of that visit, and her continued stay left me feeling unsettled, fearing she would die there. She would spend over five years of her life in two different psychiatric institutions before coming home to my grandparents. As a young woman with five children and diagnosed with manic-depression (now called bipolar disorder), she struggled to manage her moods. Later, she would remarry and have a sixth child (another son). Fortunately, she stabilized enough to complete her GED and worked for over 40 years in medical transcription. Her struggles with bipolar disorder, however, would endure.

There were many trials during childhood: severe impoverishment challenged my grandparents financially, though somehow, miraculously, they managed. I struggled emotionally as a shy, awkward child lost in a shuffle of very active male siblings. I likely would have been diagnosed with depression had there been a mental health practitioner in our rural, isolated community. Nevertheless, I went spelunking my way through life and school, and matriculated to college. It was during my college years that someone said to me, "You know, you seem sad a lot. Maybe you should check out the counseling center." Taken aback by this person's suggestion, my initial response was defensiveness. After all, I was a resident advisor in a college dormitory, performed *peer counseling*, and walked other students, some even suicidal, over to the counseling center for treatment. Now one of my peers was suggesting I, a helper, needed psychological assistance? Ridiculous!

Perhaps a year later, I had a panic attack. My heart pounded, my catastrophic thoughts raced, and my body sweated profusely. After this unpleasant experience, overt concern smashed my sense of denial. The following day, I stopped by the counseling center after my last class and made an appointment. My counselor was an affable, 30-something male who seemed to be in the Carl Rogers mode. I do not recall many specifics except his being skilled at getting me to tell my story and engage me in a Socratic dialogue. My memory of our sessions is sketchy, except for my remaining in therapy the entire semester. I recall looking forward to my weekly counseling appointments and that the counseling process improved my mood considerably. This ongoing therapeutic experience would commence what has since become a life-long experience in various segments of the mental health professions. I would again seek long-term counseling services in graduate school and for extended periods thereafter. Interestingly, being in therapy while also a practicing counselor seemed to increase my skill level, and certainly left me feeling more personally, and professionally, fulfilled.

During this long period from roughly age 20 to my early 30s, however, I would eventually lose my way in life, get divorced, be fired from a job, and almost drop out of my doctoral program. I become seriously depressed once again, and while counseling again provided the gravitas to keep going, the gains were incremental. My spirits improved during a break, upon re-reading Frankl's opus *Man's Search for Meaning*. Something within me moved, and was inspired by his writing. I began writing myself, and suddenly found enough energy to resume long-distance running. Through counseling, reading Frankl, writing, and my hour-long daily runs, my depression lifted. I also began to challenge my faulty thinking, much in the fashion of Ellis' REBT. My self-talk had been full of *shoulds*, *musts*, and *oughts*, toxic words in Ellis' theory (1999). My improved mood and energy level led to a more positive mindset (attitudinal values), and this improvement was a significant factor in my ability to complete my dissertation and doctorate degree, albeit with many challenges along the way. I doubt my story would have ended so well absent a significant change in my mindset and attitude. One way or another, our attitude becomes self-fulfilling. As my high school counselor was fond of expressing, "if you believe you can, you will, at least to some extent. If you believe you can't, you are also right." During my 25 years conducting therapy, through my own personal experience, and in reviewing research, I have found that we start to believe what we tell ourselves. Self-talk must therefore be based in rationality (example: What's the evidence for my belief?), but more positive self-talk usually precedes successful behavior (Beck, 1979). Thus, it is wise to ask yourself what attitude you would prefer to take regarding your current and future self. Revising your self-talk is a good place to begin.

I do not wish to make it sound as if this difficult phase of my life passed quickly or seamlessly due to improved thinking, although that was key. My late 20s to early 30s was the most trying period of my life, and involved a lot of therapeutic work, disappointments, frustrations, grief, and even heartbreak. I can honestly say, however, that rediscovering personal meaning and purpose was the tipping point in my recovery. I would also suggest my own experience as evidence that Frankl was correct that meaning is something encountered in relationships and through a creative, experiential, or attitudinal process, if not all three. In my case, all three of these terminal values Frankl hypothesized aided my recovery from severe depression to becoming a functional adult. Part of the challenge lies in explaining this process of transformation to others, as it can so easily be misunderstood as "Just think pleasant thoughts." I recall giving a talk to an undergraduate psychology class at a community college about Logotherapy. I explained the nuances of Logotherapy and my own process of rediscovering meaning leading to a more intrinsically rewarding life. During the question phase of my presentation, one intrepid student inquired, "But how exactly do we make our lives meaningful?" As she completed her question, young brows furrowed, with practically every head nodding. I had to refrain from my usual counselor response to a question with a question, such as "How might you begin to create a sense of meaning?" As counseling is not about answering questions for the client, but more about assisting the client to explore and discover meaning (with validated cognitive-behavioral interventions of course), I explained counseling was one way, and journaling on meaning in life, being of service as a volunteer, and so on were all examples of Frankl's developing meaning. Someone then commented about always feeling best after volunteering at the local soup kitchen. Others chimed in with various and sundry pro bono experiences. I was careful to mention, however, that habituating an ongoing sense of personal meaning would likely involve ongoing, dedicated personal growth and might involve counseling. One quick-witted fellow offered, "So, no quick road to nirvana, eh?"

Deep Listening for Meaningful Relationships

These past 15 years, I have spent extended time overseas teaching, providing trainings, consultation, and the occasional co-therapy in South Africa and in remote Indigenous Australian schools. In June 2018, I spent a month in Australia's Northern Territory providing training and consultation in remote Indigenous Catholic and public schools. At one remote Catholic school, I met Indigenous educator, activist, and Senior Australian of the Year, Miriam-Rose Baumann. Miriam was a retired remote schoolteacher and principal, as well as a visual artist. She was one of the first Indigenous school principals in Australia and is well known throughout the country. I had heard of her and her approach she used to help create understanding within her culture and the broader Australian society, which is dadirri (pronounced *da-da*). My colleague Cheryl, a psychologist whom I had worked with in remote public schools a few years earlier, accompanied me. We had a most engaging and thoughtful conversation before having to make the long drive back to Darwin.

During our conversation, I asked her to explain the essence of dadirri, and she voiced it as all about what she calls *deep listening*. She went on to explain that dadirri, or deep listening, was about presence in conversation, in mediation, and even when teaching in the classroom. "You have to be grounded in the present, with a nonjudgmental attitude and eliminate the distractions from your mind in order to practice deep listening," she said. I was struck that dadirri reminded me both of mindfulness and somewhat of Rogers' (1965) necessary and sufficient conditions for change. I mentioned this and she knew of Carl Rogers but was unfamiliar with mindfulness. After a brief explanation of mindfulness 101, she agreed there likely was much overlap between dadirri and mindfulness. She also mentioned approving of Rogers' therapeutic approach while admitting she was an educator and elder, and not a counselor. Intrigued, I asked her the same type of question the psychology student had asked me some 25 years earlier: "How does one begin to practice dadirri?" She smiled and made a mild joke about inquisitive whitefella counselors, before to expressing that deep listening is something "you just have to catch. It's something you encounter when you have the right attitude." Later, on the three-hour drive back to Darwin, I realized her statement regarding attitude and "catching" dadirri was also congruent with Logotherapy's foundation of attitude and encountering meaning in relationships (Frankl, 1986).

I was fascinated that having traveled some 10,000 miles to meet the remarkable Miriam-Rose Baumann, I learned that her concept of dadirri was closely akin to therapeutic presence, meaning, and mindfulness. Interestingly, Miriam-Rose Baumann had an intervention very similar to Rogerian principles. My most significant takeaway from this similarity was that wisdom was not a function of ZIP code, miles traveled, or of a particular culture. I also agree with Miriam-Rose Baumann that dadirri, like meaning in life, is something one encounters or catches in relationship with others when we suspend our judgment. Suspension of judgment, of course, is perhaps the lynchpin in issues regarding dadirri, Person-Centered Therapy, Logotherapy, and mindfulness. As an aside, purging one's mind of judgment towards another person based on gender, culture, sexual orientation, religion, and so forth, likely is the actual first step towards achieving meaning, dadirri, and inner peace. Perhaps judgment is like denial, that terribly effective deflector shield that prevents emotional growth, attaining sobriety, and even finding love.

In this vein of Viktor Frankl and Miriam-Rose Baumann, I have provided a number of self-reflection exercises to help readers explore and possibly *catch* or encounter meaning in their life. These exercises are by no means the only strategy towards constructing a life of meaning, but they offer opportunities for self-reflection, something Frankl considered necessary for cultivating meaning in life (1986). I would encourage readers to use pen and paper as opposed to using a keyboard or merely reading them, as writing tends to linger longer in memory (Mueller & Oppenheimer, 2014). Interestingly, I had noticed this early in my graduate school days and learned to write out all notes—albeit with a very weary, overworked arm and hand!

Judgment Towards Self and Others

In what circumstances or situations does my judgmental voice emerge? (whether towards self or others)

____

____

When I feel myself becoming judgmental towards myself, or others, how might I suspend that judgment so that I can better understand the other person?

____

____

Meaning

In what ways is meaning present in your life?

____

____

How do you sustain your sense of meaning in life? (e.g., Frankl's three types of encountering meaning through proper attitude, engaging activities, or experiences)

____

____

When do you feel your life is most meaningful? (e.g., attitude, activities, or experiences)

____

____

Was there a time when your life was more meaningful? If so, when?

____

____

If your life is less meaningful now, how could you begin to create additional meaning in your life?

____

____

If you are working with a counselor or other therapist, has your experience in therapy been meaningful? If no, what needs to change so that your experience is meaningful?

____

____

If you were to have a conversation with your younger self about creating a meaningful life, what advice would you give?

____

____

If you were to have a conversation with your future self about creating a meaningful life, what advice would you give?

____

____

If you have struggled to answer any of the previous questions, here are some suggestions for consideration:

1) Write down three ways meaning is or was formerly present in your life.
2) Each day, either when you rise from bed or before you fall asleep at night, acknowledge three gratitudes you hold (e.g., health, family, occupation, etc.).

3) Notice the times you feel meaning is present in your life. Notice what is occurring during those times, and perhaps write these thoughts down in a journal.
4) Select one daily action that you find meaningful, or simply one that lifts your spirits, and follow through with that action.
5) Find 15 minutes in your day when you can walk, do yoga, dance, jog, or do some other enjoyable physical activity.
6) Find five minutes in the day when you can breathe deeply, slowly through your nose, then exhale slowly through your mouth. When focusing on your breath, silently tell yourself, "I am enough" when you breathe in, and "I am whole" when you exhale. Feel free to play instrumental music during this time.

My Meaningful Place or Space

Some people have a specific place they call their meaningful place/space. This place/space can be a specific location or simply a concept in your mind. If you were to create this place/space, where would it be?

____

____

Meaningful Symbols

Meaningful symbols are common to all religions and spiritual ways of life. Does your meaningful space have such symbols? If so, what are they? Some people, however, prefer no symbols, and thus that understanding is important.

____

____

Journal Exercise: Encountering or Creating Meaning in My Life

In this exercise, create a journal with pen and paper or on your computer. Consider what you have read in this chapter and how meaning is or has been present in your life. How is meaning present in your life? Alternatively, how could I begin to create additional meaning in my life? A suggestion here is to be thoughtful and gentle with yourself.

Additional Drawing Exercise: Details of My Life

Some 30 years ago, I attended a workshop when we spent time drawing our past and current life, and what we hoped to create for our future. Being of the stick-figure artist guild, this drawing task posed a daunting challenge. Remember, let go of any artistic inhibitions by silencing your inner critic and just be creative using a mindful, non-judgmental approach.

1) Family: Draw your family, or if you prefer, draw your family of choice (e.g., friends). This drawing shows your connection to your family and your position in the family.
2) My World: This drawing can illustrate your broader world. Draw your friends, colleagues, career/workplace, hobbies, hopes, fears, joys, disappointments, and anything you deem relevant.
3) My Lifeline: Draw a sequence of images illustrating important marking points in your life, such as birth, education, marriage/partnership, career, etc.
4) Self-Portrait: Draw you as you see yourself.
5) Draw the future you would like to create.

Questions:

1) What have you learned from the process of creating these drawings?
2) What did you enjoy about the process of creating these drawings?
3) What did you find difficult about creating these drawings?
4) What did you find meaningful about the process of creating these drawings?

Resources to Assess Meaning and Purpose in Life

The Purpose in Life Test (PIL; Crumbaugh & Maholick, 1964) is a standardized assessment based on Frankl's Logotherapy. The PIL is a 20-item questionnaire designed to measure two dimensions of meaning in life: (1) Presence of Meaning (how much respondents feel their lives have meaning), and (2) Search for Meaning (how much respondents strive to find meaning and understanding in their lives). Respondents answer each item on a seven-point Likert-type scale ranging from 1 (Absolutely True) to 7 (Absolutely Untrue). A score of less than 50 may indicate that you are experiencing a lack of meaning in life currently. You may take the PIL for no change at www.fetzer.org.

The Meaning in Life Questionnaire is a ten-item measure of the Presence of Meaning in Life and the Search for Meaning in Life (Steger et al., 2006). There is no manual, but a link to a brief scoring guide is available online (www.michaelfsteger.com). The MLQ assesses meaning in life on a seven-point scale from *Absolutely True* to *Absolutely Untrue. The Presence of Meaning Subscale* assesses how full of meaning respondents feel their lives are. *The Search for Meaning* subscale measures how engaged and motivated respondents are in efforts to find meaning, or deepen their understanding of meaning in their lives.

The MLQ does not have cutoff scores like measures of psychological disorders might have. The instrument measures meaning in life across the complete range of human functioning. The MLQ takes three to five minutes to complete. For a scoring and interpretation guide for the MLQ, go to the following link: www.michaelfsteger.com.

Lessons Learned

"I want to show you my community so that you better understand us," my colleague said. It was June 2017, and I was volunteering at two childcare centers (AKA orphanages) in the Western Cape region of South Africa. Although I worked and played games with the children, most of my efforts focused on the staff, as they would remain after I left. I delivered numerous 1–3 hour presentations on trauma treatment, self-care, suicide prevention, and related topics to social workers, childcare staff, and area teachers and clergy. My additional duties sometimes included individual coaching sessions with staff that frequently bled into personal areas of their lives. All such sessions were confidential and became more numerous as relationships strengthened.

The first day I met a volunteer whom I will call Sofia (pseudonym). Sofia was a South African and Xhosa tribal member. She held a couple of advanced degrees, had lived in Europe and traveled the globe, something unusual for her culture, given apartheid and post-apartheid South Africa. After a three-hour presentation on a Friday morning, she drove us around the mountainous, rural community where the orphanage was located. Sofia took me to historic locations of the Boer War, beautiful vistas, and one really great little coffee shop where people made good-natured fun of my strange accent. After a snack, coffee, and social talk, she drove me over to what she referred to as the "colored and black side of town."

The term *colored*, while derogatory in the US, connotes something different in South Africa. Coloreds refer a multiethnic group native to the region who have ancestry from more than one of the various ethnic cultures inhabiting the region, including Khoisan, Bantu, Afrikaner, Austronesian, etc. The term *black*, meanwhile, refers to people of a single ancestral origin (Xhosa, for example). During apartheid, blacks and coloreds were restricted to particular lands (like our Indigenous reservations in the US), had few legal rights, were kept in menial jobs, forced to attend substandard schools, restricted in their ability to travel, and could be arrested at any time for even the most minor offense (including no offense at all). Coloreds, however, had conditions slightly better than their black counterparts did, though both lived a menial, subservient existence, sometimes living in huge, overcrowded townships on the outskirts of major cities such as Johannesburg and Cape Town. Soweto, famous for Nelson Mandela and its musicians, and infamous for its shantytown conditions, is the most recognizable of these black and colored townships, with a population just north of one million people!

Given the small town and rural location, Sofia's township community was tiny in comparison. The home she shared with her partner was on the very edge of the township. On her street, houses were small, although had running water, heat, and the usual amenities. The further we drove into the township, however, the worse the conditions. As we drove at a walking pace, small houses transitioned to shacks lacking electricity and running water. The ditches became open sewers with children playing on the very edge of these open sores. In one section, I watched a child actually playing in the sewer as if it were a wading pool! Young adults milled aimlessly about, as the unemployment rate in the country, officially 25%, likely is double. I felt myself descending into the heart of some terrible darkness. The motto above the township entrance could well have read, "Abandon hope all ye who enter."

Sofia was carefully tracking my reaction. "What do you make of us?" she inquired. Having grown up in my grandparents' small home with five siblings and later my mother, in abject rural poverty in the Ozark foothill region of Arkansas, I previously considered myself knowledgeable of impoverished conditions. I had further witnessed serious poverty in Asia, Central and South America. This shantytown, however, was an entirely new level of pain. I was honest with Sofia in my observation that the conditions with the township were abominable, while carefully noting social conditions such as poverty, post-apartheid and such were the culprits, and not the people in residence. She nodded and suggested, "Let's visit a school."

Schools in South Africa require payment. Teachers with no qualifications, other than a desire to make a positive difference, often staff township schools. She parked the SUV before a larger, shack-like, tin-roofed edifice. We entered a surprisingly clean, well-organized room with a blackboard, numerous children's paintings, and primary level schoolchildren dressed in uniforms that included blazer jackets. I met two teachers, both university educated, and residents of the more affluent section of the township. Sofia knew everyone, and children surrounded her with beatific smiles on their faces. She introduced me to the *aunties* (teachers and assistant teachers) who beamed with pride standing alongside their students as if in some university classroom. The head teacher then had the children sing several songs "for the distinguished professor from New York City!" I was equal parts touched and embarrassed at the reference and prudently opted not to correct the geographical error. The children emanated such pride, they seemed to glow. The beautiful scene before me suddenly transformed the dark, foreboding township and my eyes welling up with joy. Asked to make a few remarks, I briefly thanked the teachers and children for sharing their classroom with me, an outsider.

Saying our goodbyes, I thanked the children and the teachers once again, and Sofia drove us back to the coffee shop for a post-visit debrief. "So," Sofia began while stirring the cream and sugar into her coffee, "what are your thoughts about my township?" I was honest with her regarding my initial impressions. She nodded as I spoke of my sadness in the face of such dire poverty and desperation. Her face brightened considerably when I talked about our visit to the school, seeing the determination of the teachers and the children's pride at being students. "Look, my people have suffered greatly both under apartheid and since in post-apartheid. Too much corruption. But," and she indicated with her index finger for emphasis, "those children are our future. Somehow, we have to help them sustain the excitement in their eyes. That's tough to do when they hit adolescence and stark realities are more evident."

We then discussed how one maintains hope in what appear to be hopeless circumstances. Sofia herself grew up impoverished, yet was guided by aunties who encouraged her to continue her education, as she was a gifted student. She opined that surrounding children with elders who reinforced hope was critical. She spoke of a couple of aunties (female elders, not always a relative) who mentored her in such a manner. One such auntie modeled hope and purpose in everything she did, from feeding goats, to cooking, childcare, and her prayers of gratitude. Still, we each spoke of hoping for better times, economically and educationally, for her people and other Africans.

Another lesson herein involves the great complexity of economic and social disparity inherent in this world. The rural poverty of my childhood days in a small Ozark town, challenging as it was, is nothing close to approximating what I have witnessed in South Africa and other global locations. The familial and psychological strains on the South Africans living in the shantytown are extreme. Parents contemplate their children's future, while daily confronted with unimaginable poverty, leaving them emotionally taxed and dispirited. Yet miraculously, practically every person I met professed a sense of meaning related to family, culture, and spiritual beliefs. The false notion of the happy poor, popularized in western societies, gets pulverized in the shanty town's worst sections. Likely, those espousing such myths were themselves not living under such dire poverty. The impoverished people living in the township, and the children in the orphanage, find meaning and fulfillment *despite* their oppressive circumstances, not because of them. This is a critical point to understand, and likely one missed absent a direct experience of such circumstances. Furthermore, while the term volunteer simplicity and minimalism have established a foothold in the US and abroad, the power of choice, *volunteer as opposed to mandated*, makes a significant difference. Most westerners have a choice to make, while the residents of the shantytown do not. The choices I witnessed in South Africa are far more rudimentary than the typical westerner confronts.

Later, taking a long walk in the hill above the small South African community, I reflected on my visit to Sofia's township and the contrast between the pains of unmet basic needs contrasted with the joy on the faces of the schoolchildren. Yes, sustaining hope for an uncertain future when confronted with daily misery seems an overwhelming task. Frankl's concept of existential frustration (1986) from prolonged periods of living a dead-end existence seemed most appropriate. However, I also knew that the impact of mentors, such as the teachers, might just make the difference between hope and despair. Somehow, the teachers had discovered meaning and transcendence through the vehicle of daily service and sacrifice, through educating and protecting their students. Perhaps these women and education did represent, as Sofia believed, the best hope for the children. Maybe their daily encouragement and intervention will be enough to guide these children through circumstances stacked heavily against them. Maybe, just maybe, that would be enough, at least for some of the children. After all, it had worked for Sofia, for the teachers, and for many elders. Emotional resilience and purposeful living are critical functions in third-world communities, as the roulette wheel of one's birth is far more capricious than any casino.

Chapter 2

Neuroscience and Its Relationship to Meaning in Life

Origins

I recall first studying the brain in high school biology class. Our teacher, one of the few in my rural school who held a master's degree, stimulated my interest in the topic. He spoke of brain injuries from strokes, automobile accidents, and through dementia. He admitted that, while he had read much on the topic, brain science was in its infancy. The following summer, when my older brother returned from college in Texas, he brought along a book on the brain. I cannot recall the title, but since I was interested in the topic, he loaned it to me when he had finished reading it. "Here, better than that John R. Tunis stuff you've been reading," he said in mild sarcasm, in reference to the famous author of adolescent sports novels. Ignoring his chiding, I eagerly tore into the dog-eared paperback, only to be stopped cold by the dense prose of the first chapter. Although an avid reader, and not merely sophomoric-themed sports books, neither my literary perusals nor high school biology class had prepared me for neuroscience jargon. I was, ironically, in far over my head. My sole reason for continuing to plough through the barely decipherable text was to deprive my older sibling of any smug *I told you so* statements.

Thus, I spent the summer between my sophomore and junior year working at the school on the government CETA program, running long distances, and slowly digesting the pages of that anhydrous book. I read about the functions of the cerebellum, cerebrum, brainstem, locations of the five senses, short- and long-term memory, judgment, intelligence and the like, and the fragments of knowledge acquired were just enough to keep my interest. Fortunately, just prior my brother's return to college, I finished the book! I was so proud of having kept up my snail's pace of reading and not quitting. My brother, miserly in his compliments, admitted he was impressed with my discipline, albeit while adding his doubt that I retained much of the text's information. On that latter note, he was spot-on correct. However, the text whetted my interest for continued knowledge of how the body's most important organ functioned. My interest was sidelined, however, when studying other topics such as mathematics

DOI:10.4324/9781003168324-2

and chemistry, which, while certainly related, took me far away from my initial interest in cognitive functioning.

Then, as a college freshman enrolled in a yearlong college biology course, I reconnected with my interest in brain studies. During the lab portion, we dissected a fetal pig's brain, studying the contours and discussing them in the small lab group. My lab partner, who later matriculated to medical school and became a physician, was very helpful. Courtesy of three years of high school biology, he likely was the best student in the entire class of over 100. I leaned heavily on his knowledge, as he read all he could on the subject and passed his interest, though unfortunately not his facility, onto me. Despite being of marginal aptitude, I was a most enthusiastic student. Several times, I sought out the professor during his office hours. At term's end, he drily remarked to the class, while nodding towards me, that he wished other students had taken the interest I had.

Realizing I lacked the vocation to become a scientist, I switched my major to English and took a decade-long sabbatical from neurological studies. During my initial master's program, I switched from English to counseling after taking a counseling course for teachers. During my two years in the program, however, we did not study the brain or neuroscience. There were numerous segments on counseling, individual, group, family, children, addicts, use of the *DSM-IIIR*, and so forth, but with little attention paid to the brain, outside of topical mention in the psychopathology course. Only years later would I realize the irony of this oversight. After all, how can a mental health professional counsel people while ignoring the very organ that makes a counseling intervention worthwhile? My experience was by no means unique, as colleagues in related mental health fields voiced similar experiences. This professional deficit, however, would change in the coming years.

In 1989, I began doctoral work, and in my Advanced Educational Psychology course, the special education professor teaching the course spent extended time discussing the brain. He insisted teachers and school counselors needed more working knowledge on the brain in order to do their jobs well. He related the obvious issues of ADHD (then the diagnosis du jour), various learning disabilities, and certainly psychotic disorders. With my decade-long slumber on neurology suddenly awakened, I was as groggy and ill-informed as that famous literary character. Realizing that the winds of change were about, I commenced taking graduate psychology courses on the brain. My favorite was Psychopharmacology, taught by a very knowledgeable, engaging professor. The class was very intimate, with enrollment of less than a minyan of students, with virtually all my classmates being pharmacy majors save myself.

The Psychopharmacology course was challenging and simultaneously rewarding. At moments, I was as overwhelmed as during my summer's reading of the book on the brain. This time, however, I had help, as the professor was approachable and always happy to talk about the course. He encouraged me to continue my study of the brain, insisting that with new psychotropic drugs, such knowledge would be critical during my counseling career. Realizing the pharmacy students' course aptitude was far beyond my mean capabilities, I threw myself into study, making flash cards with different psychotropic medications, reading each chapter three times, and beating a regular path to the professor's office. He would just laugh and shake his head, explaining I was the lone student in the class who came to his office hours. Of course, the pharmacy students did not *need* the professor's help. I, on the other hand, required his constant intervention. Fortunately, it all worked out, courtesy of my diligence, the professor's capable assistance, and my taking the course as Pass-No Pass versus a letter grade. I passed the course, albeit as the worst student in the class, yet simultaneously serving as its most engaged student. More importantly, I learned the value of psychopharmacology for mental well-being and the importance of emotional regulation and dysregulation on the brain and its impact on human behavior.

Neuroscience and Well-Being

This text also represents an opus on my own enlightenment and, more importantly, on how and why meaning is so critical in the mental health field, to say nothing of constructing a fulfilling life. Therefore, some diversionary excursions are necessary to construct a strong foundation for my hypotheses. Educational beliefs require the buttress of empirical research support; otherwise, they remain unsubstantiated wishful thinking. Faith of any type, be it spiritual, educational, or therapeutic, cannot endure without facts for support. While writing this text during the COVID-19 pandemic, our former president politicized mask wearing while denigrating sound medical advice, and offered dangerous and absurd statements that the virus would simply disappear while ludicrously suggesting ingesting bleach would cure it (Brown & Sink, 2020). When it comes to physical, mental, and emotional health, research and facts matter greatly. Over 900,000 US COVID-19 deaths bear witness to a society's vulnerability to this deadly virus that many stubbornly maintain does not exist. Denial can thus be as powerful and deadly a narcotic as any methamphetamine.

During my undergraduate years, a psychologist on staff at university counseling services referenced studies on jogging which suggested sustained aerobic activity was a helpful antidepressant. I was certainly running a lot during this time, sometimes more than ten miles a day, yet remained depressed. However, I had noticed consistently feeling my best just after completing a run. The post-run period, part of the "runner's high," produced a hyper-relaxed state that lasted for a couple of hours. I asked a fellow distance runner if he experienced similar positive symptoms, and he acknowledged he did. I did not pay a lot of attention to research on the subject, but continued long-distance running. Years later, after becoming a counselor and reviewing the research, I began encouraging my clients to take up aerobic exercise. I encouraged jogging, walking, swimming, dancing, or any such activity of interest. My clients who engaged in regular exercise (say, thrice weekly for 15 minutes or more), reported at least some benefit in reducing depression and anxiety. Now, the literature does not maintain aerobic exercise alone is a recommended treatment for mental health ills, but there's no question it is helpful in supporting treatment (McGonigal, 2019).

A couple of years ago, I was listening to a podcast with health psychologist Kelly McGonigal, who was speaking on the cognitive and emotional benefits of sustained movement. She referred to movement as done in dancing, yoga, running, swimming, and other pursuits as stimulating our brain to think more optimistic thoughts and function at a higher capacity (2019). She also included excerpts from athletes who compare this euphoric state to intoxication. She mentioned distance runners who refer to the high as a mystical experience. One such runner described tears streaming down his face when undertaking a long run. Reading such entries in her engaging book was reminiscent of William James' influential *The Varieties of Religious Experience* (1902), a required text in the *Psychology and Religion* graduate course I formerly taught. Interestingly, during my monastic days, while on retreat at a monastery in the Midwest, I had what I could only describe as James' type mystical experience, not during silent meditation, but while running through the dense woods surrounding the monastery. Having read volumes regarding the flow of serotonin during extended running, I attributed this transcendent state more to brain chemistry than religiosity.

McGonigal continues with references relating sustained movement to our earliest ancestors, who out of necessity scavenged and foraged for their food, while eluding predators. Presently, running may be recreational or competitive, but its roots are possibly prehistoric (Bramble & Lieberman, 2019). The neurochemical changes running produces may have served both the function of hunting and gathering food, and increased survival odds from predators. Running may further have served as a form of early sport and pleasure. In evolutionary terms, more active people survived, passing fitness and pleasure genes through generations (McGonigal, 2019). What the average person can glean from McGonigal's and others' research is that movement helps improve our cognitive functioning and mood, as well as strengthens our cardiovascular system. Furthermore, as humans evolved, running served dually as a survival mechanism and a means of recreation. McGonigal further asserts that sustained movement likely provides a stronger sense of purpose in life (2019).

Christopher McDougall makes a similar point in his bestselling book, *Born to Run: A Hidden Tribe, Superathletes, and the Greatest Race the World has Never Seen* (2009). McDougall writes of the reclusive Tarahumara tribe in Mexico, whom he portrays as a band of super runners covering distances of hundreds of miles. After repeated injuries as a distance runner, McDougall comes away from his time with the Indigenous tribal runners convinced of two things: (1) modern running shoes are a primary problem in runners' injuries, as the Tarahumara people run in sandals; and (2) the tribe's love of running is chiefly responsible for their survival and life satisfaction. Undoubtedly, McDougall is speculating on the first point regarding orthopedic flaws of running shoes. Another possibility is that Tarahumara people became adept runners and, as it was prized as a trait, produced more adaptive runners (i.e., less injury prone), despite running in sandals. His second hypothesis, that distance running strongly correlates to tribal happiness, may hold more validity, although other factors likely contribute as well (e.g., healthier diet, traditional way of life, abstinence from alcohol or other drugs, etc.). What is not under dispute is the tribe's great love of running, one of the most highly evolved forms of movement. Even if running does not prolong life, the pleasure it brings (at least after finishing!) may be worthwhile in itself. Using myself as anecdotal evidence, in 46 years of running, my runs range from bad to euphoric, with most somewhere between these extremes. Regardless of the *quality* of my runs, however, my post-run mood is pleasurable *100%* of the time. Naturally, this effect may last but an hour or two. Yet, such a period is significant and provides an emotional boost to my day. Thus, daily gratitudes, meditation, social relationships, meaningful work, etc. help sustain what my running fueled. When I look back on my difficult and turbulent early life, running may well have been the vehicle that preserved my well-being until increased psychological and social support arrived.

Finally, Bernard Heinrich's *Why We Run: A Natural History* (2002) is my favorite book on running. Heinrich, an emeritus professor of Biology at the University of Vermont, is an international scholar in wildlife biology, focusing on insects and birds. He also is a lifelong runner, having run on the Maine Track and Cross-Country team as an undergraduate, and later a marathoner and ultra-marathoner. He has set several national records in a long running career still continuing into his 80s. Heinrich remains a firm believer that aerobic movement, especially running, is conducive to optimal human functioning. In his popular book on running, he compares humans to animals, expressing the opinion humans evolved to run and that such kinetic movement is natural. He goes on to reference a colleague's study on mice, demonstrating that mice who ran daily on an exercise wheel developed more brain cells and learned tasks faster than sedentary mice (2002). Heinrich believes running is the primary reason he remains so active at an advanced age. While I am more than two decades his junior, and far less skilled a runner, my beliefs regarding the cognitive, emotional, and physical benefits of running mirror Heinrich's.

The Power of Positive Thinking Redux

Likely, most people of my age and older are familiar with Norman Vincent Peale's popular book *The Power of Positive Thinking* (Peale, 2003). Originally published in 1952, Peale asserts that attitude is the critical ingredient for success in business, education, relationships, and everything else (2003). A critic may rightfully point out that prejudice, poverty, illness, unemployment, trauma, and other social maladies certainly can affect one's ability to think in the constructive manner Peale advocates. However, the mental health profession has demonstrated that Peale was on the right track with regard to the psychological benefits of more adaptive thinking. Specifically, the Cognitive Behavior Therapy (CBT) of Beck and Rational Emotional Behavior Therapy (REBT) of Ellis both place strong emphasis on cognitive restructuring (i.e., revising self-talk). Both Ellis (Ellis & Doyle, 1988) and Beck (1979) assert that thinking errors, principally chronic negative thinking, can lead people to poor mental and physical health. Whereas Peale spoke of positive thinking power, Beck and Ellis provided a more detailed explanation of how to begin to habituate optimistic and rational thinking into our lives. Both these notable cognitive therapy researchers validated their approach in numerous studies, and cognitive therapy is one of the most efficacious approaches to treating depression, anxiety, and PTSD, among other maladies (Beck & Weishaar, 2014).

As a counselor who has practiced cognitive therapy for over two decades, I call upon my own experiences and the feedback of my former clients in illustrating my personal support for cognitive therapy's efficacy. However, I wish to veer off in a different direction to highlight an important related construct. Psychologist Martin Seligman originally developed a model he termed learned helplessness (2006). In his studies with dogs, Seligman inadvertently discovered that one group of dogs receiving unavoidable shocks failed to take corrective action, even when escape was possible. However, the second group of dogs, who were not given unavoidable shocks, immediately took action in subsequent situations (2006). He then replicated the same experiment with humans, using loud noise as opposed to shocks, yielding similar results. Seligman subsequently coined the term *learned helplessness* to describe a belief that unpleasant outcomes are unavoidable, and consequently, the victims expend no effort trying to escape the unpleasant experience. The critical factor in people developing a learned helplessness belief system was their ingrained core belief that punishment was unavoidable.

Any therapist experienced in treating PTSD sufferers (e.g., combat veterans, domestic violence survivors, sexual assault survivors, etc.) likely has witnessed Seligman's model. However, what are we to make of those long-term trauma survivors who do not exhibit learned helplessness? For example, I recall *Beth* (pseudonym), a 17-year-old former client who had been a sexual captive for several years. An adult male family friend had kidnapped her around age 12, violating her daily for some five years. He also physically and verbally abused her and locked her in a dark basement, often bound and gagged. A plastic bucket was her toilet, her diet was subsistent at best. He frequently exclaimed, "No one cares about you." The perpetrator evidently believed he had total domination over her and began leaving her unattended more often. These unattended periods began to increase, serving to reinforce her thoughts of escape. One day he took her to a fast food restaurant for a meal. Making the excuse of needing to go to the women's room, she detoured into the kitchen, informing the manager of her desperate situation. The manager called the police, who promptly arrived and arrested the perpetrator. She later testified against him in court and he was sentenced to a long, well-deserved prison term.

Placed in foster care, she struggled mightily due to complex trauma, bouncing in and out of foster care and residential treatment programs. Fortunately, her last foster mother was able to build a trusting relationship, eventually adopting Beth. She presented to counseling as a focused, motivated client. Beth explained she had survived by dissociation, especially when being sexually violated. Dissociation is a common, natural survival technique victims employ. Beth explained, "I just go somewhere far away in my mind." Like Seligman's dogs, she could not control the circumstances of abuse. Unlike the dogs, however, she did not default into the learned helplessness model. She explained that she maintained a belief of escaping her abuser and "making him pay!" Daily, she reminded herself that her purpose was to survive until she escaped. Each day, she reminded herself that it was "one day closer to freedom." She disclosed that her religious beliefs in something beyond herself (i.e., God) helped her maintain faith in her eventual escape. Thus, her self-talk was positive regarding her survival, eventual freedom, holding her captor accountable, and thriving in her life. Thereupon, when she had the opportunity, she escaped, played an active role in holding her former captor legally accountable, and entered therapy to heal.

The lesson of Beth's experience lies in what Seligman calls learned optimism. That is, she believed in the possibility of freedom in the face of a seemingly impossible situation. I would argue, as Beth certainly did, that she had a clear purpose each day, and that purpose sustained her hope. Her religious faith provided meaning during those traumatic days and nights, further fueling her optimism. Essentially, she had found her sense of meaning and purpose through the crucible of unspeakable sexual, physical, verbal, and emotional abuse. Although I never had the privilege of meeting Viktor Frankl, each session I witnessed his spirit in the countenance of this remarkable young woman. Beth met every component of her treatment plan, completed her GED, and enrolled in the local community college, planning eventually to become a counselor or social worker. Her desire was to work with sexual abuse survivors like herself. I eventually moved across the country and lost contact with Beth. I have no doubt, however, that she achieved her goals, having already overcome extreme difficulties no academic program could (or should!) ever devise. She may well be the most resilient person I have met.

The Power of Belief: Self-Fulfilling Prophecy

Beth's poignant example exemplifies the positive psychology approach that Seligman (2006), Frankl (1986), and even Ellis (1999) and Beck (1976) addressed in different ways. Like Beth, you must believe you can achieve your goal in order to survive (Frankl, 1946), sustain hope (Seligman, 2006), and utilize adaptive self-talk on a daily basis (Beck, 1979; Ellis, 1999). Naturally, most people thankfully never have to endure long-term abuse on Beth's level (although some do). Frankl's, and later, Beth's traumatic experiences, recall the power of belief and self-fulfilling prophecy. That is, your belief system, whether you can succeed or not, lays the foundation for your eventual success or failure.

Considering Beth's case, I cannot help but be reminded of Nietzsche's famous quote, "He that has a why can bear almost any how." More inclusively, the person with a *why* has the potential to endure and transcend tremendous hardship. The important point is we all need a reason to endure, a *why* if you have it. Beth had a *why* and it helped her remain hopeful through heinous abuse until she escaped. During 25 years providing counseling with trauma survivors, I was witness to a *why* in many clients. Those lacking a clear *why* struggled far more and were more likely to discontinue therapy. The majority of my therapeutic career has involved assisting clients to discover their *why*. This entire book devoted to creating meaning in life, as evidenced by Frankl, is most succinctly about encountering our *why*. The *why*s of our life represent vehicles for our personal and professional transformation. The unspoken rejoinder to Nietzsche's famous statement is "the person who lacks a why will fall prey to almost any how." Therapists must help their clients in discovering a personal, sustaining *why* to effectively cope with and overcome life's *how*s. The following paragraph relates my foundational experience in self-fulfilling beliefs.

My rural school had among its faculty many dedicated teachers who spent decades hewing out future teachers, medical professionals, business owners, and others. One of the more unusual teachers was our school counselor. A World War II veteran who attended college on the GI Bill, he became an agriculture teacher, later earning his master's degree in Guidance Counseling through the National Defense Education Act (NDEA; United States Senate, nd). Our counselor, an alumnus of the school he taught in, Salem High School, also served grades 1–8. Due to personal interest, he had developed a psychology class many years earlier.

My relationship with him was somewhat labile, as he was hard on me, something he acknowledged after my graduation. While I did not always appreciate him, I did respect him, as he was an excellent teacher. During my senior year, I took a psychology class along with a small number of juniors and seniors. Our class, approximately a dozen students, studied the history of psychology and contemporary approaches to psychotherapy. At some point during the year, we discussed standardized testing. Our counselor and teacher had taken additional coursework so that he could administer intelligence tests. He also oversaw administration of the ACT, Preliminary Scholastic Aptitude Test (PSAT), and Iowa Test of Basic Skills, among others. During one particular class, discussion ensued regarding the validity and reliability of standardized assessment, particularly achievement assessments such as the ACT and SAT. Our counselor explained the rationale for achievement tests, then referred to as aptitude tests.

He went on to explain that colleges use ACT scores and high school grades to predict student success.

The discussion then turned to Salem High graduates' college success rates. He paused, removed his glasses, and twirled them, something he did when serious. He explained of a typical Salem High graduating class, around 15–20% matriculated to college. Of that percentage, the attrition rate was over 50% within two years. I recall our class going silent. Like all rural schools in the region, we were surrounded by severe poverty, hobbling both the school and area resources. He further explained standardized test scores correlated strongly to family income and opportunity, both in short supply in our rural, impoverished community. Just when the class seemed headed towards depression, if not desperation, he offered some encouragement. Grades and test scores are important, he reiterated, but he went on to say there was a more important variable. "I call it the *want to* factor," he said, explaining that "want to" involved motivation, resilience, and hope. "Show me someone with all three of these, and I'll show you a successful person." That is a better predictor of college and life success than high grades and ACT scores, he asserted. He concluded by remarking that if tasked with selecting people to populate a new planet, he would choose the "want to" overachievers over the high IQ-high standardized test scorers. "The reason is their demonstrated resilience and ability to beat the odds." Fast-forwarding some 46 years, with some 25 years providing counseling, 30 years teaching in universities, and over a decade providing international training, consultation, and therapy, often in remote regions, my opinion coincides with that of my late high school teacher and counselor.

Our school counselor was also quite liberal in dispensing lesson-like sayings to students. My favorite went like this: "If you believe you can succeed, then likely you will, at least to some extent. If you believe you can't succeed, you are completely right." Then he would pause for a few seconds and finish with, "Tell yourself you can succeed and keep working." I recall the very last class period before the final exam, he locked his gaze on each student and repeated the above statement. Clearly, he wanted to reemphasize a "want to" attitude that he viewed as life's most important lesson. His self-fulfilling approach suggested learned optimism long before any of us had heard of Martin Seligman or his popular theory.

The Purpose-Driven Life and Brain Neuroplasticity

During these initial chapters, I have devoted much prose to discussing meaning in life, learned optimism, self-fulfillment, positive self-talk, and resilience. I referenced the *Purpose in Life Test* (Crumbaugh & Maholick, 1964) and the *Meaning in Life Questionnaire* (Steger et al., 2006). The MLQ and the PIL provide standardized assessments to measure Frankl's meaning in life (1986). Readers having gotten this far in the text are familiar with my emphasis on meaning in life, purpose in life, resilience, learned optimism, and related constructs. Given this is a chapter on the relationship of neuroscience to meaning in life, we must examine some basic research.

Rick Hanson is a psychologist who studies the impact of mindfulness-based activities on mental and emotional well-being. He also has studied how mindfulness-based activities aid in brain development. His research suggests ongoing self-care practices such as meditation, positive affirmations or gratitudes, and positive self-talk all assist in brain neuroplasticity (2013). Essentially, the aforementioned mindfulness activities help your brain develop and function more efficiently through production of neural pathways. Hanson takes care to express that it is the habituation of these mindful practices that aid growth and development of the brain's inner circuitry.

Ongoing trauma stimulates over-production of cortisol, leading to impaired cognition and a constant hyper-vigilant state of arousal leading to distress, emotional outbursts, and social withdrawal (Van der Kolk, 2014). Mindfulness-based activities like daily gratitudes, meditation, yoga, positive self-talk, journaling on our healing, and the like can, however, promote brain development (Hanson, 2013; Van der Kolk, 2014). A valid question lies in precisely how such health self-care activities promote brain development. Evidently, magnetic resonance imaging has detected changes in cerebral flow during activities such as meditation. Wang et al. (2011) found that meditation positively affects the frontal regions, anterior cingulate, limbic system, and parietal lobes. Meditation further increased cerebral blood flow in the prefrontal cortex, and was significantly higher among meditators than non-meditators (Wang et al., 2011; Newberg et al., 2010). Whether meditating regularly actually increased a person's IQ score is uncertain. What is clear, however, is that meditation, along with aerobic exercise, increases brain plasticity (Hanson, 2013; Wang et al., 2011). Brain plasticity correlates positively with better memory and may delay the onset of dementia (Hanson, 2013).

In a similar vein, people who regularly acknowledge their gratitudes tend to be happier and less depressed (Brown & Wong, 2017). The critical question is, how much of an asset are daily gratitudes for those who struggle with mental health concerns? Brown and Wong (2017) surveyed 300 adults, primarily college students seeking mental health services at university counseling services. They randomly assigned participants into three groups. All received counseling, with the first group instructed to write one letter of gratitude to another person once a week for three weeks. The second group wrote about their deepest thoughts and feelings regarding negative experiences, while the third group had no writing requirement.

Compared with the participants who wrote about negative experience or received only counseling, those who wrote gratitude letters reported significantly better mental health four weeks later, and then 12 weeks after their writing exercise ended. This simple research study suggests gratitude writing may be beneficial for healthy, well adjusted-people as well as for those struggling with mental health concerns. Practicing regular gratitudes and journaling about gratitude practice, while also receiving counseling services, may carry greater benefits than only counseling.

An important factor in the study was that the mental health benefits of writing gratitude letters gradually occurred over time. In fact, it was after four weeks of gratitude letter writing that positive changes occurred for the letter writers. These positive effects on mood and well-being became even larger after 12 weeks (Brown & Wong, 2017). These results suggesting positive effects continuing are significant, as counseling gains often decrease over time. Possibly, the gratitude letter writers discussed their writing in counseling sessions, thereby increasing treatment efficacy. Gratitude letter writing, then, may be more helpful than verbally acknowledging gratitudes, as the act of writing may suggest a greater commitment to positive mental health (Brown & Wong, 2017). Another important finding of the study was while not all gratitude letter writers mailed their letters, there seemed no significant variation in well-being differences from those who did. Perhaps simply writing gratitudes down is helpful.

Three months after the study, Brown and Wong (2017) took results of those who wrote gratitude letters and compared them to those who did no writing, to assess if their brain activity differed. They used an fMRI to measure brain activity while subjects from both groups completed a pay it forward task. In these tasks, someone called the benefactor regularly gave individuals a small amount of money. The benefactor asked only that they pass the money on to someone if they felt grateful. The participants then decided how much of the money, if any, to donate to a worthy cause. The gratitude letter-writing participants experienced greater neural sensitivity in the medial prefrontal cortex, a brain region associated with learning and decision-making. These results suggest that people who are more grateful may also be more attentive to how they express gratitude. The gratitude letter writers also displayed greater activity in the medial prefrontal cortex three months after writing the letters. Expressing gratitude, and habituating gratitude expression, may have lasting positive effects on the brain. Possibly, journaling on gratitudes may improve brain elasticity, and likely leads to an overall sense of mental and emotional well-being. Thus, habituation of gratitude practice, both verbally and via journaling, is likely therapeutic for clients struggling with depression. My personal and professional experience is daily gratitudes increase one's sense of meaning and purpose.

These studies, among others, suggest meditation and seemingly additional mindfulness practices stimulate the production of blood flow, which increases serotonin and lowers cortisol. Mindfulness-based practices such as meditation, gratitude practice, and philanthropic acts also seem to enhance emotional regulation (Zhang et al., 2019). A full reading of these research studies reveals neuroscientists are just beginning to scratch the surface on the positive impacts of mindfulness practices such as meditation. My observation is that mindful practices such as meditation, daily gratitudes and the like strongly correlate with meaning and purpose in life as well. The important factor for therapists is to encourage clients to habituate regular, ongoing practice of meditation, gratitude acknowledgement, and related mindfulness-enhancing activities (e.g., yoga, exercise, healthy diet, etc.).

Conclusion

Undoubtedly, regular practice of mindfulness-based activities will be an asset both in counseling and in daily living. As previously stated, my belief is that mindful practices strongly correlate with meaning and purpose in life. I make this leap between mindfulness correlating to mindful and purposeful living, albeit while admitting it is a leap. Furthermore, I must of necessity caution readers that mindfulness and counseling are likely more therapeutic than mindfulness alone. It bears mentioning that while mindfulness-based practices such as meditation, daily gratitudes, and body movement (e.g., running, swimming, cycling, etc.) are important components of a healthy lifestyle, they are unlikely to cure depression, anxiety, PTSD, etc. However, they may assist clinicians to treat these and other mental disorders, postpone dementia, increase meaning and purpose, and be a positive asset to regular and ongoing counseling.

Lessons Learned

It was March 1984, and I had recently begun graduate school. Having completed my bachelor's the previous May, I spent the fall as a substitute teacher back in my rural Ozark community. I loved teaching, though admittedly had little idea of *how* to teach. My plan had been to take a semester off, then commence graduate school in January. Through serendipity, I landed a scholarship that took me some 2,000 miles to the Pacific Northwest. Having never been away from Arkansas for more than three months, filled with excitement, and an equal measure of anxiety, I journeyed west.

As a fitness enthusiast, I had been working out at the university fitness center in addition to six or seven days of running per week. The fitness center had a robust social atmosphere, as college fitness centers tend to. I made several friends through the fitness center, regularly spending time with them during workouts and over post-workout coffee. One person of interest was an undergraduate co-ed engineering major. She was intellectual, witty, and an uber-fit runner. Just prior to spring break, she invited me to attend a lecture delivered by a biochemistry professor. Admittedly, I had no real interest in the lecture. My interest lay in spending additional time with her. Therefore, I enthusiastically accompanied her, expecting a very forgettable, terminally boring lecture. Although nearly 40 years has passed, with my once-robust memory having deteriorated, I remember the basics of the evening.

The lecture was held in an aged, cavernous auditorium. I had been in the auditorium a couple of times for the one-dollar films shown most Friday nights. My sketchy memory suggests some 50 persons showed, mostly a collection of professors, graduate students, and an assortment of others. I recall being pleasantly surprised that the professor giving the lecture was such a gifted speaker. While I remember only fragments of his talk, one part of his lecture has remained in my consciousness since. He mentioned that if you take a sample of a lab rat's tears, then reinject them back into that rat, the rat would show signs of depression. He went on to say tears are likely one of the body's natural methods of releasing toxins. He went on to say crying should be encouraged, especially in men who have embodied a stoic, stiff-upper-lip approach to grief.

While I found the notion of crying as therapy interesting, I gave the matter scant additional thought after the lecture. However, the idea of tears being a natural way of purging toxins returned to me a year later when matriculating into the counseling program. The lecturer's counsel has become firmly entrenched in the decades since. My lifetime observation is the seemingly universal cultural norm that "men don't cry" has done great destruction to men's emotional and physical health. Film, literature, sports, and politics all evidence ridicule of men crying in grief and disappointment, often terming them "cry babies." Sadly, even tragically, men's appropriate outlets for grief and sorrow seem to have been through the anesthetic of alcohol use and abuse. Such has especially been true of first responders like paramedics, military veterans, and law enforcement. I recall a friend, a now-retired police officer, telling me of the after-hours gatherings in a bar to drink away job-related stress. "Gathering at the bar was our therapeutic support group," he stated, before admitting that alcohol further compounds the job-related grief and trauma.

Years ago, during one of my international service projects, I spent five weeks in several South African orphanages. One orphanage was particularly large, with some 175 children and adolescents. In addition to my usual presentations on trauma treatment, self-care, and the like, I consulted with the director, treatment team, childcare workers, clerical staff, and groundskeepers. I also spent two full afternoons meeting with children and adolescents on grief and trauma issues. The most significant encounter occurred, however, when meeting with the social work supervisor and several childcare workers.

Evidently, some of the adolescent males continued to struggle with nocturnal enuresis. Their emission resulted in a malodorous aroma, leaving the childcare workers frustrated and their peers angry. Their peers and the childcare staff harshly ridiculed the bed wetters. The childcare workers, all of whom were female, were generally a supportive group of professionals who had a good relationship with the children. Some, however, would berate and ridicule the bed wetters before their peers, even using pejorative names for those suffering enuresis. This "teasing," as the head social worker framed it, resulted in some of the boys crying, thus increasing the ridicule. The issue had come to a flashpoint between the older sibling of a bed wetter and another adolescent in the way of a nasty fight. One of the childcare workers then approached the head social worker with her concerns over enuresis. As the fight occurred just days before my arrival, and because I was an outsider, the head social worker asked me to address the matter. I agreed to meet with her and the childcare workers regarding this delicate and traumatic issue.

There was an added complication to my task. I was a Caucasian from the US, while the childcare staff were all Xhosa women. Thus, in addition to the enuresis conflict among children and staff, there was a potential cultural disconnect complicating the meeting. Anytime I volunteer providing training, consulting, and therapy, I work to make sure to present with an attitude of cultural humility. After all, the various cultures I have worked with in Asia, Africa, and remote Australia are far older than my own and have suffered significantly since colonization. Given that these disparate cultures have continued to survive despite various attempts at genocide, marginalization through stealing their sacred lands, polluting their waters and cultural grounds, and via racist name calling, visiting westerners must tread lightly.

With the above in mind, we met in the group room. There were perhaps ten childcare workers in attendance, the head social worker, and myself. The head social worker laid out the issue and conflicts involved, then solicited my opinion. My eyes surveyed the room, revealing everyone gazing expectantly at me. In the moment, my mind flashed back to the long-ago lecturer's opinion that a rat's tears are a means of natural purging. Taking a breath, I acknowledged the unpleasant odor of enuresis. I then went on to express that bed wetting strongly correlated with anxiety. I further suggested many of the children suffered from PTSD, and that criticizing such a child for bed wetting increased anxiety, and would likely increase the occurrence of enuresis. Recalling, although not mentioning, the rat tears example, I suggested bed wetting was the mind and body's reaction to trauma, and that "teasing" would further traumatize said child, and increase bed wetting.

Pausing, I noticed some childcare workers nodding their heads, while others appeared to be considering my words. One of the childcare workers asked, "What do you think about boys crying?" At this point, the room quieted, ticking clock audible for the first time. I explained the rat's tears story from decades back, and that tears were the body's natural mechanism of purging toxins. I also opined that crying itself likely was a healthy response to grief and other emotional pain (such as trauma). I acknowledged having grown up in a "boys don't cry" culture, and that I had come to view that norm as unhealthy. In their case, boys being shamed for bed wetting likely worsened the trauma and the enuresis. My suggestion was that the shaming cease, and if so, the enuresis likely would lessen over time.

There was an extended silence, leaving me wondering if I might be shunned. After all, I was an outsider, and a whitefella with little understanding of their Xhosa culture. Just as I began to sweat, an older childcare worker from one of my workshops spoke up. "I agree with Professor Shannon," she began. "I see the damage the shaming has done and I would like it to stop. Maybe then, the bed wetting will be less too." Her words created a domino effect as several others joined in, mentioning their own struggles with the shaming and the doubts they harbored over it. At the meeting's end, the childcare workers were united against shaming boys for wetting the bed. They agreed to meet with the social work staff for a new intervention, noting that "old practices die hard," as another elder childcare worker put it.

The following day, the childcare worker who initially spoke up pulled me aside after my last workshop. "You know, my younger brother wet the bed. My father used to whip him something fierce," she said, eyes watering. "I've always known this was a bad practice. Tell me, does shaming boys happen in your culture?" I explained it certainly did, and with similar results. "So, you see crying as good?" "Yes, I do." "Me too!" she said, and then abruptly threw her strong arms around me, temporarily leaving me breathless, and certainly surprised at her acceptance.

My most significant lesson learned is that we all are human, regardless of culture, nationality, gender, sexual orientation, religion, etc. While we are all the same species and experience the same basic emotions, however, cultural expression varies considerably. The similarity I have discovered through decades of counseling, teaching, and training is all people wish to be respected, love and be loved, and to be understood. The adolescent boys wetting their beds were suffering the residual effects of trauma. They clearly were feeling misunderstood, shamed, and further traumatized, implicitly or often explicitly accused: *you're at fault*. Such callous rebukes are emotional boulders that crush the very life out those most vulnerable and in need of compassion, and further complicate matters for all involved.

How often have you witnessed trauma victims accused with hurtful words like *what were you wearing, why didn't you leave, you made me do it*, etc.?

Chapter 3

Who Am I? The Meandering, Washboard Road to Self-Hood

With over 30 years of university teaching experience and 25 years providing counseling, the notion of the self is never far from cognition or discussion. During counseling, the exploration of the self is a natural part of the personal growth process (Rogers, 1961). Carl Rogers placed great emphasis on assisting the client's self-exploration phase of therapy, viewing self-examination as a natural part of personal growth. Socrates championed a similar process, opining that an unexamined life was not worth living. For Socrates, life examination occurred when a teacher addressed critical thinking questions to a student. His *Socratic Questions* require the learner to think more critically, reevaluating previously held opinions. Socratic dialogue is widely used in Cognitive therapy, where the focus is on modifying thinking and facilitating behavioral change (Clark & Egan, 2015).

Example:

CLIENT: "I am a miserable failure!"

COUNSELOR: "What is the evidence you are a miserable failure?'

CLIENT: "I was just fired from my job."

COUNSELOR: "Lots of people are fired for many reasons, some of which are unjust. How does losing a job equate to you being a failure?"

CLIENT: "I was raised with the idea that good people don't get fired."

COUNSELOR: "You know the media is full of people unjustly fired for many reasons. Now, could you tell me what makes someone a good person?"

CLIENT: (Pause) "Well . . . I'm not sure." (Laughs) "Guess I have thought more about what a good person is not."

COUNSELOR: "Perhaps we might then discuss what qualities a good person might possess."

CLIENT: "Sounds like a good idea."

In the previous example, the critical focus is on the exploration process, not simply arriving at particular answers. In the example, the client begins by stating, "I am a miserable failure." Through the Socratic process, however, the larger issue uncovered is that of being a good person. Then, the counselor

DOI:10.4324/9781003168324-3

suggests a focus on what makes a good person. Then, the client deconstructs this "good person" ideal. Under Socratic dialogue, one seeks a more rational belief regarding the self (Clark & Egan, 2015). Culture, family, religion, and situation, among other factors, determine a person's underlying beliefs. Therefore, the emphasis in this chapter focuses on the *process* of personal self-discovery, something meaningful in itself.

Fritz Perls likened self-discovery to peeling away the layers of selfhood (1969), whereas Rogers (1961) compared growth to potatoes. Regardless of metaphor, we are eventually discussing a process towards that self-discovery. In Buddhism, all teachings reference Dharma, meaning truth and law existing in one's heart and mind (Thittila, 1958). A person may discover Dharma through managing one's thoughts and purification of toxic emotions, such as resentment, long-term anger, and revenge. Then, one can begin to live a more peaceful inner existence and send out loving kindness to those in the outer world (Thittila, 1958). Dharma involves meditation, a minimalist lifestyle, and understanding the *Four Noble Truths*. These four truths emphasize that life involves suffering, suffering being caused by desires, that suffering is temporary, and that suffering is ameliorated through meditation and ethical living (Thittila, 1958). Dharma has many equivalents across cultures. Navajo (Diné) culture intertwines truth, harmony, and meaning with family and cultural cohesion (Frankland et al., 2004). The phrase *walking in beauty* implies being strong in culture and living in harmony with nature and Navajo ways. The important factor to realize in these different cultures is that self-understanding involves a process, usually with a mentor, guide, shaman, clergy, teacher, or therapist.

In Chapter 1, I posed questions such as *Who am I* for the reader's consideration. A significant difference between the initial chapter on meaning in life and this one on meaning and self-discovery is that these processes are complementary, yet different. The process in this text involves active participation. That is, reading theory and an author's opinions are typical methods of peeling the onion of self-hood, to use Perls' metaphor. Active engagement with what one is reading involves a higher thought process, as one must use self-reflection to assess their level of understanding and actual practice. To engage readers in meaningful self-reflection, consider the upcoming exercises. I recommend readers sample exercises in whatever order they deem helpful. Furthermore, readers are encouraged to review their answers periodically to assess how their thoughts, opinions, and practice evolve.

My Self-Story

In a journal, either on a computer or paper, commence a weekly account of the journey towards self-understanding. Begin by silencing your inner critic and write without fear of grammar or literary quality. This journal is your opportunity for free expression. You might consider beginning each entry with the sentence fragment, *Today my self-story involves . . .* as a springboard. The suggestion is to write two or three times per week with whatever length you deem appropriate, as this is your journal. In one month, read what you have written. Ask yourself, "What have I learned about myself through writing this journal?" If a close friend were to inquire, "How has writing this journal increased your self-understanding?" how might you answer? Naturally, feel free to continue the journal indefinitely. Some people spend a full lifetime writing their journal. Like the PRN abbreviation in medicine, journal as often as necessary.

Questions for Self-Examination and Understanding

You are encouraged to answer these questions in writing. Keeping a record is essential for assessing self-growth. Some questions may be a repeat from Chapter 1. The interesting comparison is to examine differences in your answers. In some cases, you may not have an answer, and that is okay. The important part, then, is to reflect on how you might answer the question.

1) If someone were to ask, "Who are you?" how might you answer? Consider answers beyond the typical name, occupation, where you grew up, etc.
2) Where are you? This may involve geography, relationship status, spiritual self, life meaning, etc.
3) What do you consider your core mission in life?
4) Regarding the previous question, how often do you reflect on that core mission?
5) What would you like people in your circle (e.g., family, friends, colleagues, etc.) to understand about you?
6) What is the most important lesson life has taught you? What makes that lesson so important?
7) Who has been most influential in your life and why?
8) Core values are those we hold to be most significant (e.g., honesty, ethical living, being nonjudgmental, etc.) What is your most important core value?
9) Consider a challenging time in your life (e.g., death of a loved one, divorce, job loss, etc.). How did you address that challenge? What did you learn during that process?
10) What would you most want to change in your life? (e.g., behavior, lifestyle, career, etc.) How might you begin to make that change?

Daily Gratitude

Decades ago, while contemplating becoming a Trappist monk, I attended all-day Saturday meditation sessions at a monastery. During a break, our guide suggested a daily gratitude practice. He suggested acknowledging gratitudes anytime between waking and bedtime. He further encouraged habituating gratitudes, especially on the days when *not* feeling grateful. More than 30 years of daily gratitudes since has proven him right. Each day I rise from bed, wipe the sleep from my eyes, and then quietly acknowledge three gratitudes. Acknowledging gratitude is easy when one's career, personal life, and physical and emotional health are robust. The challenge lies in acknowledging daily gratitudes when health concerns arise, or depression rears its dark head, and when relationships are failing. The even harder challenge is acknowledging daily gratitudes each day for a lifetime. Having navigated many personal and professional life challenges, daily gratitudes were often my *why* in rising from bed.

The term gratitude derives from the Latin *gratia*, meaning graciousness or gratefulness. Gratitude is a thankful acknowledgement for what has been received. The gratitude process provides an opportunity for reflection on goodness received and renewal for acknowledging such appreciation. Some research suggests daily gratitudes may increase one's level of optimism (Brown & Wong, 2017). So, what are three gratitudes (or blessings) in your life? Examples might include a loving family, meaningful occupation, close friends, a home, etc. Again, consider habituating daily gratitudes for the remainder of your life. Such is monastic discipline!

Here are some additional ideas to cultivate gratitude on a regular basis:

Send out thanks to someone: Mentally, or in writing, thank an individual who has done something kind for you.

Keep a gratitude journal: On a daily or weekly basis, write down your gratitudes. Perhaps elaborate on how such gratitudes have positively influenced your life.

Write thank-you notes or emails: Write a note expressing your appreciation to someone (e.g., family member, friend, colleague, etc.). Make a habit of writing and sending one such message monthly.

Meditation: Meditation involves focusing on the present moment without judgment and with wisdom (Kabit-Zinn, 2017). Many use a mantra for focus during meditation, while others simply focus on their breath. Find what works for you. Even brief meditations during the day are helpful.

Loving kindness thoughts: When you are meditating (or praying), send kindness to those in need. If possible, send out loving kindness to those with whom you are angry. Loving kindness thoughts do not absolve another person of responsibility, but represent an opportunity for self-healing. Emotional preparation is certainly required for this most difficult gratitude practice.

Healing prayer: For those who practice daily prayer, give thanks and ask blessings for those less fortunate and who need emotional, physical, sexual, and other healing.

Reflective exercises such as these can provide an ongoing process of self-discovery. Ongoing self-reflection is necessary, as there is no point in life where we are *done*, due to life's dynamic nature. Just as one can never wade into the same river twice, we are constantly growing and changing; ongoing evaluation is necessary. When I began these self-reflections 30 years ago, my answers were quite different. In my early 60s, I think differently than I did in my 20s. My takeaway learning is that the process represents the most important part of self-reflection, more important than particular answers, although answers can be significant also.

Meditation

I already mentioned meditation under the previous *Daily Gratitude* section. However, I wish to provide more information, as much confusion exists regarding meditation. Meditation is not a religion, but has been practiced by Buddhism, Hinduism, Christianity, Judaism, and other religions for over two thousand years. There are many variations on meditation, with some involving mantras, prayers, particular postures, eyes closed or open, and so forth. Most important is discovering what works for you. While taught a particular approach at a monastery, I have deviated over the decades, while keeping vestiges of that teaching.

In his seminal book *Thoughts Without a Thinker*, psychiatrist Mark Epstein discusses how Buddhist philosophy and meditation helped manage professional demands (Epstein, 1996). When I originally read his book, I was director of a small college counseling center, carrying a significant caseload alongside clinical supervision and administrative responsibilities. I was frequently pulled in various directions between counseling, supervision, managing crises, psychoeducational presentations, and consulting with faculty and staff over students' concerns. Unfortunately, my former daily meditation practice slipped to a couple times a week, increasing my stress level. Reading Epstein's book fortunately reawakened my mindful brain. He spoke of how daily meditation helped him manage a full and challenging patient caseload. He even suggested setting aside as little as 60 seconds between patient sessions. He recommended this "mindful minute" practice was helpful in preventing carrying issues from a just-completed session into the following one. Epstein's Zen boundary was a siren call. In following this one-minute-between-sessions meditation, I found myself more emotionally fresh, better focused on the current session, and able to release information from the previous one.

For meditation practice, find a time in your day and begin your practice. For me, usually it is the end of my lunch period. I return to my office, closing the door for a five-to-ten minute session. Focusing on my breath, I take a slow, deep intake through my nostrils, then slowly release air through my mouth. Usually, I close my eyes. When my mind wanders, as it can, I simply focus on my breath. Sometimes I use a mantra, but the primary focus is the breath. These brief, mindful respites are not magic, as they do not *fix* concerns, but they help manage daily challenges and responsibilities. Furthermore, after these brief sessions, I am more relaxed, with life seeming more manageable, even meaningful. Perhaps most meaningful of all is the discipline of daily meditation, as it involves a mindset of temporarily setting aside all responsibilities. When the meditation is completed, I reengage with those responsibilities. Simple as this sounds, much like the one minute between sessions, brief meditation in my workday helps improve my mood and attitude.

There are many variations and schools of thought on meditation, and numerous books available on sitting meditation. Walking meditation is a variation worth mentioning, as it has provided me a viable alternative. During my monastic phase, we occasionally took meditation walks. One Saturday after lunch, our master took us on a two-hour meditation walk through the woods. His instructions were to focus on the breath, and to notice anything our five senses picked up. How did our feet feel walking on the soft earth? What did we see, such as birds, trees, other animals, etc.? What sounds did we hear, smells did we notice? He even suggested we consider how our post-walk snack might taste. During this ambulatory experience, I discovered it easier to lose myself in the flow of walking than while sitting. I polled my fellow meditators discovering roughly half of a similar mindset. Thereafter, I began to take regular meditative walks in a wooded area near my residence. Years later, while on an hour-long run with a monk, he suggested I might take benefit from meditative runs. On select Saturdays, I take a one-to-two-hour meditative run (*very slowly!*).

Meditation, Daily Gratitude, and Meaning

My experience for the past 30-something years is that daily gratitudes and meditation have improved my mood, helped me manage numerous challenges, disappointments, and relationship challenges, and kept me emotionally healthy during some very difficult periods. Admittedly, my experience may not be the experience of people reading this book. The current research on meditation, however, suggests it may be helpful in managing anxiety and depression (Kabit-Zinn, 2017; Newberg et al., 2010); gratitudes seemingly help sustain an optimistic, hopeful mood (Brown & Wong, 2017), while physical activity appears to promote optimism (McGonigal, 2019). Thus, I feel justified stating mindful practices like daily gratitudes, meditation, and moving the body (walking, running, dancing, etc.) are important outlets in our well-being. Likely, regular practitioners of these mindful practices find life more meaningful as well.

Summary

As I wind up this chapter, a disclaimer is required for ethics' sake and good sense. There is nothing magical about daily mindful practices. Mindful practices will never cure depression, PTSD, grief, disappointment, estrangement from loved ones, and other traumas. Mindfulness will not lift us from poverty, feed hungry children, or create a safer neighborhood (a worthy idea in violence reduction perhaps!). Mindfulness practice will not cure terrible diseases such as cancer, ALS, HIV/AIDS, etc. Rather, mindful practices such as meditation, daily gratitudes, reframing thoughts, movement, etc. *can* help us manage difficult circumstances such as disappointment, disillusionment, anxiety, depression, and grief. Mindful practices do not erase emotional pain, as such is part of the human experience. Moreover, there is something liberating in acknowledging honest grief, pain, and disappointment. The worst misunderstanding potentially arising from reading this text is the false belief that emotional pain is optional. Recalling the Four Noble Truths, the first involves acknowledging suffering. The second is that desires cause and worsen suffering. The third, however, is that suffering is temporary, and fourth, that meditation and ethical living are the pathway through suffering's dark valley (Kabit-Zinn, 2017). Pain will occur, but a pathway out exists.

Mindful practice has been my journey to a more meaningful life, even when depressed, anxious, grief-stricken, and disappointed. We experience the full range of human challenges and emotions in a life cycle that one day ends in our death. Although we hold no power over mortality, we retain the freedom to choose our attitude, and in doing so reclaim a sense of personal, spiritual, and psychological liberation (Frankl, 1986). This liberation likely represents the vehicle towards meaning and fulfillment, even when our lives are not proceeding as desired. Perhaps more importantly, mindfulness can help us achieve the most important objective of all: namely, in becoming ourselves in a world that desires and tempts us to become so much we are not.

Lessons Learned

"You see, I don't like myself," James (pseudonym) sobbed as he sat on my couch. During my scholastic career, I spent a decade supervising university residential communities. James represented an outlier in this particular living group. He was obese, socially awkward, and very isolated. You only needed to observe him in a social setting to understand his struggles. At a kick-off social function the community held at the beginning of the academic year, I observed him standing on the periphery of the wider social circle, unsure of how to proceed. Social anxiety is scarcely new to mental health professionals, of course. Unfortunately, pharmaceutical companies have figured out anti-anxiety drugs are a big market, and have capitalized on people's need, fast-forwarding through side effects, naturally. Left unsaid is that a variety of non-medical therapeutic interventions (e.g., CBT and others) can help people achieve similar results without unpleasant side effects. Regardless, James was grappling with severe social anxiety, leaving him very lonely and depressed.

His floor resident advisor (RA) and I, the resident director (RD), had been his chief relationships. Both his RA and I had listened with him on numerous occasions. Naturally, as a credentialed counselor, I had broached the topic of seeking university counseling services, even volunteering to walk him over. He steadfastly refused, stating a desire to "work it out myself." Clearly, he was not working it out. As the RD, I made extensive, albeit limited, use of my training and experience, reminding residents seeking my assistance that actual counseling would not be ethical given our relationship. During my RD career, I made scores of referrals to counseling services at the two institutions I attended, performing crisis intervention on a number of occasions. James was turning out to be one of my less successful mentees. He would knock on my door almost weekly, with me limiting our time at 30 minutes. I explained he needed more in-depth assistance from a counselor. "But you are a counselor," he would protest to my refrain, "But not in this role."

This particular evening, he was especially upset. "Nobody wants to be my friend," he complained, wearing his sadness in his large body, exclaiming, "Who wants to be friends with an overweight slob?" Sadly, given society's pejorative values on optics over substantial issues like integrity, honesty, ethics, kindness, etc., there was sad truth in his words. Society is full of lonely people, with college campuses being petri dishes of loneliness. In a decade of staffing university counseling services, I have counseled many isolated, lonely, depressed students like James. My years supervising residential living communities had provided me an even clearer picture of human isolation. James was one of the most socially isolated students I had encountered in my career. I had broached his joining a student organization based on his interests, referring him to the Student Activities Center for more information in his doctoral area of computer science. He followed up, but claimed the organization rejected him. I was becoming very concerned about him, especially as he disclosed a suicide attempt several years earlier. Unquestionably, he was depressed, lacking a support system, and pessimistic regarding his future, what mental health professionals consider three predictors of suicidal potential. Concerned for his well-being, and mentioning his survival, I again voiced professional therapeutic help, but he again refused. In desperation, I had sought out a colleague in counseling services, someone whom I had referred many students with positive results. The counselor sympathized with my plight, but admitted what we both knew: James would have to want his assistance.

My helping at a cul-de-sac, an opening emerged. "James, if you were to make a friend, what would that person be like?" He glanced up through red eyes and a tear-stained face, momentarily hesitating before replying, "I'm not sure? I've never had a real friend." For a man in his early 30s, this was a startling admission. He then continued. "You know, back in high school I was in the TAG program (Talented and Gifted). We had this Scholars Bowl competition for area schools. I was on our school team and we placed second in a state competition. It was one of the few times I felt accepted." He paused and then continued. "But we don't have a trivia team here." Suddenly, admittedly late, there was a viable opportunity. "What about starting one?" Naturally, he rejected my suggestion outright. "I tried as an undergrad, and no one wanted to join." When I suggested another try, he shook his head, replying, "One of the worst rejections I've experienced." James was an expert marksman in shooting down viable ideas.

I grew frustrated with his continued refusal to seek counseling services or try new approaches to making friends, all met with his, "I tried that before and it didn't work," deflection. He even accused me of not caring, listening to him only because RD responsibilities dictated. His words held some truth, as time with James was unpleasant, not because of his obesity, but rather his chronic negativity. Having grappled with depression from adolescence onward, I had learned the value of positive self-talk and the support of friends. I did maintain human compassion for James regardless of my frustration level with him. Just as things seemed bleak, another idea sprang forth. Offering suggestions to James was like hitting a tennis ball into a wall, the rebound effect being difficult to manage. "What if our community were to hold a weekly trivia night? Perhaps others might be interested?" I had a history in this endeavor, having been a key player on several trivia teams. Furthermore, James had been a good trivia player and a weekly social event might just be the vehicle he needed. Just as importantly, a lack of interest could represent my failure and not James'. James was interested, but given his history, wary.

Regarding the matter, I spoke with the staff. All agreed that a weekly trivia night seemed worthwhile. The hall president believed trivia would be popular, given the *Jeopardy* show's popularity among hall residents. Buoyed by encouragement, we posted flyers publicizing our inaugural Trivia Night, offering small prizes for the winning and runner-up teams. The hall president even offered to play moderator. Excited, James had a bounce in his step. However, the following day he defaulted to his typical depressed self. "Nobody wants to be on my team," he said, looking despondent. "Okay, I will be on your team," I said, half expecting, ironically, he might reject me. Surprisingly, he agreed, adding, "But we need four members." I explained that two others had approached me about being on their team. After James left, I immediately begged the duo onto our team. The only cloud of uncertainty was whether community members would show up. Apathy had been a stumbling block for much of the hall's social and educational programming.

The big night arrived, and I felt weighted with anxiety. I breathed a hefty sigh of relief as the room filled with teams poised to battle for prestigious prizes! First place netted a $10 gift certificate at the campus bookstore, while runner-up teams would receive a $5 certificate. As each team had four members, trivia was the draw, not the paltry prizes. Each team had a name and we asked James to pick our moniker, as he was Team Captain (on my suggestion). He chose the Razorbacks as our name, mascot of my alma mater, the University of Arkansas. That done, the heated competition ensued. From the tipoff question, James was the dominant player, exceptionally well-read beyond his field. That night, he carried our team to the finals, where we emerged victorious. Everyone cheered the prize winners as well as all participants. The hall president, bless him, proclaimed James the Most Valuable Trivia Player and presented him an MVTP certificate. Everyone cheered the lonely, awkward man who suddenly found himself the object of admiration, not ridicule or rejection. James beamed, overwhelmed at the goodwill his peers showered upon him.

Relief that the inaugural trivia night had gone so well buoyed me as much as James. Yet, given his melancholy nature and habit of finding the dark cloud amongst sunshine, my confidence level that he might sustain his newfound mood elevation was low. How would he feel when our team lost and someone else was MVTP? Finding out took one week, as the previous week's runner-up edged us out on the final question. Anxiety high, I watched James closely as the victorious team captain accepted the MVTP award. To my astonishment and relief, James led the community in a round of cheers for her and her teammates. Their captain, a young Chinese woman, was impressed, expressing that next term she wanted him as a teammate.

The weekly trivia night continued throughout the term, with the Razorbacks and our arch-rival (I cannot recall their name) battling as if they were a Yankees-Red Sox rivalry. More important was James' newfound pride and his peers' respect. He even made a couple of friends and joined a cadre of students who watched *Jeopardy* and competed while doing so. At term's end, as the community cleared out for the break, someone knocked at my door. It was James. I welcomed him in, hoping his visit was not a last-minute crisis, something quite common in collegiate residential communities. He sat in his usual place on the couch, but this time it was to thank me. "I know you put together the Trivia Night for me." He smiled, something unforeseen during our past conversations. I inquired: "What did you learn from the trivia experience?" He considered the question a long moment. "You know, I have spent too much time trying to be someone I wasn't. I suppose it's a reminder to embrace who I am."

I liked his answer, but wanted to tease a little more information from him. "Who do you say you are?" He smiled again. "I'm someone who is just beginning to entertain that question. Funny it never occurred to me previously." He rose, offered his hand, and left my cramped apartment. We continued Trivia Night through the year, and while attendance and enthusiasm abated somewhat, it remained our most popular event. James continued as the best player, closely shadowed by his newfound friend and arch-rival, the Chinese student. Unfortunately, I left the job as RD for a position at counseling services, losing touch with James.

The most obvious lesson learned was attitude and social connections are crucial, especially to lonely people who feel defeated by life. Yet, a positive attitude and friends do not come easily to many. In my long, meandering road as counselor, professor, and student affairs professional, I have witnessed too many like James. These otherwise intelligent, gifted persons may comprehend theoretical physics and other heady topics, while simultaneously being socially illiterate. Perhaps my most significant takeaway lesson is that nothing, neither IQ, money, nor degrees, can soothe the sting of human isolation. Winning at trivia certainly was important to James, but the social component of his trivia prowess, namely friendships, were his tipping point. As counselors, therapists, and other professionals, we must teach the Jameses of the world how to create healthy friendships. In doing so, we may have accomplished our most important therapeutic success.

Chapter 4

Wandering in the Wilderness

Facing Existential Challenges

Existential theorists like Maslow, Rogers, May, and Frankl have had a significant influence on the counseling profession (Corey, 2017). While differing in their particular theoretical orientation, all accommodated the belief that an existential approach to counseling required assisting the client in examining her or his life. This examination involves addressing core issues of life meaning, relationships, occupational challenges, and facing mortality, to name some of the more pertinent areas. Two very different books for recommended reading are Irvin Yalom's *Staring at the Sun: Overcoming the Terror of Death* (2009) and Mark Epstein's previously mentioned *Thoughts Without a Thinker: Psychotherapy from a Buddhist Perspective* (1996). Epstein and Yalom's books provide different views on existential issues affecting all humans. Most importantly for those in the therapeutic community, the books provide an opportunity to view two master therapists and creative thinkers addressing life-and-death issues with patients. Most significantly, both authors accomplish their task without seeming either pithy or clichéd. Unfortunately, these two books were published long after my stumbling into the counseling profession. I would like to say my entry into the mental health profession came about after prolonged, sober, intense self-examination. Such a statement would, however, be patently false.

During winter term of 1985, I enrolled in a graduate course titled *Counseling Skills for Teachers*. This was during a phase when I entertained hopes of becoming a professor of literature. My motivation for enrolling in the course was my job as a resident advisor (RA) for a small university co-operative student residential community. As an RA while an undergraduate, I had taken a similar course, but desired additional training, as mental health and addiction issues were so ubiquitous among college students. A doctoral student in the Counselor Education program taught the class, with my classmates an assortment of P-12 teachers seeking a second master's degree. My memory is sketchy, but it seems we had around ten students in the class, which ran from 7:00–10:00 PM one evening per week. The instructor briefly explained his background and that he worked from an existential orientation similar to Rogers and Maslow. He encouraged us to view human nature with an orientation of seeking first to

DOI:10.4324/9781003168324-4

understand the client. He spoke of the need to bracket off our judgment, especially when value conflicts emerged between the client and ourselves. Introductions were made, each student explaining his or her rationale for taking this course. Motivations were similar: namely, to be a better teacher, parent, or friend. After going over the syllabus and a brief orientation to the profession, the instructor opined that each of us were commencing a journey. That journey had taken some far from their origins, as two of us had traveled over 2,000 miles for graduate school. The instructor emphasized, however, the more significant journey was internal, as opposed to any distance we might log in miles.

I didn't make too much of our initial class other than being pleased to be learning skills that could assist me become a more skilled listener and guide for the undergraduate students in our living community. Weekly practice included basic skills such as reflection of content, paraphrasing, summarizing, open-ended questioning, and body language, among others. The course built on my previous undergraduate training and the instructor praised my performance. That said, my skills were rudimentary, and good listening and a timely referral to counseling services were the best tools my training provided. My classmates noticed my facility, and during a break, one commented, "You should become a counselor. You're a natural." I thanked her but explained my long-term goal of being an English professor, and commented that listening to people's problems all day was not my ideal career.

I did not give a career change additional thought until term's end. Our capstone project involved a ten-minute mock counseling session. My partner was a veteran teacher in the area. We would counsel one another, switching roles after ten minutes. I cannot recall anything of her session with me, but I will never forgot my mock session with her. The day of our final class, her marriage was rendered apart. Somehow, after gamely navigating through the session as my counselor, she unleashed a torrent of grief and anger, lasting well beyond the prescribed time. The instructor eventually stopped the session and requested the class take an unscheduled, extended break. My unfortunate partner was in full, and understandable, emotional meltdown.

I do not recall what happened to my partner, although it seems a friend came and took her home. What I do recall was my debriefing with the instructor. As we were the last dyad, he dismissed class quickly, thanking everyone for their sensitivity and understanding during our classmate's very tough time. During the debriefing, he was effusive in his praise of my ability to be present before such animus. My years running collegiate residential communities had provided numerous opportunities to remain present before anger, hurt, grief, suicidality, and similar emotional maladies. He then made his pitch for me to apply for the master's in counseling program. I thanked him for his confidence and conveyed my appreciation for teaching us valuable counseling skills. I did not immediately agree, however, to apply for the program. That came more, honestly, due to the realization few English faculty jobs were available. More than anything else, my foray into the counseling profession reflected occupational anxiety, representing a *Hail Mary* act of desperation.

Mystics, Everyman and Everywoman Seekers

Growing up under my grandparents' tutelage, weekly church attendance and Bible study were strongly encouraged. I read of Moses leading the Jewish people in the exodus from Egyptian slavery, Jesus' itinerant rabbinic wandering about with his disciples, and various and sundry additional Midrash tales from the Judaic *Tanakh* (Old Testament) and Christian New Testament. I was, however, unschooled in the vision quests of other spiritual sages. Fortunately, I took a graduate philosophy course taught by a phenomenal teacher and scholar, Marcus Borg, a well-known scholar on the historical Jesus. Our course, however, focused on other religious mystics. My favorite was Herman Hesse's evocative and lyrical opus *Siddhartha* (1951). Hesse's novel was an account of Siddhartha's journey of self-discovery and eventual enlightenment, eventually becoming Buddha and the genesis of the Buddhist movement.

Hesse's story takes place in the Nepalese area of what is now Tibet (China). Siddhartha, an affluent young man, makes the difficult decision to leave his wife and young child in the hope of attaining spiritual illumination (one wonders what his family thought!). He becomes an ascetic beggar, wandering throughout the region. Accompanied by his friend Govinda, he fasts, renounces all possessions, meditates long hours, and seeks out the famed teacher Gautama. Later, he separates from Govinda and Gautama, arguing personal meaning comes only in solitude and without a teacher. He wanders throughout India, encountering scores of pilgrims and sadhu (holy men), encountering much resistance when bucking the rigid caste system, preferring to meditate and beg along with the untouchables (the Dalit), rejecting the nobility's (Brahmin) assertion that sacredness emanates from societies' upper crust (Hesse, 1951). He eventually attains enlightenment, not through seeking, but rather while sitting quietly under the Bodhi tree. Interestingly, perhaps ironically, his enlightenment occurred not in deep meditation, or chanting in a monastery, but in a quiet, prosaic moment.

All great spiritual teachers have their own journeys towards enlightenment. The important issue for the purposes of this text, however, is that one does not have to be a guru, start a movement, wear sack cloth, visit a holy land, or retreat to a monastery to confront existential questions. Siddhartha's lesson might suggest existential realities occur under natural circumstances. Existential questions regarding the meaning of life, our purpose in life, meaning in life, death and nonbeing, and whether life continues beyond death, remain persistent questions. For Frankl, May, Yalom, Epstein, and many others, it is engaging with the existential givens, unsettling as they can be, that make life so personally enriching. For therapists, the ability to engage a client in exploration of existential matters possibly represents life fulfillment, as both life and death anxiety pose persistent questions (Yalom, 2009). Therefore, of necessity, we as clinicians of all persuasions must take a deep dive into an exploration of death anxiety.

Fear of Death: A Natural Human Phobia

In his richly written text, *Staring at the Sun: Overcoming the Terror of Death* (2009), Yalom begins with a description of fear of death. As death represents the finality of human life, this fear is entirely natural, and certainly, there is nothing *unnatural* about death, unless it is an unnatural death (i.e., homicide or suicide). Perhaps the greater fear, then, is our perception of loneliness regarding death and separation from loved ones forever (depending on spiritual beliefs). Yalom explores the human capacity to examine our own existence and impending demise, imagining the painful details of the death process, thereby creating a terror of death. Nearing death awareness, he illustrates, poses a constant threat to our enjoyment of existence and casts a life-long shadow from which we can never truly step out. In reaction, society has manufactured various methods of distraction from mortality, like plastic surgery, a multi-billion-dollar cosmetic industry, an entertainment industry obsessed with youth, and cryogenic preservation, to mention but a few of the death-denying smoke screens. Regardless of these concentrated efforts, death denying as a defense mechanism is doomed to fail, as the natural life cycle proceeds and physical and mental decline will occur regardless. Buying stock in death denying, whether through surgery, cosmetics, revising our age, or marrying a much younger person is like investing in a commodity guaranteed to fail at some future point. Yalom's approach is to focus on addressing client despair, and assist them in overcoming their terror of death. Ironically, having patients address death is required to lessen their fear of death (Yalom, 2009).

Raised by grandparents whose social circle was that of elderly friends and relatives, I attended funerals in my primary years. I watched as death rituals played out before my immature eyes. Women wailed while men sat and stood in rigid stoicism, eyes desert dry, while the minister eulogized the decedent, while stirring in eternal-reward promises. What confused me was the outpouring of grief from the women. If the departed was in a better place, should we not be happy for them? Yet, I seldom noticed any merriment at funerals in our tiny Ozark town. During the funeral of an elderly relative, I asked an aunt why people were crying if our loved one was in Heaven. She replied, "Because he has died, child." Thus, there was both a finality in his death, and simultaneously the gift of eternal life, a disconnect I found perplexing. While my culture bought into the reality of physical death, they made their wager on eternal life, provided one professed a Christian belief. Like my grade-school classmates, I accepted life after death, yet remained perplexed at the morose atmosphere. Only in adult years would I shed the stiff-upper- lip male approach for the cleansing grief expression of women. My spiritual beliefs would also undergo a significant transformation during my 30s.

Unquestionably, death is all around and about us. While writing this book, a global pandemic that has cost millions of lives ravaged the world. In the US, despite more than one million deaths, many people clung to the tragic misbelief that the COVID-19 virus was a hoax. A former president gave wings to this false paradigm, politicizing social distancing, wearing face masks, and disparaging proven medical science. Clearly, the capacity for denial wages strong in the human psyche, sometimes at great cost both to the individual and to society. Then there are the overworked, exhausted medical professionals, doctors, nurses, and others who grapple daily with the effects of the virus, many succumbing to its deadly effects during the process. Medical professionals being derided by politicians and misguided others for dispensing sound medical advice is bad enough. Risking their health and lives treating COVID-infected patients who refused vaccinations represents one of the most tragic, senseless themes of the pandemic. A doctor friend remarked on patients dying of COVID occasionally uttering, "But COVID doesn't exist."

Despite death denial, the existential reality of death endures. That death is always so close is, in my mind, the very reason many take life for granted, kicking the can of death down the road, so to speak. I recall an Ash Wednesday service I attended with several graduate students some 35 years past. The priest smeared ash on our foreheads and uttered the oft-repeated words, "from dust you came and unto dust you shall return." This *memento mori* drama (death reminder) scarcely created a ripple among us. Afterwards, we retreated to a pub where we quaffed beer, laughed, and celebrated life, as young adults would do. At some point, however, I realized we had not mentioned the ancient death ritual we had just participated in. I inquired regarding thoughts on the service, especially the intention to confront our mortality. Faces of confusion, shoulder shrugs, and rolling eyes were the reply. To my friends, participation in the service amounted to checking a cultural box. "It's just what we do," one replied off-handedly. Our gathering then returned to talk of frivolity, future dreams, hopes of completing our dissertations, and landing academic jobs thereafter. "We are young, alive, and hopeful for the future, so let's be happy and celebrate" was the message. Such a death-evasion refrain is decidedly common in a society where many have been raised on the mantra of *you can be anything you want*, itself another fallacy.

I certainly understand the sentiment echoed by my friends and greater society. We become so preoccupied in pursuing our dreams, careers, raising a family, and enjoying life that the reality of death seldom crosses our mind, *until it does*. As a longtime counselor, having witnessed clients struggle with addiction, anxiety, and depression, zest for life so evident in their struggle to overcome adversity, death may well seem an afterthought. Even when addressing suicide, death often seems less real, as many clients echo just wanting to be out of pain without giving thought to death's finality. Later, when the imminent suicide phase passes, most clients have expressed being glad to be alive, even if in pain.

I recall one expressing, "I really didn't consider death as *death*, you know?" Many other otherwise suicidal clients have offered, "I came in because I didn't really want to kill myself." Among people actively entertaining death, death as the end seems unreal. Even with death confronting us at funerals, treating suicidal clients, smeared ashes, or another cultural ritual, our ingrained capacity to look past death persists. Unquestionably, focusing on our lives is helpful in creating happiness, and hope is a strong buffer against suicide (Beck, 1976). As Yalom (2009) and others maintain, facing our own mortality is nevertheless a healthy part of our emotional growth.

Writing About Death

During the previously mentioned death and dying course, we were required to keep a journal on our beliefs regarding mortality. As our professor reviewed the syllabus regarding this assignment, discomfort was evident on many faces throughout the room. After class, another student taking the course pulled me aside. "Doesn't the death journal seem morbid?" he asked, furrowed lines etched across his forehead. I explained it seemed very natural given the course topic, and likely helpful in our future counseling careers. He shook his head in disbelief. For my part, I found the assignment oddly invigorating, and actually looked forward to the process. Twice weekly I wrote several pages regarding my exposure to death, thoughts, fears, hopes, spiritual beliefs, disbeliefs, and in a later entry, how I hoped to die (I maintain a desire to live healthily beyond 100 years). During the final, in lieu of an examination, the professor facilitated an engaging discussion on our experience regarding the course. While the overall sentiment was quite positive, many voiced that the mortality journal as the most difficult assignment. "I had to confront and reflect on my mortality in ways I've been able to avoid previously," one admitted to a room of nodding heads. The professor opined that journaling, due to the in-depth, self-reflective nature, required a more active engagement in a subject than reading, watching a video, or participating in a discussion. This seems especially true when handwriting on paper over keyboarding on a computer (Mueller & Oppenheimer, 2014). My experience was that journaling on death, while certainly uncomfortable at times, was life-invigorating for me as well. In discussions with classmates, my experience in this regard was not unique. I came away from this course on thanatology with a renewed purpose for my life. More than two decades later, reading Yalom's book on death (2009) was a reintroduction, once again, to life affirmation. In other words, understanding life is finite provided meaning and purpose to my life.

Now, my experience in the thanatology course did not match that of many of my classmates, any more than my thoughts on death coincided with my friends at the Ash Wednesday service, or my profoundly meaningful experience journaling on my mortality. People differ in personality, occupations, avocations, and outlook; cultural lenses change perception; and the nature of life experiences (e.g., upbringing, religion or lack thereof, interests, etc.) serves to help create the person we become (along with genetics). My own opinion, however, lies close to that of Yalom, in that confronting and exploring death lessens the existential anxiety and the emotional pain accompanying death. In Yalom's book, recalling counseling a terminally ill client named Susan, she expressed concern for her incarcerated son George. Yalom inquired what will provide meaning, especially given George's inability to fill the role of her son (2009). Her focus, however, continued to be on her son's future. Even with the dimming of our life beacon evident, people remain life-focused. In Susan's case, her focus is a wayward son and the scant time remaining in her own life. Likewise, journaling on my mortality, culminating with envisioning and chronicling my own death, awakened some slumbering life force within. That I continue to reflect on a graduate thanatology course completed over 35 years ago illustrates the influence of active reflection on life and death matters. My recommendation is that all counselors, therapists, medical professionals, clergy, and others engage in a similar process of confronting their mortality in a supportive environment (e.g., therapy, support group, journaling, etc.).

Meaning in Life and the Reality of Death: Paths Differing

Recently, I read Paul Wong's critique of Yalom's *Staring at the Sun: Overcoming the Terror of Death* (Wong, 2009). Having found Yalom's book insightful and instructive, Wong's critique of Yalom's book was also thought provoking. Both Wong and I concur with Yalom regarding the cathartic value of actively engaging with our mortality. All therapists, clergy, and medical professionals would be wise to read Yalom's book, as these professions encounter death. Like Wong, my primary disagreement with Yalom lies with his blanket dismissal of all spiritual and religious beliefs regarding death. He even refers to fear of death as the foundation for all religion (2008). One can almost hear Marx's famous words regarding religion as "the opiate of the people" echoed in most of Yalom's prose. Unquestionably, many do use religion as a narcotic, insulating them from baser realities, much in the way others self-medicate with alcohol or other drugs. However, not all, nor even most, are guilty of such. Furthermore, many people misuse psychotherapy, with some therapists using patients for their own needs.

Now, given my long spiritual and religious history as a member of an organized religion, albeit not walking in lockstep, Yalom and Marx have much to teach religious people regarding healthy skepticism. Too many wars are the tragic result of religious intolerance, or where religion is used to garner war support. There is the clearly extravagant lifestyle of many religious leaders, notably televangelists, siphoning donations from supporters living on fixed incomes. We witness corrupt political leaders manipulating the religious masses, while their own lifestyle runs antithetical to moral and ethical living. Freud considered religious belief to be a neurosis (1995), and Ellis referred to some religious beliefs as irrational (1985). In my 25 years providing counseling, I have had a front row seat to the aftermath of religious extremism, treating adult survivors of physical, sexual, and emotional abuse perpetrated by religious leaders, while evangelical Christians proclaim mental health professionals like myself as "false teachers," with known church leaders maintaining religious faith as being sufficient to heal depression, anxiety, mental illness, etc., and finally, known pastors ordering traumatized women to remain in their abusive marriages. Because I have worked in rural and remote areas of the US and abroad, I have at times taken the brunt of such intolerance and ignorance. Growing up in the rural south, I recall the Bible used as support for racial intolerance, sectarian violence, and even slavery! Without question, religious belief certainly can be intolerant, an opiate, irrational, and a threat to healthy life, something we can observe with pastors actively deriding wearing facemasks, social distancing, and vaccinations, all of which help save lives.

Having scribed the previous paragraph, however, I have worked as a pastoral counselor and along with colleagues provided low-cost and pro bono counseling services for the needy. Religious organizations often provide needed community services such as donating money and time to feed and house the homeless, and some leaders such as Martin Luther King, Jr. win Noble Prizes for peace and justice work. Most religious belief correlates with optimism and meaning in life and clearly helps in grief remittance, addressing anxiety, depression, and combating suicide (Frankl, 1986; Tomer et al., 2008). While there is much disagreement regarding 12-step programs such as Alcoholics Anonymous (AA), a large number of people have achieved and maintained sobriety through involvement in AA, an organization with a spiritual core. Thus, regarding religious faith, how well it works for the individual believer likely is the litmus test in whether such is a *healthy* versus irrational belief. Interestingly, when referring to his client Paula, a cancer survivor, Yalom confesses a desire to requisition a small corner of his natural skepticism for some of Paula's grace. Yalom acknowledges that no one, religious or skeptic, can really know whether or not a supreme being exists (2009). Here Yalom and I stand on the same shaky ground of unknowing. Specifically, no one can really *know* whether God (or another supreme being) or an afterlife exists. Likewise, no one really knows that God or life after death *does not* exist. Regarding addressing existential questions of mortality, religion, or skepticism, William Glasser's iconic question is my guide: How's that (belief/nonbelief) working for you? (Glasser, 1998). We all, counselors, therapists, teachers, etc. would do well to ponder Glasser's question from time to time.

Conclusion: Understand Thyself

E. M. Forester wrote something of how death destroys a man, but the idea of death actually saves him (1910/2002). Yalom follows this strategy throughout his text. His belief that focusing on and exploring death anxiety as a means to lessening our fear of death is the thread running throughout his book. Recently, re-reading Yalom, the philosopher who most comes to mind is Epictetus, who wrote that man is not disturbed by events, but rather his perception of those events are disturbing. Essentially, as we explore death and the dying process, we lose some of our fear and become more conscious of our life. Given their intertwined relationship, both conscious living and dying are the pathways to a more meaningful life. Existential approaches to counseling have as their essence exploration of what brings meaning to life. What brings meaning to one person's life, for example religious faith, may be completely meaningless to an atheist. Conversely, another person's atheism is not the meaningful road for a spiritual person. What is critical for therapists lies in facilitating clients in exploring their personal meaning regarding existential questions of living and dying. Below are a few questions regarding meaning in death and dying for exploration. Some questions are a variation on previous questions, as entertaining the same basic question multiple times may provide more insight.

Reflective Questions Regarding Meaning in Life and Death

1) What brings personal fulfillment and meaning to your life?
2) What would you rate as the most significant lesson you have learned? If you cannot select just one, what are two or three significant life lessons you have learned?
3) How has acknowledging your death brought meaning to your life? Alternatively, how might acknowledging your mortality bring meaning to your life?
4) What is your greatest fear about death?

Journaling on Meaning in Life and Death

I mentioned the requirement in my thanatology course to keep a journal of my thoughts and emotions regarding my own death. You might consider keeping a journal on your mortality. Specifically, consider what brings meaning to your life and how meaning is manifest in your life. Furthermore, scribe on your own mortality, including any relevant thoughts, feelings, hopes, and fears regarding your death. How might death bring meaning to your life? Finally, given the reality of death, what actions might you need to undertake to prepare yourself and loved ones for this eventuality? I suggest keeping the journal for at least 30 days, writing at least twice per week. If possible, keep the journal for two to three months, and then review it. Your last entry could involve entertaining the question, "What lessons has journaling on meaning in life and death taught me?"

Lessons Learned

Summer 1980 was panning out as an otherwise hot, humid, uneventful respite from college. Returning home to save money, my mother found me a job as an orderly at our small-town nursing home. As two male orderlies had just quit, the nursing home was understaffed. Despite the area's chronic unemployment, few seemed interested in this thankless, physically challenging, privacy-invading, and all-too-often depressing job. My oldest brother had briefly worked as an orderly, so I understood the drill. I was to assist residents with basic needs, helping them at the toilet, cleaning them when they soiled themselves, getting them dressed and in their wheelchair or another seat, dispensing medications, assisting at mealtime, and applying restraints. As a young undergraduate, *I didn't know what I didn't know*, as the saying goes. What I did understand was that summer was likely to be long, hot, slow-moving, and unpleasant.

I was prescient in some regards: the summer was the hottest in years, the job physically and emotionally taxing, and my tiny, isolated hometown as uneventful as one would expect in a small, isolated outpost. I worked swing shift five days a week, a schedule that seldom gave me two consecutive days off, occasionally called in to cover a colleague's shift. Perhaps the most difficult part of the job, harder even than cleaning someone having soiled themselves, was watching previously capable people descend into the black hole of dementia. One patient who had been a close friend of my grandmother's, and knew me well, now thought I was her sibling, always referring to me by her brother's name. Another, a woman in her early 90s, would pinch my derriere ("Don't turn your back to her," a shift partner had advised too late), while a few patients in the throes of dementia would swing their canes at me. One smacked my shinbone, raising a hefty bruise. My colleagues were mostly a collection of well-intentioned nurses, nurse's aides, maintenance staff, and cafeteria workers. The staff included my mother, who worked in medical records, and my college roommate's father, the nursing home administrator. Recognizing everybody had a difficult job, with patients possessed of severe cognitive, affective, and physical limitations, I resolved to endure the physical and emotional burden to the best extent my 20 years allowed. Come September, back at college, I could turn the page on this unpleasant occupational interlude. As I would learn, however, life had other plans for me.

I cannot recall the elderly man's name, and he was not a person previously familiar to me. One afternoon, the head nurse requested my assistance in transporting a patient from his room to the covered porch. I shall call this resident *Paul.* Paul was in his late 80s and confined to a wheelchair. Although my memory is sketchy after 40-plus years, I recall him as short in stature, with no discerning physical characteristics other than being elderly and confined to a wheelchair. After lifting and placing him in the chair, I wheeled him to the outside porch, locked the wheels, and turned to leave. "Wait a minute, young fella," he said. "You can spare five minutes with an old man." Figuring the staff could see me through the glass windows, a few minutes chaperoning him seemed acceptable. Expecting my charge would simply fade in silent memories, I was surprised when he posed a thoughtful question. "Young man, what do you want out of life?" "Huh?" I snorted in a most inarticulate manner, unprepared for such a weighty question from this aged man. He continued: "When I was about your age I wanted everything: a wife, family, money, and a good paying job. You look like an ambitious fellow yourself." Nonplussed, I examined this patient in a more studious way. While his body was failing, he was lucid, and his piercing blue eyes suggested having witnessed much in life. He smiled and crossed his arms, clearly awaiting my answer to his question. I replied something vaguely like, "Finish college and get a job." He smiled, nodding his head. "When I was about your age, I had just landed a good-paying job in Kansas City. Got outta my small, dead-end town. After I'd been working at the factory for a few months, an older coworker asked me what I just asked you." He paused as if assessing me. "What did you tell him?" I inquired. "Can't recall exactly, but likely it amounted to about what you said." He smiled again. At that moment, a nurse requested my help, interrupting our unusual dialogue.

As with most shifts, there were too many patient needs to address and few idle moments. Several days passed before I had additional contact with Paul. My second encounter came at bedtime. "Paul's asking for you," my shift partner said, looking bewildered. I helped Paul into bed and he requested I linger a moment. "Thought any more about what you want from life?" I replied no, feeling sheepish. "An old man like me understands the value of free advice," he added. "But see, you don't talk much, but somehow you strike me as someone who wants more outta life than the regular nine to five job." I recall thinking Paul had overrated me, as my life goals were nebulous at that time. "Well, I had my goals, made good money and all. Now here I am," he added, with a tired smile. Realizing he was weary, I turned off the light, tucked him in, then attended to other patients.

Despite my being young, immature, and directionless, Paul had awakened something slumbering within me. I made inquiries about him but unearthed only rudimentary information. He was not from the area and seemed to have no close relatives anyone knew about. He had relocated to the area after retirement. Health failing and living alone, he had moved to the nursing home only recently. "He's likely just an old, lonely man slipping into dementia," one of the nurses counseled me. Paul was old, and likely lonely, but he seemed in command of his faculties, leaving me even more curious about him. Soon thereafter, we spoke again. "Have you read Hemingway's *The Old Man and the Sea*?" he asked. I replied that I had read it several years earlier. "Well, that's one of my favorites. I'm like Santiago, losing what I set out to gain. You understand?" I recalled the story but failed to comprehend his meaning. Evidently noticing my blank look, he advised: "Young man, life's short and it's not about money or a big name. It's about your journey. Be thankful every day." Then, he abruptly turned over for his nap.

Thereafter, my interactions with Paul became more transactional, with mundane conversation centered on medication reactions, diet, and bowel movements. He would smile and shake his head at me occasionally, but his eyes were alive and they met his wrinkled smile. Nearing summer's end, I informed him of my impending return to college. He slowly nodded his head in understanding, or perhaps approval. I voiced having enjoyed our time together. "Have you reread Hemingway's fish story?" he inquired. I said no, but intended to do so. Suddenly an insight occurred to me. "What does the story mean to you?" I inquired. "Life, my life," he replied calmly and succinctly. "You understand Santiago? Well, that's my life. You understand?" I nodded, but my 20-year-old self was simply unable to grasp Paul's message. Perhaps I was too distracted by the vicissitudes that accompany youthful restlessness. I bade him good night and left his room. Monday, I was back at the university, my thoughts consumed with exams, papers, work schedule, social engagements, and pressing occupational and emotional struggles.

Given immediate demands, I quickly closed the book on my nursing home summer, forgetting Paul. It would be decades before some vestigial memory would return him to the forefront of my consciousness. On an international trip somewhere, a local angler was showing us his trophy catch of a huge marlin. Beaming with pride, tourists photographed the fisherman and his catch. Suddenly, cognitive gears shifted in my head and memories of Paul emerged. Upon returning to the US, I belatedly reread *The Old Man and the Sea.* Hemingway's thoughtful statement regarding how a man can be destroyed yet never defeated (Hemingway, 1995) particularly reminded me of Paul. Had Paul seen himself as Hemingway's aged character Santiago, struggling with life weariness, bad luck, with life having slipped past him? Did he view me as a Manolin, a young protégé in need of mentoring? Had I been simply someone who provided him essential human connection, or was I a stark reminder of his long distant and disappeared youthful potential? Did Hemingway's novella represent Paul's finding meaning and transcendence at life's end as his personal and private victory? Paul, while inform and elderly, seemed neither defeated nor destroyed. Rather, he appeared mostly curious at what a young man like me, merely passing a summer earning college money, desired from life. Paul seemed as full of unwavering determination as the literary character Santiago. Possibly, his pride emanated from his never surrendering hope, despite being elderly, physically infirm, and isolated, with death winging closely about.

I do not know the facts regarding how Paul found such power in Hemingway's metaphoric tale of the unconquerable human spirit. I wonder, however, if the answer lies at the end of the story. After sharks have devoured the prized marlin Santiago fought so valiantly and exhaustingly to catch, he apologizes to his nemesis, the marlin. He has ruined them both, he concedes, by sailing beyond what was safe for a prudent angler. When considering his misfortune he decides he has simply ventured out too far for his own good. Like Santiago, Paul had an intense pride and an inner strength that belied his age and circumstances. Paul was not like the maniacal Ahab, blindly chasing after what could only destroy him. Rather, I believe Paul saw himself having ventured beyond safe waters, losing what he sought to gain, yet somehow in that loss, ironically finding the only meaning he could ever keep. I believe this was the lesson he was attempted to teach me, but either his rudimentary instruction, my immaturity, or that gulf spanning nearly 70 years between us, was too great to bridge. Despite his cameo appearance in my life, over 40 years later he remains visible in my mind's eye. I can envision my future self in three decades, life light fading, weary, still grappling with that great existential mystery regarding the meaning of my life, defeated perhaps, yet not destroyed.

Chapter 5

Wisdom vs. Mammon

Healing the Divided Life

When I wrote the draft for this book, my spouse reviewed it and exclaimed that mammon seemed an archaic term, one likely misunderstood due to its religious etymology. Her concern may well prove correct, yet the term seems perfectly fitting to me. Mammon generally is a biblical term describing the debasing influence of material wealth. In his Sermon on the Mount, Jesus famously opines, "No man can serve two masters . . . You can't serve both God and mammon" (Matthew 6:24). One needs no religious inclination to recognize mammon as another term for greed. This ancient term likely originates from the Hebrew or Aramaic language. Mammon appears in the *Dead Sea Scrolls* and the *Talmud*, so we are going back some 3,000 years. This epoch of time illustrates materialism's long, problematic history.

The other misunderstood word my spouse troubled over was wisdom. Wisdom also heralds back to many spiritual traditions: Judaic (e.g., the Wisdom of Solomon), Christian (the Gospels), Islam (corresponds to the name of God), Buddhism (knowledge achieved experientially), and likely is a thread through all spiritual traditions. Defining the term is far more complex than the opposite (mammon), however, and potentially more nebulous. Having spent a lifetime grappling with inchoate terms, I shall continue occasionally employing them, given they convey a long history of strife and struggle. Now, of necessity, let us attempt a definition of wisdom.

Perusing the vast space of the internet, numerous definitions for wisdom emerged. Most relate to judgment, insight, knowledge, attitude, teachings, discernment, sagacity, sapience, etc. Molecular biologist, mindfulness instructor, and author John Kabit-Zinn includes wisdom in his definition of mindfulness, describing mindfulness as awareness arising through paying attention, on purpose, in the present moment, non-judgmentally, and with self-understanding and wisdom (Kabit-Zinn, 2017). Faced with a legion of definitions, numerous variations, some at odds with one another, I defaulted to my usual practice of Occam's razor. That is, the simplest definition is likely the most accurate. The *Cambridge Dictionary* defines wisdom as the ability to use your knowledge and experience to make good decisions and judgments (Anonymous, n.d.). Given

DOI: 10.4324/9781003168324-5

that making good decisions, and even more so acting upon them, can be challenging, the *Cambridge Dictionary*'s definition seemed appealing.

Now that the messy aspect of defining wisdom and mammon are over, we move on to the more significant part of the title: namely, bridging the chasm between these competing forces. First is wisdom being the ability to use one's knowledge to make good decisions and judgments. For those of us in the therapeutic community, self-reflection is an essential component of therapeutic success for both therapist and client. Success will involve reflecting back on our experience and asking ourselves critical questions like, "What went well? What went poorly? How does this knowledge help me with this client, issues, situation, conflict, etc.?" Self-reflection is a necessary step in decision-making and thus an unnamed component in applying wisdom to our judgments. Given my current age at the time of writing (61), having taught for over 30 years, counseled people for 25 years, and led numerous professional trainings and retreats for 35 years, I have learned the great value of self-reflection. Looking back on my formative education, however, self-reflection was seldom part of my training. Socialized from junior high onwards to take copious notes when the teacher, professor, and trainer were speaking, I filled reams of notebooks (when we actually wrote with pens!). In preparation for examinations, I read and re-read my notes, utilizing rote memory for recall. In my haste, I seldom thought to analyze this time-intensive process until graduate school. Moreover, rarely did any professor suggest a variation on the process. I wrote mindlessly and regurgitated said knowledge on exams—that is, until confronted with a different approach.

During some counseling course in graduate school, I have forgotten which, the professor asked us to cease note-taking one afternoon. He posed the question, how often do you actually consider what you are writing? I recall feeling confused. My entire educational experience consisted of taking notes and then reviewing them in preparation for exams. My memory is foggy, but the professor's words went something like this: "We seek guidance everywhere except from within ourselves. Listen carefully to your instructors, but also ask, 'What do I think, feel, and believe?'" As a professor and international trainer, it often seems my students and trainees seek particular answers. This is natural, given trainings on significant mental health concerns such as PTSD, depression, anxiety, suicidality, and so forth. The reality is a reservoir of knowledge and experience to draw from; the more significant work likely is getting our audience to engage the material on a more intimate level—meaning, heeding our own inner voice of wisdom. Challenging our inner critic as well as that of the trainer can be very important. In CBT, we ask, "What's the evidence for that belief/thought?" This discernment process is a function of wisdom. In fact, one wisdom definition used the very term *discernment*. I will illustrate this discernment process in the next paragraph.

During my master's program, one of our internship instructors was a doctoral student from California. She had spent some 25 years as a child and adolescent therapist working with Child Protection Services and other agencies. I will refer to her as Sally. Sally had a natural gift for educating students and helping them develop clinically. She provided constructive criticism in a manner both educationally sound and palatable. During one grand rounds discussion, a student inquired about how to proceed with a client when we felt stuck. Sally began with the obvious answers of listen well, stay within your scope of competence, seek out your supervisor after the session, and so forth. She then paused and became more philosophical. "Each of you are developing an inner counselor. That inner counselor is a combination of education, training, and experience, but also personal insight. Heed that inner counselor." Sally was suggesting that our most significant asset as a counselor was within ourselves, and not something external. Make no mistake, Sally emphasized good training, coaching, and supervising, all critical in the development of any therapist. However, she was advising us to tune in to that inner guide within ourselves, and not to ignore or discount it.

Of the scores of my undergraduate and graduate courses and many professional trainings covering nearly 40 years, Sally's counsel has been the most sage in my career. Heed your inner counselor and give voice to what s/he is saying to you. Now, this has relevance for therapists, in that clients will face existential issues requiring unpacking the minutiae of their lives and leveraging acquired knowledge with decision-making. Sally's advice recalls for me a former client. I shall call this former client Grace. Grace was a young college student enrolled as a pre-med major. She was bright, hardworking, likable, and poised for a bright future. Grace, however, was grappling with her self-confidence. Despite being an A student and a recognized leader among her peers, she confessed being plagued by self-doubt. She stated that others' expectations of her—parents, coaches, professors, and peers—was creating unbearable pressure, so much so that she had begun thinking of suicide. Such dire thoughts frightened her and were her impetus to seek counseling services. Achieving considerable progress in therapy, she joked it was her goal-oriented nature. During an early session, she mentioned occasionally keeping a journal and finding that helpful. I encouraged her to journal about her experience in self-understanding, explaining everyone else had expectations for her, but what were hers? She admitted she had scarcely considered setting her own, being so focused on those others had set.

Naturally, she jumped into the assignment with aplomb, practically filling a notebook in one week. The following session we discussed her journal. I began with a direct question. "So, what has this journaling experience taught you?" This gifted young woman sat back in thought momentarily. "I suppose that I have spent so much time trying to meet others' expectations for me that I scarcely considered my own. What's my purpose? I have filled a notebook but don't know." Her insight became the driving force in our session. By session's end, she decided pursuing her own sense of meaning and purpose was her primary goal, not just being an A student, varsity athlete, or future physician. Her following journaling focused on living an authentic life. She this authenticity required living purposefully. Naturally, being a physician certainly could be a very purposeful life, yet purposeful living was not exclusive to medicine. Opening her Pandora's Box, for the first time she questioned why she wanted to become a doctor, realizing she had never before considered the matter. Her facility in math and science, high SAT test scores, family and teacher encouragement, and social prestige had been the driving forces in pursuing a medical career. "Everyone else seems to have plotted my career except me," she added.

Before graduation, Grace informed me of her acceptance to medical school. However, she had chosen to defer matriculation for a year to further consider the matter. She acknowledged her parents and professors were concerned she might change her mind and, more difficult for her, her parents were disappointed. "I do not like disappointing my parents, as they have invested so much in me (she was an only child). Ultimately however, it's my life." She graduated and we lost touch. What remained, however, was this very intelligent, likable, athletic natural leader had always put others' plans before her own. Finally, her inner voice screamed so loudly she could no longer ignore it. I am reminded of Parker Palmer writing that we listen for guidance everywhere except from within our own self (2000). Grace had learned the lesson Sally had taught my classmates and me earlier: Heed others' counsel, research matters carefully, but attend to your inner guide as well.

The Divided Life

Several years ago, having just returned from a busy six months as a visiting scholar and volunteer worker in remote Australia, I collapsed on the sofa for an afternoon of binge TV. I selected a documentary titled *Minimalism: A Documentary about the Important Things* (2016). The film focuses primarily on the lives of two 30-something-year-old friends, Josh and Ryan. They grew up together in Ohio, going separate ways after graduating from high school. After college, Josh became a highly successful sales representative, regularly working 70-hour weeks. Then, in one month, his mother died and his marriage ended. Suddenly he was confronted with an existential crisis a high salary and nice home could not solve. He makes a statement something like riding in the passenger seat of his life for too long (D'Avella, 2015). He reconnects with Ryan, who had become disillusioned with corporate life and quit his job. After a period of discussion regarding what is essential in life, they author and self-publish *Minimalism: Live a Meaningful Life* (2011). They jettison their contemporary lives with few possessions, start a blog, and later a vlog (video blog) about the philosophy of minimalism. Eschewing personal wealth, they focus on relationships, health, self-growth, and contributing to the good of society. Now, they do emphasize using frugality to meet basic needs.

During the process, they hit upon the idea of a national speaking tour promoting minimalism. They shrewdly focus on bookstores, as they can promote their book and philosophy. On an early stop, less than a handful of people show up. Undaunted, Josh and Ryan give the tiny gathering their full attention. In time, after radio and internet interviews, they slowly build a following. Late in the documentary, they are speaking to overflow crowds, with ages ranging from millennials to the elderly. The film includes interviews with scholars, a media correspondent, and several others. Director Matt D'Avella, whose previous directorial experience was in filming weddings and Bar Mitzvahs, mortgages everything he owns and films on a very lean budget. After initially rejecting it, Netflix places the documentary on their site. Over time, millions have viewed the film, promoting the message of essentialism to critical acclaim. Josh and Ryan then commence a vlog titled *The Minimalists*, where they espouse their essentialist philosophy of simply living.

Most noteworthy about Josh and Ryan's story was that they described living a divided life. Raised on the classic American dream of hard work equaling personal and financial success, Josh speaks of enthusiastically embracing this myth to the exclusion of any personal life outside work. He reported earning a high six-figure salary, but ironically sinking deeper into debt. Only when his mother dies of cancer and his marriage abruptly ends does he question the high cost of his corporate values. Reconnecting with Ryan, both admit losing their faith in a competitive, materialistic system that holds little regard for a life of healthy balance. In so many words, both admit to having lived a divided life. The divided life is that chasm between the life we are living and the one we wish to live. No doubt, a high corporate salary with competitive bonuses held alluring rewards for Josh, but it was destroying his life. Watching the film, I could not help but be reminded of the competition between Meaning vs. Mammon (for many, God vs. Mammon). Josh and Ryan went on to experience much success amid many hardships on their journey from corporate materialism to becoming essentialists (now their preferred term).

I must add that not all holding vast sums of wealth are evil, greedy, callous people. I suspect most wealthy persons are not. There is little question, however, that corporate success requires long hours and an opportunistic mindset, often at the cost of others' misfortune. Working 70+ hours, six to seven days a week, carries a high cost on relationships, physical, and emotional health. Still, I have met wealthy people who have good family and friend relations. One family member founded a business in his garage, growing it into a multimillion-dollar business over seven decades. I shall call him Sam. Sam worked long hours seven days a week, spending little time with his wife and two children. I inquired how he was able to keep up his strenuous pace for so many decades (he was in his mid-80s then). He attributed his productivity to genetics (his mother died at 99), his daily walks, and the sense of purpose from building and growing a company. When I inquired further regarding the meaning part, he explained that working for others seemed like drudgery. When he created something of his own, however, making sacrifices was much easier, as he had a clear purpose: namely, to create success, provide for his family, and help society. On becoming wealthy, he supported worthy causes like the arts and college scholarships, donating millions of dollars. All the while, he lived in a small, simple home, owning one car.

Years later, when I knew Sam better and we had a more established relationship, I inquired how his wife and children viewed those years when he logged long hours establishing his business. He admitted his family did not get much of his quality time. He emphasized that providing them a nice home in a safe neighborhood with quality schools, and later paying for college, was his focus. He deferred most family responsibilities to his wife; his spouse and children viewed the situation differently than he did. Over time, Sam worked to build a stronger relationship with his children and grandchildren, with general success. Interestingly, Sam lived a life of simplicity. His ranch-style house was comfortable, though small and located in a decidedly middle-class neighborhood, nary a McMansion in sight. He wore old clothes purchased on sale, and drove an American-made sedan more than a decade old. His prize possessions—other than his company—were subscriptions to various thought-provoking periodicals (e.g., *Scientific American, The Economist, The New York Times*, etc.).

There is little question, however, that *volunteer* simplicity differs greatly from inherited poverty. Growing up poor in an inner-city ghetto provides few real choices other than the quest for survival. Sam, raised in a ghetto, become wealthy as an adult. Volunteer simplicity is, ironically, a luxury many in this world simply cannot afford. Sam did retain strong social justice values, donating generously to worthy causes dear to his core values, namely that of education and racial justice. Of course, Sam *chose* simple living, and having such choice is liberating. I would assert, however, that Sam, unlike minimalists Josh and Ryan, was not living the same type of divided life between wisdom vs. mammon. For Josh especially, he freely confesses to a former life of materialism prior to his awakening. Sam, although quite rich, was *never* a materialist. Yes, Sam became uber-wealthy, but lived simply, using his earnings for worthy causes. Sam thus had a strong sense of meaning and purpose, and despite affluence, and through conscious, simple living, managed to refrain from tasting the shiny apple of mammon.

The Client Who Sought Wisdom

While working in a university counseling center, a young undergraduate came to my office, having scribbled *seeking wisdom* as his reason for seeking counseling. I pondered his novel answer, then commenced the intake interview. His scores on the Beck Depression Inventory-II, drug use screener, and interview suggested no presence of a mental disorder. His academic grade point average (GPA) was very robust, as he was an honor student. Given that he appeared well adjusted, and being the first client seeking wisdom, such became our starting point. I shall call this former client Sean.

He explained his minor was philosophy and he was studying major philosophers such as Plato, Socrates, Kierkegaard, and others. He mentioned growing up in a nominal Protestant family. Having become dissatisfied with organized religion, he had selected philosophy as his minor due to disinterest in anything else. Describing his family as affluent, he found the business world and pursuit of money unappealing. He described struggling with his sense of purpose for some period and had been considering counseling. Recently, he had attended a panel discussion where I had been one of the speakers. Evidently, something I mentioned regarding meaning in life resonated with him. I asked, "So what does seeking wisdom mean for you?" He paused and then replied something like, "Well, I don't really know. I just know my life seems empty and devoid of meaning."

Likely every client I have counseled, regardless of age, has in some manner said, "My life is less meaningful." I recall grade school children, despondent over their parents' divorce or death of a grandparent, essentially conveying as much. Elderly clients have remarked with post retirement and the death of a spouse their life is over. Vast numbers between ages 25–55, addicts, ex-convicts, those with mental disorders, unemployed, suicidal, and so forth had commonly voiced a loss of meaning and purpose. Sean, then, resided in an existential vacuum with plenty of company. I inquired whether there had been a time when he felt life was meaningful. Shaking his head, he outlined a lonely childhood with little in common with his siblings. He reported his parents, both successful professionals, had little time for him. Playing high school soccer had been his primary outlet, and while he played on an intramural team, he no longer enjoyed it as he previously did. He went on to express finding my comments on meaning in life during the panel interesting. His comments provided a roadmap for the session.

I inquired, "What do you find appealing about meaning in life?" He then explained that his parents, decent people, honest, non-abusive, essentially kind-hearted types, seemed to have a primary fixation on acquiring wealth. He reported their entire focus was on materialism, something he found emotionally shallow and unfulfilling. I asked, "How is meaning present in your life?" To which he answered, "It isn't." I had learned that when I am unsure of what to say, I remain silent. Remaining silent, clients tend to fill that vacuum. Sean added, "I hope searching for wisdom will be meaningful in itself." "What might your life look like if you were to find it meaningful?" I asked. He replied, "I would be happier and feel more a sense of purpose." At session's end, I gave the homework assignment of journaling on meaning and wisdom. Instead of giving focus questions related to the topic, I suggested he journal four to five times a week on topics of meaning in life, life purpose, and wisdom. I encouraged him to feel completely unconstrained regarding length, as perhaps two sentences might prove as fulfilling as a page. We made a follow-up appointment for next week.

The following session, he brought his journal, desiring to share a couple of entries. He had been faithful in daily journaling. His most insightful passage revealed having never considered what constituted a meaningful life. Instead, he had focused on what was *not* meaningful in his life. He made some statement regarding "gazing through the wrong end of a telescope." Inquiring, "If you were living a meaningful life, what might you be doing?" He smiled and replied, "Probably just what I'm doing now. Exploring meaning through counseling, journaling, and speaking with friends." We then unpacked his statement. He had checked out Viktor Frankl's, *Man's Search for Meaning* from the university library. His roommate had noticed him reading the book, and commenced a long conversation over the topic of meaning. He disclosed coming to counseling and the journal he was writing on meaning. What he and his friend decided, after a discussion peppered with occasional disagreement, was the very discussion on meaning had been very meaningful. He speculated a meaningful life was possibly composed of meaningful activities that filled the soul. Sean completed therapy soon thereafter and created a small weekly discussion group focused encountering meaning in life. He contacted me prior to graduation, expressing our focus on meaning in life had paid good dividends. He planned to take a gap year traveling and working odd jobs, possibly joining the Peace Corps thereafter.

Ikigai: Living Through Purposeful Activity

In their rich tapestry of a book, *Ikigai: The Japanese Secret to a Long and Happy Life*, authors Hector Garcia and Francesc Miralles discuss the Japanese concept of ikigai (2016). Ikigai translates roughly as the happiness of being busy (Garcia & Miralles, 2016). The authors clarify happiness is not simply being busy at something, but rather finding a way to make work purposeful. They further illustrate this ability to reframe work to a higher purpose (e.g., providing for family, assisting colleagues, an ethical focus, etc.) as being the difference between a job and ikigai. The authors mention that on the island of Okinawa, there are 24 people over the age of 100 for every 100,000 inhabitants, a ratio far exceeding the global average (Garcia & Miralles, 2016).

Living a longer life is not entirely a function of ikigai. Significant influences include genetics, diet, exercise, social support, and good medical care, to cite a few important variables. Perhaps the more important part of longevity is living longer while healthy and having a life of purpose. The philosophy of ikigai incorporates an attitude of contemplation and living in harmony with nature, unlike the western mindset emphasizing a mastery over nature and the environment. According to many Japanese people, everyone has ikigai, roughly, what Frankl termed a sense of meaning (1986). This personal ikigai lies within everyone, awaiting liberation. Thus, ikigai is an intrinsic property, nothing occupation, social status, money and possessions—all externals—can provide. Many people, perhaps most, are still searching for their ikigai, or continue the illusion that meaning emanates from accumulating material possessions. We need not look far to view the result of this *hungry ghosting* or living through our desire, grasping at what we do not have. Our ikigai is embedded somewhere deep within, and discovery requires a patient search, much like my former client Sean. Garcia and Miralles (2016) emphasize that Okinawans believe ikigai is the reason for rising from bed each morning.

Having provided counseling to children, the elderly, university students and those unschooled, wealthy clients to the indigent, those in the US and abroad, hundreds of depressed, often bored and purposeless clients explained struggling to rise from bed. All exclaimed in some fashion that they "had no reason to rise from bed." Ikigai, then, is akin to Frankl's meaning in life theory. That is, the person with a reason to rise from bed is in touch with their personal ikigai. Nowhere in my extensive readings of Frankl have I encountered the term ikigai, but if he were alive today, Frankl would make this connection. Although ikigai is a Japanese concept, the notion of meaningful, purpose-filled life likely transcends all cultures. The critical question becomes, how does one get in touch with their ikigai? (Alternatively, meaning, purpose, etc.)

While my former client Sean could encounter meaning in therapy, in discussion with friends, and journaling about it, meaning (ikigai) was always within himself. No doubt, Sean's process involved self-reflection and a social connection with others, activities promoting the encounter with ikigai. Frankl asserts that meaning kept many of his fellow inmates alive, and occasionally led them to sacrifice their own life to save another's. Frankl also seems to believe encountering meaning is the liberation of an existing capacity within the individual. This inner meaning (ikigai) may be liberated thorough study, personal reflection, journaling, or engagement with others. Garcia and Miralles mention the term moai, or close bonds within a community. The moai evidently had its origins during difficult times, when farmers would meet to support each other during a poor harvest. Members of a moai make assisting the needy a priority through financial assistance, social support, donating food, or any number of additional ways (Garcia & Miralles, 2016). Likewise, Frankl recounts inmates sharing their own meager food rations with a needier person. In my own spiritual tradition, the fishes and loaves story in the New Testament serves as another example of moai, the catalyst for people to come together in collectivist groups to assist others. While Sean found journaling quite meaningful, the rich discussions with others were the tipping point of encountering meaning. When he created a discussion group focused on meaning, he discovered a greater purpose to his life. No question, then, social engagement strengthens meaning, ikigai, moai, etc.

Other methods for encountering ikigai occur through doing good works, either individually or collectively. There are any number of good works to undertake, either a single act (e.g., changing a flat tire for someone), volunteering as a tutor or in a soup kitchen, teaching a child to read, etc. Very likely, as with Sean and the people Garcia and Miralles chronicle, uncovering ikigai will also involve self-reflection. Honest self-reflection likely leads to living a life more in harmony with nature. For example, I have been following the small house movement. People from millennials to the elderly are choosing to live in small and sometimes tiny houses due to financial exigency or environmental sustainability. Bryce Langston, a New Zealand resident, has a YouTube show titled *Living Big in A Tiny House* (www.livingbig inatinyhouse.com). A former actor, Langston travels throughout the world interviewing people living in small homes, posting videos on his YouTube channel. In every interview, in addition to affordability, residents articulate a desire to live simply and sustainably. A number voice that simple, sustainable living has increased their sense of meaning and purpose. There appears to be a connection to meaning or ikigai, and simplicity, environmental harmony, and social connection. Interestingly, many small house communities are cropping up in the US, New Zealand, Australia, Japan, etc. and appear to be increasing in popularity.

No doubt, there are endless methods people of all cultures utilize to discover the meaning embedded within their mind and soul. The important measure for many is that the search process couples with some type of human contact. In ikigai, self-reflection plus helping others is the human arithmetic to solving the existential vacuum. In my life travels, I have met people who have encountered meaning and purpose through work, volunteering, meditation, yoga, gardening, and many other activities. Discovering one's own personal ikigai is a critical task for seeking to live a purposeful, fulfilling life. As one 95-year-old woman remarked to me, "The key to living a meaningful life is living a life of meaning."

Questions for Consideration

This book represents both a narrative regarding creating a meaningful life, and a resource for therapists, teachers, medical professionals, parents, and anyone else. The following questions may assist readers in exploring their own ikigai/ inner meaning. While the questions may not provide readers inherent meaning, they may facilitate a search for meaning. I suggest readers consider writing down responses to the following questions. Retake the test(s) in a week or so to evaluate changes in your score(s). Naturally, positive changes are desirable, although some fluctuation of scores in either direction will occur. Your scores may also decline due to life circumstances like grief, job loss or dissatisfaction, divorce, etc. I retake some of these assessments once or twice a year as an existential check-up.

1) What types of activities seem to bring meaning and fulfilment for you?
2) What is the most important lesson you have learned in your life? Why has that lesson been so important? How has learning that lesson changed you?
3) If you were to write a short story with yourself as the protagonist, what would you write?
4) Was there a time when your life seemed more meaningful? If so, what was different about that time?

5) What accomplishment are you most proud of? What did this success teach you?
6) What has been your biggest disappointment? What has this disappointment taught you?
7) What brings you joy? What lessons has joy taught you?
8) What leaves you feeling sad? What lessons has sadness taught you?
9) Has there been a pivotal moment in your life that transformed you in some manner?
10) If you could give your younger self advice, what would that advice consist of?
11) If you could speak with your future self, what might you say?
12) If someone were to ask, "How can I live a meaningful life?" what advice might you provide?

Naturally, answers depend upon many factors such as age, life experiences, occupational and financial situation, overall health, home security, present circumstances, and much more. My experience, personally and as counselor, is that exploring such important, reflective questions is inherently meaningful in itself, regardless of the answers. I would encourage readers to perhaps engage with these questions and, if you enjoy it, journal on these questions and your subsequent answers. Then, share and discuss these questions with someone you trust, as Frankl postulated that meaning was both an intrinsic quality and acquired or enhanced in meaningful contact with others (Frankl, 1986). A further caution is that we should refrain from judgment towards others whose worldview is in contrast with ours. A good part of living a meaningful, purposeful life requires respecting contrasting viewpoints.

Additional Resources for Consideration and Reflection

Clearly, I am interested in self-assessment. Assessment has provided both my clients and myself a format for self-exploration. When considering important topics such as meaning and purpose in life, assessments operationalize these sometime amorphous terms. Standardized assessments can also help us measure our sense of meaning in life. Meaning and purpose are constructs correlated with life satisfaction and inversely correlated to depression. I recommend the following fair-use assessments for further exploration and discussion. The assessments below assess your present state of mind. I find them useful as a pre- and post-test measure in counseling, training, and consultation encounters.

First is the *Meaning in Life Questionnaire* (MLQ), by Michael F. Steger (2010; http://michaelfsteger.com). The *MLQ* is a ten-item questionnaire, with five items focusing on the *presence of meaning* and five items focusing on the *search for meaning*. The MLQ will provide a scale to score these two subscales.

Next is the *Purpose in Life Test* (PIL), by Crumbaugh, J. C. & Maholick, L. T. (1964). The PIL is a 20-item self-report attitudinal scale designed to measure the extent a respondent perceives a general sense of meaning and purpose, or inversely, suffers from Frankl's existential vacuum. It consists of 11 items focusing on the respondent's mood, three items addressing life goals, and three items addressing the meaning of life itself. https://link.springer.com/referenceworkentry/10.1007%2F978-94-007-0753-5_2336

Next is the *Subjective Happiness Scale (SHS)* by Lyubomirsky, S. & Lepper, H. S. (1999) (http://sonjalyubomirsky.com/subjective-happiness-scale-shs/). The SHS is a four-item scale of global subjective happiness. Two items ask respondents to characterize themselves using both absolute ratings and ratings relative to peers; the remaining two items offer brief descriptions of happy and unhappy individuals, asking respondents the extent to which each characterization describes them.

Finally, I suggest the *Toronto Mindfulness Scale* (TMS) by Lau, M.A., Bishop, S.R., Buis, T., Anderson, N.D., Carlson, L., & Devins, G. (2006). The *TMS* consists of a 13-item Likert scale consisting of two subset scores: (1) Curiosity score, and (2) decentering score. Once again, the TMS is a thoughtful measure of a thoughtful term (mindfulness) that is often misunderstood. (www.ocf.berkeley.edu/~jfkihlstrom/ConsciousnessWeb/Meditation/TMS.htm)

Lessons Learned

Australia's Northern Territory is a large, remote region twice the size of Texas, yet populated by just over 250,000 people. Remote school counsellors, like my colleague Cheryl, cover as many as eight schools, some being so remote that flying out is required. Two extended summer service projects, one with the Katherine Remote Group Schools in 2013, and another with the Catholic Education Office in Darwin in 2018, have sent me scrambling all across the far reaches of this remote, wild, mesmerizing land.

Australia's Indigenous people have historical roots going back at least 40,000 years, with some estimates putting the figure closer to 70,000 years (Blakemore, 2019). You can view remnants of their ancestry ("Our Mob," as Indigenous people refer to it) in over 5,000 rock art paintings across northern Australia. These amazingly resilient people have survived their land being forcibly taken, their people being slaughtered, forcible relocation, being denied citizen rights until recently, and the further indignity of the *Terra Nullius* decree, which proclaimed that prior to Europeans arriving, the land was unpopulated!

I have witnessed much pain in remote Australia, while at the same time met very resilient, talented elders, teachers, and artists. Unfortunately, bad news generates sensational headlines, and there is much bad news: various studies report Indigenous Australians are 12 times more likely to be incarcerated than white Australians, their life expectancy is ten years shorter than white Australians, the rate of Indigenous children in out-of-home care is exponentially greater than other Australians, Indigenous youth are at significantly greater risk of dropping out of school than other Australians, and Indigenous Australians have one of the world's highest suicide rates.

This somber news represents the backdrop of a distant, sparsely populated, antipodean land of great contrasts. The Northern Territory has remarkable, unusual beauty, with rock mesas that glow and change colors from sunrise to sundown. There is the unusual wildlife, most native only to Australia: kangaroos and other marsupials; the echidna, an egg-laying mammal; over 400 species of birds, including parrots, galas, and wedge-tail eagles; several of the world's most venomous snakes; and the salt water or estuarine crocodile, the world's largest and most aggressive reptile. Having traveled the world over, including to Antarctica, no place has seemed as exotic as the Australian Outback.

In 2018, I returned to remote Australia to provide training, consultation, and occasional counselling in remote Indigenous schools. In 2013, I spent two months working with Cheryl, a remote school counsellor and psychologist based in the Katherine area. We visited ten schools where separately and conjointly we gave trainings on traumatized youth, self-care and destressing, suicide prevention, addressing behavioral disorders, and other related issues. Then, while a visiting professor at the University of Canberra in 2016, I spent my spring break providing, training, professional coaching, and doing the occasional co-therapy at a very remote Indigenous school in Arnhem Land.

With excitement and trepidation, I deplaned at Darwin International Airport, totally spent after a 35-hour journey that originated in Buffalo, New York. It was thankfully Sunday, providing a recovery day. On Monday I jumped into meetings with teachers, well-being staff, remote school principals, and administrators. On Tuesday, I flew to the Tiwi Islands on a tiny plane, where the lone pilot provided flight safety procedures (oxygen mask, seat belt, flotation device, etc.) prior to the 20-minute flight to Bathurst Island, just across the Timor Sea. My colleague, a psychologist serving at the school on Bathurst Island, added with a wry smile, "Don't worry about your flotation device, the crocs will eat us if we go down," in that all-too-casual manner Aussies employ when referencing mortality.

We landed around noon, and after lunch at the middle school cafeteria, we delivered three one-hour presentations. Boots on the ground and immediately commencing work had been the norm in my previous NT sojourns, and 2018 was no different. I preferred this approach, as it helped me adapt quicker. After my last presentation, two teachers waited to speak with me regarding student behavioral issues, and thereafter, exhausted, I returned to my room for rest. I would spent two very full days training, visiting classes and doing mindfulness meditation, yoga, and talking about the US. On Friday, I flew back to Darwin, and the following Monday the busy cycle resumed.

The second week was one of my most fulfilling. I accompanied Cheryl to Daly River, where I would provide my usual trainings on self-care, suicide prevention, working with traumatized children and such, visit classes where I would teach meditation and yoga, and meet with teachers. At day's end, Cheryl approached me with good news. Miriam-Rose Ungunmerr-Baumann, an Indigenous teacher, principal, and artist, said she would be pleased to visit with us after my morning training the following day. The next day, after a mindfulness training with grade school and middle school children (e.g., meditation, healthy self-talk, and yoga) we walked over to visit Ms. Baumann at her home just off the campus.

Miriam-Rose (how she introduced herself) was born in Daly River, raised by an aunt and uncle, attending the very school where she would become teacher and principal. A member of the Ngangikurungkurr people, she speaks four languages. She was one of the first Indigenous school principals in Australia. She is a recipient of the Order of Australia, and Senior Australian of the Year in 2021, among others. During her retirement, she has promoted what she calls Dadirri (pronounced "da-da") to her people and others across Australia. Dadirri means deep inner listening and quiet, still awareness. I was most curious to speak with her regarding dadirri and its similarity to counseling.

Renowned also for her paintings, as we approached her home, she sat on her veranda, painting with meticulous brush strokes, face serene as a monk. After Cheryl made introductions, we commenced our visit. She spoke of her people, their connection to the land, her family, and finally her years as teacher and principal. She smiled remarking, "I expect a whitefella like yourself didn't come all the way from New York to hear me speak of the past. You want to talk about dadirri." I replied being pleased to talk of anything with her, but I had a particular interest in deep listening. She explained the philosophy of dadirri, that it weaves her people's culture, dreaming (origins), and spirituality together. She described dadirri as that wellspring inside us. Curious, I inquired how one might encounter dadirri. She replied one needed the correct attitude. That is, you must be still and remain in silent awareness when the wind passes through the trees, or while sitting on a riverbank, or simply being present to someone in grief.

Further intrigued, I mentioned her approach was somewhat akin to that of psychologist Carl Rogers. Miriam-Rose nodded in agreement, being familiar with Rogers' work. She did express dadirri being somewhat distinct from humanistic psychology, as dadirri remained grounded in the collective spirituality of her people, not in a particular therapeutic approach. She regularly provides dadirri trainings across Australia to young children, university students, and leaders in business and industry. I explained my brief foray into monasticism, which led me into meditation some 30 years ago. She acknowledged dadirri was very much a mindfulness, present-oriented approach, similar to meditation.

She inquired what I thought of her people, meaning the children in the school. I explained my experience the past two days working with the children and that the trainings I delivered to the teachers and staff being very fulfilling. I was particularly impressed the children were well versed in meditation. She chuckled, adding she "guessed so," given her extensive work in teaching dadirri. She pressed me further: "But what do you really think about my people?" she repeated, studying me carefully. I paused, thinking of the depressing statistics regarding Indigenous incarceration, suicide rates, sexual offenses and domestic abuse rates, and the decade-shorter life expectation. Fortunately, I recalled the scores of resilient youth, teachers, community leaders, and elders who had warmly welcomed me into their community all across the Northern Territory. I recalled a meditation while sitting at the base of Uluru, that iconic monolith and deeply sacred site. I explained having seen much beauty and pain, resilience and resignation, but also that there being something ineffable about her people and the NT itself. She nodded her head in understanding and replied something like, "No need to struggle too much with words, sometimes it's enough just to be aware of what you are experiencing. That's dadirri." She paused again before continuing. "I have seen much in my years. Enough pain for several lifetimes. Too many of my people on the drink, forsaking our culture, our sacred ways, hurting one another, dying from the inside out. Dadirri is a way of healing that pain and catching that wisdom within." I could think of nothing to say in reply, but thought back to Sally, my graduate school supervisor who spoke of the inner counselor; Sean, my former client who sought wisdom; and all *seekers* I had encountered in my travels throughout the globe.

After an hour, with Cheryl and me facing a three-hour drive to attend a meeting in Darwin, we regretfully said our goodbyes. I expressed the desire to attend one of her dadirri workshops. She said I would be most welcome anytime. On the three-hour drive back to Darwin, back roads wound serpentine through remarkably remote, exotic, wildly beautiful country. At some point Cheryl inquired about my experience at Daly River. I described a most positive experience with the school staff and children, but that visiting with Miriam-Rose was the highlight. While we had just over an hour's meeting, her words and very presence left a profound impact on me. One of the last things she said lingers still: "Careful now, when that red dirt gets into your skin there's no way of getting it out." She was prescient, as that NT red dirt definitely remains in my skin and I have no desire to cleanse it.

I have learned many lessons during my overseas projects. I have witnessed the aftermath of colonization, destruction of traditional ways, lands forcibly taken from Indigenous people, loss of cultural pride, judgment from a callous society, the alluring anesthetic of alcohol and drugs, a sense of rootlessness, depression, domestic violence, cultural and geographic alienation, and ultimately, an early death, often from suicide, fills this cultural void. Fortunately, I have witnessed talented artists, exceptional teachers and elders maintaining cultural traditions, artists, dancers, and storytellers, to cite a few. I have seen

the resilience of a battered people, ignored and slighted, who simply refuse to wither and die. Perhaps as Miriam-Rose Ungunmerr-Baumann has, they have discovered their dadirri, calling it forth every day. Regardless of culture, finding one's meaning within perhaps represents the most important lesson of all. Those who find their dadirri, their why, meaning, ikigai, survive and thrive. Those who cannot find their dadirri likely substitute with alcohol, drugs, hopelessness, and a premature death.

Chapter 6

The Transforming Power of Failure and Its Lessons

When progressing through childhood and adolescence, authority figures such as teachers, coaches, family, the media, etc., spend much time extolling the virtues of academic, athletic, familial, and financial success. The mass media bombards us with successful actors, athletes, politicians, and business leaders. The messages are clear: Our society is about winners, and one must aspire to high achievement to be important. In high school, one teacher exclaimed, "Everybody in class should aspire to be number one," index finger pointing true north while stalking before class as if Patton addressing the troops. Realistically, few actually make millions, get elected to high office, or become great athletes or artists. The principle refrain seemed to be, "Work harder, and you too can become anything you want." Growing up, I bought into this line of thinking, much to my significant cognitive, emotional, and spiritual misfortune. After all, only a limited number can achieve number-one status at any particular time, nor can we become everything we desire.

Like many, my formative years were spent spelunking through school (especially math), disappointing my coaches, and feeling like a failure. I wanted to stand on some dais as someone important, a model of discipline, hard work, and talent. Unfortunately, such accolades were not to be part of my upbringing. Believe me, I worked hard, and likely few peers studied as many weekly hours nor trained as much for their sports. There were to be no awards for me, no recognition of my academic or athletic prowess, nor was anyone pointing to me as the embodiment of what one might aspire to become. Like most of my peers were, I was simply another average person. In a society valuing the exceptional, being average can become a crushing weight leading to a profound existential crisis. The unspoken message "*If you had just worked harder*" was virtually audible. Carrying the guilt of unachieved promise was emotionally debilitating. After all, failure is awful and terrible, *isn't it?*

During college, while working as a resident advisor (RA) in a residence hall, I was required to take a three-credit course for RAs. Co-instructors taught the class, one of whom was a doctoral student in counseling. During class discussion one afternoon, the topic of student success emerged. All RAs spoke of the academic and social pressures on students, with suicidal ideation an

DOI:10.4324/9781003168324-6

ever-present concern. Many identified fear of failure, either in the minds of the students or their parents, as a significant cause of stress. At some point, the instructor studying to be a counselor remarked something like, "Well, perhaps our students need to define success for themselves." I was most surprised, even shocked, at his statement. Someone then followed up with a question regarding failure. Our instructor, who I will call Jim, stated that trying to live up to others' expectations, while common, was potentially very destructive. He went on to express that most of the suicidal students he had counseled were distraught at having failed some arbitrary standard set by parents, teachers, or society. I recall further debate, with some in agreement with Jim, and others voicing concerns regarding the importance of a unified standard. Intrigued, I sought Jim out after class. Realizing I was struggling with anxiety regarding perceived lack of achievement, he suggested a colleague at counseling services.

As a young adult of 20, I entered counseling. My treatment plan focused strongly around my ongoing self-image as a failure. My counselor Steve (pseudonym) helped me peel away the layers of the success myth I had carried since childhood. Oddly enough, I had never given serious thought to how unrealistic and unhealthy these internalized messages had become. My initial therapeutic experience was very liberating, as for the first time I questioned what success and failure actually meant for me. Like practically all my peers, I simply accepted what authority figures had said I *should* achieve: namely, high academic success, athletic accomplishments, being a leader among my peers, etc. Yet, these *should*s were causing me significant emotional and psychological pain. I recall my counselor posing the question, "Okay, what's so bad about failure?" In fielding his question, I stumbled about verbally, unable to articulate a cogent response. His thoughtful question was novel to me, as all authority figures had stressed that achievement was good, failure was bad. "I would encourage you to consider developing your own standards," he suggested. Realizing he was right, this became the focus of therapy.

Albert Ellis, founder of Rational Emotive Behavior Therapy, developed a number of shame-attacking exercises to address moments when people tend to catastrophize some perceived error or egregious failure (Ellis & Doyle, 1988). Ellis wanted people to take healthy risks, succeed and fail, and in the process realize both success and failure can be liberating and even enjoyable. Some examples of shame-attacking exercises are walking down the hallway at work singing your favorite song, dressing in a garish outfit, or asking a question during class or at a conference, even when you fear appearing foolish. The risk only needs to be something activating your sense of shame. These shame-attacking exercises held relevance because I felt like such a failure and believed others saw me as such. During therapy, Steve helped me brainstorm a list of healthy risks I might take. One involved dating. I had had only a couple of dates in my life due to fear of rejection. (Guess what healthy risk number one was?) Steve also employed the question "What's so bad about being rejected for a date?" Ellis, who borrowed from Epictetus, said people are disturbed not by events, but rather our by perception of those events (i.e., failure). My homework was to ask one person out before our counseling relationship ended. Steve prepared me for both success and failure. Success was easy, of course, but failure triggered my shame button. Steve suggested success lay in the asking, however, not in the object of my affection's acceptance. I found such a concept appealing, but expected I might struggle with assimilating such, given a lifetime of converse conditioning.

After much coaching, I asked someone for a date and she accepted! I was happy, but in a sense disappointed, being well prepared to employ shame-attacking strategies and the new reframing strategy. (Interestingly, I prepared more for failure than success.) Resolving to keep asking women out until rejections came my way, I quickly achieved success! No question, rejection remained unpleasant but not awful nor terrible, and I could move on to someone else. I continued reframing success as making the effort, even when results were disappointing. My therapeutic experience helped me begin turning my life around by viewing myself as successful rather than a failure. Naturally, there would be many times when struggle and disappointment were revisited. Fortunately, counseling provided tools that would help. Later, however, I would need to expand my emotional toolbox.

Kintsugi: Filling the Cracks

As someone who has studied philosophy, I have learned a great deal from both eastern and western philosophers. Candice Kumai is a popular chef and author. In her book *Kintsugi Wellness: The Japanese Art of Nourishing Mind, Body and Spirit* (2018) she explores the important message behind ceramic art. Kintsugi is the Japanese art of mending broken pottery pieces with gold. Built on the philosophy of embracing flaws and imperfections, it allows one to create an even stronger, more beautiful work of art. Each break is unique, and instead of repairing an item like new, the 400-year-old technique actually highlights the shards as a part of the new design. In repairing our brokenness we may actually create something even more special, resilient, and beautiful.

Kintsugi holds relevance for contemporary societies and peoples the world over. Whether one is grieving death of a loved one, a divorce, job loss, or any other personal tragedy, kintsugi represents a process to reframe hardships and a reminder that brokenness does not imply failure. Rather, kintsugi suggests we can heal through our tragedies and traumas and come out stronger, more resilient, even more beautiful (Kumai, 2018). Kumai suggests people do not reach their full potential until they negotiate that journey through painful times. This healing process requires we do ongoing emotional work, as brokenness will reoccur. For readers who are counselors and other therapists, reading this talented culinary artist will sound much like reading a psychotherapy text. No question, the kintsugi metaphor is a mindset that can work very well for therapists counseling clients, or in mending our own cracks and fissures.

Kintsugi has many applications. One in particular stands out to me. More than two decades ago, I had a colleague who was a longtime addiction counselor, whom I will call Mary. Mary was a high school dropout and former drug addict who achieved sobriety, finished her GED and then an associate's degree in addiction counseling, became a counselor, and raised a family. She was one of the most naturally skilled therapists I have ever met. One of her standard interventions was assigning her clients to make a collage of their life by cutting photos from magazines. Midway through counseling, they would create another collage based on changes since entering therapy. Finally, prior to graduation from therapy, they would create another, focusing on their self-view at the conclusion of therapy and sobriety. Clients would compare and contrast these three collages. She explained that clients often remark that their collages tend to get more optimistic with each successive creation. As part of the graduation ceremony, the now-sober clients would speak about their addiction and their lives prior to treatment. They would address the stark pictorial representation of themselves before, during, and after treatment. Mary reported that many graduates would offer that the collage process was the most significant part of treatment. Over two decades later, it seems Mary maintained a philosophy similar to kintsugi. Her view was that only in embracing our brokenness could we begin to reassemble and glue together the shards of our shattered lives. This psycho-emotional-spiritual reassembly process involves merging and mending these disparate pieces of our lives to create a gestalt of healthy selfhood. This newly mended self, with broken parts fused with gold representing the healing process, conveys a beauty and resilience previously unobserved. It involves acknowledging our broken selfhood, such as trauma, addiction, incarceration, etc. as painful and unfortunate, but a past we have learned from and healed. Having done our intensive therapeutic work, healed and learned our lessons, we can then move forward in a healthier, more adaptive manner.

As a counselor who has worked with addicts, traumatized youth and adults, the mentally ill, ex-convicts, and university students, in the US and abroad, some of whom seem to have jettisoned all hope, kintsugi represents the opportunity to create a newly healed self, made far more beautiful through the healed scars. This healing is what we in the mental health profession call post-traumatic growth. This is where clients can reclaim their unabridged story at 12-step meetings, public forums, interviews, blogs, etc. Part of what needs reframing in society is redefining beauty not as cover shots on magazines, supermodels on the runway, or actors in film and TV, but ordinary people who have healed and learned through their trauma and brokenness. An important distinction herein is not that we praise abusers for providing pivotal growth opportunities, but rather *despite* abuse, addiction, and poverty, we are able to seek out help, do our healing work, and overcome challenging obstacles. Listening to Leonard Cohen's evocative song *Come Healing* (2012), I think of my former colleague Mary and her natural ability in shepherding seriously traumatized, self-medicating clients through the healing process.

In considering the lessons of kintsugi, counselors, therapists, teachers, plumbers, etc. must necessarily self-reflect on their lives. All mental health professions have a code of ethics that serves to protect the public as well as provide guidance through challenging clinical situations. From 2011 to 2014, I served on a task force that revised the *American Counseling Association's Code of Ethics* (American Counseling Association, 2014). This three-year period produced a new ethical code for our profession. The collegial relations forged through that crucible of long monthly conference calls and annual in-person gatherings made the sacrifices worthwhile. The code specifically posits self-care as an ethical obligation (Section C: Professional Responsibility, C.2.g.). My own experience, based on 35 years in the field, leads me to believe self-care, or *lack thereof*, is the most violated ethical mandate. Friends and colleagues in the sibling professions of psychology and social work have confided similar concerns to me as well. Part of our professional responsibility, then, lies in ensuring that we professionals are maintaining ethical practice by developing and being actively involved in ongoing self-care. Maintaining licensure and certification in various states and territories requires ongoing continuing education (CE trainings) in treatment modalities. However, there is no such equivalent requirement in self-care to maintain one's credentials. Ethical codes may specify self-care, but there is no specific requirement, unlike a prescribed number of continuing education hours. There are of course, CE trainings on self-care, but professionals are not required to have any CE hours in self-care. With all this in mind, here are some reflective questions for your consideration:

1) What type of personal self-care program have you developed? What does the plan consist of? Remember, it need not be running marathons. Three days of walking for 30 minutes are sufficient.
2) Many consider meditation, prayer, singing, drumming, or another such mind-spirit outlet an asset in good self-care. Which of these, if any, have you found helpful? (If you have a similar practice, how has that worked for you?)
3) If you needed to debrief about something important (outside of spouse or partner), would you have at least two friends with whom you could share your concern?
4) What is one hobby or activity you engage in weekly that helps you de-stress? (e.g., swimming, yoga, singing, etc.)
5) Regarding kintsugi, and creating beauty from flaws and imperfections, is this philosophy represented in your life? If so, how?

The idea is not to promote any sense of guilt for all-too-busy professionals, but instead to encourage busy mental health clinicians, professors, and graduate students (and anyone else) to optimize their health. Our professions exist in large part to assist people in constructing healthier, more fulfilling lives. Because modeling behavior is the best teacher, and due to the high levels of stress and burnout in the field, mental health professionals need active self-care plans, especially in this pandemic era.

Reframing Defeat

As the title of this chapter reads *The Transforming Power of Failure and Its Lessons*, this is a good place to offer a tale related to transformation. It was summer 1987, and I had recently graduated with my master's in counseling. I had performed very well academically during the program (rare for me!), received strong reviews on my internship, and felt optimistic nearing graduation. As life will sometimes dictate, however, my dreams began to crack and finally shatter. With my classmates seemingly hired weekly, I was getting thin envelopes in the mail. (Prior to the virtual era, job rejections principally came via mail.) Naturally, this occupational non-success weighed heavily on me. During this challenging period, peers, faculty, friends, and others offered ample advice, little of which proved helpful. One colleague accused me of not wanting a job badly enough, while another speculated that perhaps subconsciously I was sabotaging my chances due to unresolved issues.

In reality, I was putting out significant effort in searching for jobs, utilizing university career services for resume, cover letter, and interview assistance. When I did manage to land interviews, most of which seemed to go well, no job offers emerged. I could sense discouragement in my body and finally understood how people could "wear their defeat." After graduation, while still working my survival job in retail sales, I continued with career services for more coaching and inspiration. The career counselor assisting me, who I will call Jane, was a seasoned veteran, having taught and counseled prison inmates prior to her current university job. She was most definitely of the tough love school; she thoroughly analyzed my resume and cover letter before putting me through an exhaustive series of mock interviews. Despite her intervention, I continued jobless in the field. While my memory is hazy and I cannot recall her precise words, I recall the generalities of one particular meeting lucidly.

After yet another review of my resume and cover letter and another mock interview, she leaned back in her chair, removed her glasses, and shook her head. She expressed bewilderment at my non-success, having assisted several of my peers in being hired at schools and agencies, a statement leaving me feeling even more like a failure. She then made a statement that seemed totally out of character. "Look," she began, "I'm not much of a spiritual person. However, perhaps the right job or situation just has not yet arrived. Maybe the universe moves when it's time." I had no idea what to make of this statement, nor did it seem in any way helpful. She recommended I read Richard Nelson Bolles' popular book, *What Color Is Your Parachute* (1970-current). I had previously read this popular text, finding it a creative take on job searching, but had not found it particularly helpful. As Jane had put a lot of effort into assisting me, however, I vowed to read it again. Perhaps I had overlooked something on my initial perusal.

Feeling equal parts desperate and discouraged, I checked the book out from the university library and commenced a rematch with Bolles' iconic text. Initially, my retry seemed unhelpful until reaching a particular section. In this section, the author wrote regarding the power of reframing. He suggested readers reframe each job rejection as *one rejection closer to success*. Suddenly, something in my psyche clicked. My lack of employment success had left me feeling discouraged, and consequently my self-talk was negative. The cognitive therapy approaches of researchers such as Albert Ellis and Aaron Beck came to mind. Bolles was essentially applying cognitive reframing to the job search. Thus, while in the midst of abject disappointment and even depression, a paradigm shift occurred in my thinking. I would revise my perspective regarding my unsuccessful job search. Henceforth, each rejection would teach me something important, namely, that it would be *one rejection closer to success*. Some refer to this type of thinking as *failing forward*. I simply refer to it as reframing my self-talk. Some might see it as cognitive distortion, but the question then becomes, *how is that working for you?* Well, after adopting Bolles' reframing strategy, my mood improved significantly. Honestly, I remained disappointed when rejected for a job, but I was no longer catastrophizing. A couple months after this epiphany, my job search ended with success: I was hired! There was nothing magic in my newfound attitude, as I endured several more rejections prior to success. However, my reframing those rejections from "failed search and I'll never get hired" to "Okay, that was a successful failure and I'll be a stronger candidate next time," provided a significant emotional lift. My new belief system was a variation of the self-fulfilling prophecy: If you believe you can succeed, you are more likely to eventually be successful. Conversely, if you do not believe you can be successful, you likely are correct as well. Choice of attitude is powerful!

Buoyed by this success, I returned to the career services office to inform Jane. Walking into her cramped office, stacked high with books and papers, she was busy as always. She brightened up immediately upon seeing me. "You've been hired. I can tell by your body language." We held a celebratory conversation regarding the dips and valleys of my job search. She asked what advice I might pass along to graduates struggling to land a professional job. I explained reframing and that critical section in Bolles' text as the genesis of my new mood. A few additional employment rejections challenged my new-found belief, but my attitude of feeling more prepared with each non-success kept me upbeat.

Jane nodded in agreement, recounting the challenges in assisting soon-to-be paroled convicts in landing employment. Her experience was that attitude and the resilience that follows were the critical ingredients. Rising to leave, I thanked her again. Walking across the street to the university library to return the library book, I considered that of the book's 300-odd pages, creative drawings, charts, and advice, success had come down to one page concealed within Bolles' magnum opus. This is not to suggest that the rest of the book was unimportant. Rather, the treasure I needed to find was that *one* particular page that spoke to me. Others would perhaps find different sections of the book helpful. In fact, soon I would use Bolles' popular text in an adult job club setting, with most participants finding the text helpful, although I do not recall any client mentioning the page that had been so transformational for me.

Now, here is a lingering question that has nagged me: What if I had not reread Bolles' book and thus never read that page, or if reading in haste, I had missed that critical information in Bolles' book? I would like to believe something else would have caught my attention, but such oversight would have extended my sense of failure. Jane was instrumental in my taking another crack at reading Bolles' text. For reasons of veracity, I must express that while stating a reframe silently or aloud is quite simple, ongoing disappointment in a job search, promotion, relationship ending, etc., is much more challenging. I expect we all can recall disappointments that left us feeling emotionally crushed and fragile. The crux of the matter, perhaps, is reframing failure when our heart just is not into it. It is a bit like staying fit. Beginning a fitness routine is easy, but sustaining that healthy routine, be it walking, jogging, swimming, etc., requires the discipline of habituation when one is not motivated. My personal experience, and that as a counselor, is that success likely lies more in the discipline of reframing (or exercise for that matter) than the reframe itself. Habituation is critical in maintaining good mental and emotional health and in all successful ventures. The healthy habit approach is what has most transformed most of my former client's lives from dire to fulfilling, to say nothing of my own.

The 35 years since my *a-ha* moment of reframing have not always been easy. Times of failure and disappointment have certainly boomeranged back. Reframing various life disappointments has been a large part of working through that disappointment. The working through process has often been difficult, painful, and full of doubt, leaving me wondering if fulfillment was illusory. There were desired jobs I did not get, promising relationships that ended abruptly, and scores of manuscript rejections, to mention a few. Fortunately, if we can just keep climbing, regardless of how incrementally, those dark, lonely valleys lead upward. Rest when you must, seek emotional support (e.g., family, close friends, counseling, etc.), work your self-care plan, and maintain healthy self-talk and prosocial behavior. This risks sounding all too much like dispensing clichés, but the reality is attitude, self-care, social support, and spiritual support for many makes a huge difference.

The following section may help prepare readers for challenges in managing disappointment and failure.

Learning From and Transforming Failure

I encourage readers to answer the questions below using a pen. Some research suggests writing with a pen or pencil over typing on a laptop improves memory and aids with cognitive development (James, 2017):

1) Consider a disappointment or failure you have had either recently or sometime in the past. Describe that experience in as much detail as possible, including any associated feelings, thoughts, and sensory impressions you may have experienced (in your skin, stomach, smells, sights, etc.).
2) What does failure represent for you? Where does your conception of failure come from?
3) No question, failure and disappointment are unpleasant. Disappointment, however, can teach us important lessons that may help us in the future. What important lessons did your failure/disappointment teach you? (Say, one to three lessons learned.) If nothing comes immediately to mind, then give the matter more time to see what lessons emerge.
4) Regarding the lessons failure taught you, how might you use that knowledge to become more resilient? How might these lessons help you become a better therapist, health care professional, teacher, supervisor, parent, etc.?
5) How have lessons failure has taught you aided your emotional, personal, and occupational growth?
6) What would you want a client/patient (or family member, friend, etc.) to understand regarding failure and how to transform it?
7) What key goals would you hope to meet within the next one to five years?
8) Failure will close some doors (at least temporarily), though it may open others. What opportunities or doors has failure opened for you?
9) How much anger do you hold because of a significant failure? How might you address that anger in a constructive manner?
10) If you feel angry with yourself regarding a significant failure or disappointment, how might you begin practicing self-forgiveness? If you are angry with someone else, do you wish to forgive that person? If so, what could you do to begin the forgiveness process? Remember: Forgiveness does not absolve someone of responsibility for hurting you. It is more about your healing. If you are not ready to forgive, a question to consider is "How is my holding this anger towards another person working for me?"

Failing Forward

A few years ago, while idly scrolling through LinkedIn, I came across a posting that caught my attention. Someone had posted an article on the topic of failing forward. Intrigued, I clicked on the link, hoping it was not just time-wasting clickbait. Fortunately, the philosophy of transforming failure was a significant part of the author's message. While I have forgotten the author and exact wording, it inspired me to research the topic. I recently ran across one such article in *Forbes* (Childs, 2019). The article states the obvious: while failure poses difficulty for everyone, it simply is a matter of doing business in any field. The author quotes NBA legend Michael Jordan, who speaks of having missed over 9,000 shots, lost almost 300 games, and 26 times having been trusted to take the winning shot and missed. Jordan goes on to discuss failing numerous times, while adding the ironic postscript that his failure was why he was successful.

The concept of learning from our mistakes is centuries old and cuts across all cultures, religions, and occupations. Business leaders, psychologists, and many others have written on this topic, including John Maxwell's text with the apt title *Failing Forward: Turning Mistakes into Stepping Stones for Success* (2007). Maxwell suggests that business leaders who foster a culture of learning from mistakes, and not *never make a mistake*, are more likely to be successful. Maxwell's philosophy took me back a few decades to a lecture in a graduate school. A guest lecturer, who ran a large mental health agency, stated his philosophy was to encourage healthy mistakes. He quoted from the best-selling book *In Search of Excellence: Lessons from America's Best-Run Companies* (Peters & Waterman, 2007). Specifically, the authors of the popular text quote the CEO of a successful corporation encouraging employees to make sure they generate enough healthy mistakes. Someone in our class inquired as to an example of a healthy mistake. Our guest lecturer opined that healthy mistakes are the ones we learn and grow from in the process of taking a healthy risk, failing, and then self-reflecting on failure's lessons. He further illustrated with Thomas Edison's famous statement that success in creating the lightbulb required some 10,000 mistakes. One *Harvard Business Review* article suggested that business leaders must buy into the philosophy of succeeding through or even because of failure. The critical factor is corporate executives creating a no-blame game, thus empowering employees to become comfortable and responsible for learning from failures (Edmondson, n.d.).

Okay, if Fortune 500 CEOs, famous athletes and inventors, and esteemed publications such as *Forbes* and *Harvard Business Review* have embraced failure, why is failure generally looked upon as being bad? Much of the answer perhaps lies within society's highly competitive, winning-is-the-only-thing mantra. Glance at corporate CEOs, athletic coaches, college presidents, and other leaders, and you will see success formulated on wins, not losses. We can review famous quotes on the topic. General Patton's "Americans will not tolerate a loser," Vince Lombardi's "winning is the only thing," and Knute Rockne's, "show me a good and gracious loser, and I'll show you a failure," are among some of the most famous (or infamous) quotes on failure. On my high school basketball locker room door, someone had scrawled in black, "Losing is worse than death because you have to live with defeat." My teammates collectively thought the quote absurd, yet it remained prominent from grade school beyond my high school graduation. That no coach or PE teacher removed this absurd quote suggests more than mere coincidence.

No argument, when fighting Hitler and the Nazi threat, there could be no room for loss, as the consequences were too severe. Setting that extreme example aside, however, one might ponder, what exactly is losing? We all understand when our sports teams lose, and it is disappointing. Yet, only one team gets to win the Super Bowl, World Series, NHL championship, etc. Does this mean the runner-up is a loser? In 2007, the New England Patriots finished a season with just one loss, but that lone defeat was in the Super Bowl. Patriots coaches, players, and fans naturally were deeply disappointed. The larger question to me, however, is: Should this loss in the title game negate 17 straight wins? I would be curious to hear a round table conversation on this type of example. Sports is an arena where wins and losses are easy to evaluate, record-wise. However, success is not always so clear, even in the sports world. I will cite a sports example close to home for illustration.

In the academic year 2019–2020, prior to the COVID-19 pause, Niagara University men's basketball faced a trying stretch of bad news. Ten days prior to the start of the season, their much-prized new coach resigned abruptly, citing personal reasons. Thrust into the role of head coach was a 31-year-old assistant who had never been a head coach. To add unneeded additional calamity, injuries hit the youthful team hard, leaving just nine players, and no player taller than 6'6". Due to foul trouble and necessary rest periods, the team occasionally played with no player taller than 6'3" on an NCAA Division I basketball team! (For readers unfamiliar with college basketball, this is shocking.) The losses piled up, and a much-anticipated season turned quickly to gloom. Yet somehow through the trials and setbacks, the team discovered cohesion and went on a winning streak, even defeating the conference best team (who held a significant height advantage) by erasing a significant deficit with under 15 seconds to play. The young head coach and several players commented that hardship helped them toughen up and support each other. When it seemed they would finish dead last in the 11-team Metro Atlantic Athletic Conference, they finished in sixth place, and won their opening game in the conference tournament before COVID-19 concerns shelved the tournament. Their record of 12–20 was not what one would typically consider successful. However, given the myriad of challenges the team endured, including losing their head coach just prior to the first game, 12 wins was miraculous! In recognition of this improbable feat, head Coach Greg Paulus won the Joe B. Hall Basketball Award for Best First Year Head Coach. No, the team's record was hardly stellar, with several more losses than wins. Wins and losses, however, were not the sole measure of the team's success. I would assert this simple lesson from a basketball team has far broader implications, principally illustrating that a one-size-fits-all measuring stick does not fit all contingences.

Transforming Failure: A Three-Step Model

As mental health professionals, we assist clients in reframing and redefining thoughts when they cause or exacerbate anxiety and depression. I think of that classic Reality Therapy question: "How's that working for you?" (Glasser, 1998). Too often, our society views success in a binary win-lose mindset. If you do not win—in fact, win every time—you are a loser. This distorted and unattainable definition of success and failure can leave us feeling depressed, dissatisfied, and like failures. Yet failure is simply a realistic part of the developmental life process, and learning to deconstruct it in a healthy, proactive manner is important for future success and emotional well-being. For example, Niagara's college basketball team redefined the term "successful season." Thomas Edison redefined his failed experiments as necessary for his enormous success. This author redefined his numerous job rejections, viewing each rejection as bringing him closer to being hired. In all cases, redefinition, or reframing, was essential for eventual success. Therefore, redefinition require regular and ongoing revision of our self-talk to be more rational and realistic (Ellis & Doyle, 1988). In my workshops on mindfulness-based self-care, reframing our self-talk as the basketball team, Edison, and this author did is the starting point for any training.

Transforming and redefining failure also requires that we separate ourselves from failure. Often, the tendency is to define our self-concept from our accomplishments or failures. If we succeed, we are "winners." If we fail, we are "losers." My recommendation is the basic cognitive approach by Ellis (Ellis & Doyle, 1988). That is, we are disturbed more by our perception of failure than failure itself. The first step is revising one's self-talk, as in the preceding paragraph. Instead of telling ourselves, "I'm a failure for being fired from my job," we might instead express, "It's unfortunate I was fired. However, this gives me the opportunity to find a job that better fits my talents." There is a big difference then between *having* failures and *being* a failure. Edison mentioned his 10,000 failures and then his huge success. Who would call him a failure? Again, the crux of the matter is perspective, and this is where professionals such as counselors and other therapists play a significant role.

To expand on this topic of reframing, Ellis (2000) created what he labeled the A-B-C Framework (Later the A-B-C-D-E Framework) to attack and reframe irrational and problematic thinking and behavior. **A** represents a disappointing event or experience, or an inference about an event by an individual. **B** is the person's belief about **A** and largely creates **C**, the emotional consequence of that thinking, which can be healthy or unhealthy. An example of A-B-C is a person whose marriage has failed. The divorce represents the activating event (**A**), which causes the belief (**B**) that the person is a failure, and leads to the consequence of depression (**C**). Fortunately, there is **D** (disputing), leading to **E** (or new, more effective philosophy) (A. Ellis & Ellis, 2011). Cognitive counselors and therapists such as myself and others have made extensive use of Ellis' A-B-C Framework to assist clients in reducing depression and anxiety and in leading healthier, more fulfilling lives. I encourage clients to view each day as an opportunity for practicing this healthy mindset Ellis developed. This A-B-C model is very effective (A. Ellis & Ellis, 2011), easy to implement, and fits well with a healthier outlook.

Resilience is the third essential ingredient in transforming failure. Thomas Edison again represents the epitome of resilience by never giving up despite a long list of failures. Albert Ellis sometimes joked he was turned down roughly 100 times before he had his first date. Like Bolles' advice in *What Color Is Your*

Parachute (1972-current), Ellis reframed each romantic rejection as one step closer to success. Reframing correlates with resilience, as the person who reframes failure as temporary, even helpful, is far more likely to achieve success. As my high school counselor often opined, "If you think you can succeed, you're right. If you think you can't succeed, you're also right." In the early 1950s, Norman Vincent Peale published his huge bestseller *The Power of Positive Thinking: A Practical Guide to Mastering the Problems of Everyday Living* (Peale, 2003). Peale emphasized that one had to cultivate an attitude of belief in one's ability to succeed. That belief (a.k.a. positive thinking) led to action and eventually success. If you read his popular book (Peale was a Christian minister and his ecclesiastical language will challenge some), you may notice it sounding very similar to cognitive therapy. Peale encourages reframing failure and being resilient through cultivating a mindset that success follows a positive attitude and ongoing effort. Now CBT, REBT, DBT, and so forth provide a more defined structure, but Peale's positive thinking concept is definitely related.

Before moving on, a cautionary message regarding resilience and positive thinking is necessary. No question, positive thinking is essential for successful counseling, and all cognitive-oriented counseling approaches promote it. Viktor Frankl (1986), Albert Ellis (2000), Aaron Beck (1963, 1979) and many other researchers have all illustrated the value of reframing negative cognitions. Positive thinking, however, is not *magical thinking*, and likely will not lead to fame, wealth, and the trappings that go along with such (much of which may not be healthy). Reframing is about revising negative self-talk for more *rational* thinking and behavior. Rational implies realistic and responsible thinking and behavior. Responsible thinking suggests that the downsized worker reframe her depressed self-talk that a better job is ahead, not that the better job will make her a multi-millionaire. A positive attitude is essential, reframing negative self-talk such as "I'm a loser" to "That's one loss closer to success," and necessary for resilience. Responsible thinking is not "I can achieve anything!" This overstatement would imply that people of my age and ability could play in the NBA, become a neurosurgeon, an Academy Award-winning actor, etc. Some people do indeed achieve these rare feats, but they possess significant talent while also beating long odds. One must not confuse being a star in sports, the film industry, business, education, or the therapeutic community with a meaningful, fulfilling life, as we all know rich, talented, famous people who remain unhappy despite significant accomplishment. Civilization has a long history of famous, talented, financially successful people whose lives were full of misery.

To Recap, the Three-Step Model of Transforming Failure:

1) Reframe negative self-talk. Example: "I am a failure because I did not get the promotion" to "I failed to get this promotion but the experience has prepared me for future promotions."

2) Separate yourself from failure: This step is a repeat of Step 1. "I'm not a failure. I just failed at this particular thing. However, I will be more prepared for success in the future."
3.) Practice cultivating rational and realistic self-talk as in Step 1. More importantly, practice rational self-talk each day for habituation.

Summary

Transforming failure in order to succeed is an essential task for mental health professionals and everyone else. This transformation is vital in counseling work with clients and important in our own lives. With some 25 years counseling experience in many venues, including overseas, I have had a role in helping clients achieve their treatment goals. I have also experienced many failures with clients, and at times experienced distress and guilt over the consequences. Good clinical supervision, along with reframing, has helped transform those failures into a failing forward mentality, much as in my job search foibles. All therapists will struggle with some clients or patients, occasionally questioning their ability to effect healthy change. Kintsugi is a helpful metaphor for addressing our human imperfections, especially ones that arise in our professional work and in our personal lives. Thus, while failure on the job and in our own lives can feel catastrophic in the moment, adopting an attitude of failure as transformed success can become the catalyst for a growth mindset while laying a foundation for future success. All counselors, social workers, psychologists, medical professionals, and such have challenging roles in assisting struggling patients in reframing and working through mental disorders and life challenges. Learning that failure is temporary, and may even be instrumental for future success, can transform our clients' lives as well as our own.

Reflective Exercises

1) What was the most important concept in this chapter?
2) When you consider the concept of kintsugi and making beauty from imperfection, can you think of a time in life you have done this? How did you accomplish that?
3) What do the terms success and failure mean for you? How are your views of success and failure working for you?
4r) What have been your most significant successes and failures? What did you learn from your success and failures?
5) If asked to give a keynote speech on what you have learned regarding your successes and failures, what would you tell the audience?

Lessons Learned

I shuffled down the hallway, footsteps heavy, as if a condemned man approaching the gallows. I was on my way from the Communications Building to the

Registrar's Office to withdraw from college. As the fourth of six children (all boys) raised by our grandparents, they had instilled the value of education in us. They wanted more than rural poverty for us, and while on a meager budget, they made whatever sacrifices possible for our sake, nurturing the value of education for social mobility and personal transcendence. Given their intervention, I felt terribly guilty having wasted their hard work and sacrifice. During high school, our school counselor warned us that anyone matriculating to college would need to be prepared to work hard. He mentioned that typically only a fourth of our high school's graduates attended college, with the attrition rate of those attending near 50%. His words sounded a warning siren. Thus, I resolved to work hard and make my grandparents proud. I would graduate from college and move on to a successful career, vowing not to become one of the 50% who dropped out.

Now my shattered dreams and expectations lay scattered about in shards. Instead of an educated person on his way to graduate school and future success, I was simply another failure, joining that sad, illustrious line of hometown college dropouts. I recall one such person in particular. Returning home, he sat forlornly on the steps of the County Building staring forward at nothing in particular, defeat etched on his formerly hopeful face. Now I would take his place, another casualty of dreams crushed in the vise of reality. My every slow, weighted step seemed to beat out a terrible cacophony: *You are a failure. You are a failure. You are nothing.*

My failure was not due to poor study habits or a lack of discipline. I was majoring in Chemistry, having enjoyed the subject in high school, and was considering becoming a high school science teacher. College chemistry and physics were a far different experience, however. Furthermore, the Bachelors of Arts program of study required one year of a foreign language. My small-town school had offered no foreign languages during my years of study, and college French had proved very challenging. Skating just north of academic suspension with no direction or confidence while feeling most sorry for myself, I wandered down the hallway as if a somnambulist in some ongoing nightmare. Unfortunately, it was no dream.

Just as I was approaching the double doors that would lead to my demise, a sharp, familiar voice beckoned: "Mr. Hodges, I have been looking for you. Come to my office right now!" It was my French professor. She was a tall, imposing African American whose voice could have commanded armies. She was cultured, intellectually gifted, demanding of students, and a force in any classroom she occupied. Honestly, I was scared to death of her. Like a buck private, I turned and followed my general to her office. Interestingly, I recall being even more fearful of her than my impending sad-looking life. She led me into her office shut the door, then took a seat behind her desk. Peering over her glasses at me, face like granite, she began having her say.

"I want you to understand something right now. I have watched too many otherwise promising students become discouraged and quit. You have that look of quit about you, and I want to know why." Suddenly, my fear ebbed and waves of puzzlement ensued. Did she have me confused with someone else? After all, I had been the worst student in her classes for two consecutive semesters. "Well, I am waiting for an answer," she replied in a firm, impatient tone. *What does she want me to say?* I recall thinking. *That I'm just an ignorant hayseed?* Unable to articulate a cogent response, I sat mute. Thus, she continued.

"I have been a professor a long time and understand students struggling with a subject. I am certainly not blind to your struggles with my class, but also notice you attend every class and keep trying. Some of my better students skip. I want you back in my class in spring. I will help but will not tolerate any quitting, understood?" I nodded, still aphasiac in shock of my improbable rescue from the scrap heap of life. Finally summoning my voice, I inquired, "Why would you want a student like me?"

She looked away for a moment, staring at nothing in particular, but evidently thinking. She then recounted coming from a small Georgia town before going off to college in the big city. She confessed to feeling overwhelmed and lost. *She understands*, I realized. I sat up higher in my chair, pointing out having skipped her final exam the previous day, figuring passing was impossible. "Nonsense, you will take the final right now." With that, she whipped out a copy of the final and handed it to me. "You have an hour. I will be right here grading papers if you have a question." I took the paper and commenced my Sisyphean effort. After vainly grappling with the exam for the better part of an hour, I handed forth my paper, shame returning due to my pathetic performance.

She took my exam, slid her reading glasses on and spent what seemed a long time reading my exam, yet making no marks. When she finally peered up, I felt ready to faint. "Alright, a couple in the class actually did worse. You passed. Now, next semester you will do better, right?" Recognizing a rhetorical question, I nodded, shocked at having passed, wondering who possibly could have performed worse on the exam than myself.

Realizing my professor had given me a reprieve from a dead-end life, my lightheadedness lingered long after leaving her office. Resolving that next semester things would be different, I vowed to find a pathway out of this dark valley. Instead of shuffling to the Registrar's Office to drop out, I walked purposefully across campus to the Fulbright Arts & Science Hall to change my major to English, selecting it due to my love of reading. That accomplished, I then headed to the Counseling Center to schedule an appointment. Having looked into the abyss of hopelessness, and having that dark void staring back, change was not only necessary, it was vital for reclaiming my life.

The following semester, working and studying was my life. I was working more than full time, 20 hours on campus in a lab and roughly 20–25 on the weekends delivering pizzas from afternoon until the wee hours of the morning. Often weary, I poured myself into the most significant task of my young life, my survival. Spring term's conclusion arrived, and my performance in my new major (English) significantly outpaced my previous anemic results. I did make noticeable improvement in French class, although far less than my professor or I would have liked. I attended all classes, went to all assigned language labs, and beat a path to my professor's office weekly for help. Still, my efforts resulted only in marginal gains. My professor may have been the only person more frustrated with my struggles than myself. She wore an expression of exasperation anytime I spoke in French. I was passing her class, though barely.

With my strong performance in other classes, there was no danger of my flunking out of college, but my French grade was for pride. I was already feeling guilty for letting down my grandparents; I was not eager to add my formidable professor to the list. Unsurprisingly, I was the last student left in class during the final exam. I had put in quality time studying in a group and alone. Still, my efforts yielded little promise, as the exam was tough. As I stepped forward to hand in my exam, she peered up from grading. Her expression suggested, *Well?* I thanked her for all she had done and turned to leave. "Not curious how you did?" I turned as she was gathering the exams. "Let's go," she replied. I followed her back to her office. She shut the door and commenced marking my paper. I fidgeted anxiously as her face registered a continuous frown, red pen dancing about like a Middle Ages court scribe scribbling out an order of execution. Mercifully, she rested her pen, and slipped off her glasses. "Better," she offered, to my immense relief. "Better" was not necessarily cause for celebration, as she certainly had gifted me a pass the previous term. Gathering my fleeting courage, I inquired if I had passed. She smiled and replied, "Congratulations!" extending her hand across her desk. Winning the lottery could not have matched my elation at that moment!

There are marking points in our lives, times when we know we have approached some Rubicon from which we cannot simply turn back. These are life-defining moments whereby we either proceed with purpose or retreat in utter defeat. I have witnessed this in the faces of former clients and students on many occasions. I have seen myself in their struggles and successes, joys and crushing pain. Looking back more than 40 years at that chance encounter with my French professor, frequently I have wondered how my life would have evolved had she not seen me and taken time to care. More surprisingly, how she found any vestige of promise in likely her worst student remains a mystery. Just as it appeared I would slip off into oblivion like so many others, she stepped in. No question, her timely intervention offered a reprieve that changed the direction of my life. Years later, when passing through the area, I stopped by her office, hoping she remembered me. Remarkably, she did. I expressed my gratitude but sought clarity. "Why did you help me, the worst student you had?" She smiled and in a moment of levity offered that there actually were a couple of worse students before answering, "I helped because you were worth it."

Many periods of struggle lay ahead for me, and more yet await me still. The lessons learned from this tough, demanding, yet ultimately kind woman lie in sustaining the belief in possibility and nurturing it in vulnerable others. Yes, I had experienced failure before her intervention, and have failed *many* times since in the past 40-plus years. The difference now lies in understanding that experiencing failures and being a failure are distinctly different. The difference between these two poles lies in our attitude regarding failure and success. That my professor took time to care for the least of her students was a powerful and transcending lesson. I have tried to pay it forward with my own students and clients.

Finally, in my personal and occupational life, I have failed often. Yet, my attitude remains that I am one disappointment closer to success. This simple reframe grounds my being, strengthens my resolve, helps me dust off the detritus of disappointment, and continue forward. Because frankly, I *am* worth it.

Chapter 7

Finding Meaning Through Essentialism and Sustainability

Packing my car with my personal belongings was a task taking all of 20 minutes, given my minimalist lifestyle. It was a dark, cold, snowy morning with a very long drive ahead. I was leaving my job as director of Clinical Services at a rural eastern Oregon clinic for my new position as director of Counseling Services at a small, rural Minnesota university. I squeezed two suitcases in the trunk, and added my desk lamp, Zen-style meditation bench, and a sack of groceries. After a quick stop at the coffee shop for coffee, my next life adventure began solo with no need for even a U-Haul.

My life had always been about simplicity. During childhood, our grandparents raised my four siblings and me in their compact Ozark home. By necessity, we lived with little privacy and much shared ownership of the little we possessed. I shared a bed with my younger brother in what for several years was a dirt-floor basement, heated by a wood stove during winter. My grandparents, having survived two world wars and a depression, were adaptive people who gardened, canned food, wore the same clothing for years, and lived necessarily in simplicity (actually poverty). What my formative years taught me, however, was not a feeling of deprivation, but rather an appreciation for a simple lifestyle without clutter. When asked in childhood by a relative what I planned to do as an adult, I recall answering, "Live in a small house and ride a bicycle." I have not strayed far from that early sentiment. The reason this chapter exists because of my anecdotal experience that simple living, with a smaller carbon footprint, fewer material possessions, and less debt, generally equates to fewer headaches and more personal fulfillment. More personal fulfillment, moreover, holds a strong correlation with life meaning, personal satisfaction and happiness (Seligman, 2002). Simple living, however, will vary depending on a person's needs: for example, a single person versus a couple, or someone living with dependents and extended family. The more essential component of simple living, moreover, likely lies in the attitude one takes regarding simplicity and material possessions (that *attitude* thing again). Simplicity likely represents more a *being* versus a *doing* in life. The former term suggests a presence grounded in a present moment of sustainable living, as opposed to the mindset that more

DOI:10.4324/9781003168324-7

material possessions equates to a better life. There is no question, however, that voluntarily living a minimalist lifestyle in a small home or apartment is distinctly different from enforced poverty.

As mentioned previously, *Minimalism: A Documentary About the Important Things*, directed by Matt D'Avilla (2015), a mid-20-something filmmaker whose previous cinematographic work had involved filming weddings and Bar and Bat Mitzvahs, highlighting two early thirty-something friends, Joshua Fields Milburn and Ryan Nicodemus, helped spawn an entire movement. Joshua and Ryan, whose moniker is "The Minimalists," feature prominently in the film, but are also accompanied by economists, a popular news anchor, artists, musicians, corporate leaders, and everyday people. The film explores how Joshua and Ryan, two corporate dropouts mentioned in a previous chapter, take viewers on a cross-country road trip through America to promote their recently self-published book, *Minimalism: Live a Meaningful Life.* Sandwiched between cameos of different interview clips with economists and others are Joshua and Ryan's talks in bookstores, cafés, and various gathering places.

Joshua and Ryan were childhood friends from the rust belt who wearied of the Skinner box approach of corporate America. Despite making high salaries and achieving promotions, a title, office, and money did not equal fulfillment or happiness for them. Throughout the film, Joshua, Ryan, and many others deconstruct the American Dream myth of success (i.e., money) by posing questions like: Can authentic happiness and success be measured solely by wealth and possessions? What is the cost in global human and environmental terms of consumer culture? What is the alternative to corporate American life? Viewers hear of Joshua and Ryan's radical simplification from houses to small dwellings with few material possessions, which they call minimalism. Both are quick to acknowledge there is no precise amount of possessions required to be a minimalist. Rather, the minimalist movement requires a sense of consumer conscientiousness and an encouragement to refrain from impulse buying. Both Joshua and Ryan encourage people to meet their basic needs and provide for their families, while simultaneously emphasizing the need to simplify your life whenever possible. The documentary illustrates simplification of life by different people in a number of ways.

One person featured in the film travels the world with all his possessions in a backpack, living in simple habitations (cheap motels, hostels, with friends, etc.) Another is a woman who runs a concept she calls Project 333 (Becker, n.d.). The idea in Project 333 is to wear only 33 articles of clothing for the next 3 months. All clothing, jewelry, shoes, and outerwear count towards your number. Exceptions include underwear sleepwear, furniture, and workout clothing. Others profiled have downsized from sizable homes to studio apartments and off-grid, small habitations. News anchor Dan Harris, perhaps the most famous person featured, had an on-air panic attack brought about by a consuming pressure, resulting in a mindfulness-based lifestyle involving daily meditation.

The documentary also includes a small homes designer, a former Wall Street Broker, and many others espousing a scaled down, more simplistic lifestyle. In various ways, these people profiled in the film are saying something similar: namely, that a materialistic, monetary, and possessions-oriented way of life results in a sense of purposelessness, or as Frankl termed, the existential vacuum (1986). In fact, every person interviewed in the film describes a sense of life disappointment, even crisis, brought on through a life of chasing more financial success and social status, all vain attempts to fill a void in their lives. Reviewing the film, I could not help but wonder what Frankl would have made of it. The thread running throughout the documentary, Joshua and Ryan's book, and later podcast, is a sense of meaning derived through essential living. In fact, both Joshua and Ryan have mentioned that essentialism is likely a more appropriate word than minimalism. Perhaps the question becomes, what is essential with regard to meeting one's personal, familial, and professional needs?

While authoring this book, the world has been in the grip of a pandemic the likes of unseen in a century. As of this writing, more than 6 million people have died worldwide, and more than one million in the US. COVID-19 brought shutdown and isolation, followed by a slowdown, huge layoffs, and leaving others working remote. Initially I was working from home, later moving back to my campus office, teaching and communicating via Zoom and email. Although busy teaching, advising, and writing two books, my recreation has consisted of reading, watching films, and working out. One of my favorite viewing subjects has been the small house movement. One of the most popular channels on YouTube is Bryce Langston's *Living Big in a Tiny House* (www.livingbiginatinyhouse.com). Langston, a New Zealander and former actor turned small house advocate, travels the world filming brief (around 10–15 minutes) segments of people who live in small to tiny homes. Owners range from young, single adults to elderly couples, those downsizing from large homes, others formerly homeless, and an itinerate few who live in converted school buses and vans, constantly on the move. Motivations for this lifestyle run the gamut involving freedom from prohibitive mortgages to wanting more economic and personal freedom. Virtually everyone. Langston interviews mentions an interest in simplicity, sustainability, and personal fulfillment as motivations for their small house lifestyle. Several have specifically mentioned finding more purpose and meaning in this basic lifestyle.

The contemporary simple living concept likely has its genesis in the counterculture movement from the 1960s and 1970s. In 1981, Duane Elgin's bestseller *Volunteer Simplicity* advocated the virtues of a scaled-down, simplified lifestyle. A simple living philosophy, however, is scarcely a modern concept. Buddhist and Catholic monks have been entering monasteries and living communally, performing simple tasks such as gardening, winemaking, and copying manuscripts for over 2,000 years. Their desire in joining religious life and living separately from society was to find a more purpose-driven, spiritually enhanced, fulfilling life. The small house movement documented by Bryce Langston likely represents a modern, secular, simplified approach to minimalist living that originated some two millennia previously. While monasteries and intentional religious communities remain, the majority of small house residents appear to be seeking a simplified, purposeful life untethered to a particular religious approach. Many acknowledge being spiritually oriented, just not formally religiously inclined.

Global Environmental Challenge

Bill Gates, in his recent book *How to Avoid a Climate Disaster: The Solutions We Have and the Breakthroughs We Need* (2021), makes a robust case that sustainable, simplified living may save the planet from destruction. Gates outlines the serious threat of human extinction, and advocates for a net-zero emission of greenhouse gases. Finally, he lays out a concrete (he is literally working on zero-emission concrete) plan for achieving this most challenging zero-emission goal. While he admits the irony of a high-tech billionaire mogul advocating zero carbon emissions through simple, sustainable living, he is investing billions of dollars to support environmentally sustainable cities.

Some readers may possibly be wondering about the inclusion of this chapter in a text for mental health professionals. I maintain that all professions must continue strong, sustained advocacy for global carbon-zero emissions. While not an environmental scientist, there is much agreement in the scientific community that global warming represents a dire threat to humanity's survival (Gates, 2021). Gates makes the point that without sustained reversal in our huge carbon output, temperatures will continue rising, resulting in global droughts, catastrophic wildfires, polar caps melting at alarming rates resulting in major cities being flooded, and desertification of greater tracts of formerly sustainable land, culminating in the demise of humankind and numerous species.

Some voices, particularly those on the conservative side of the political spectrum, decry Gates as a doomsayer, much as they have done with the scientific community and medical professionals; witness the denial of COVID-19, anti-COVID-19 vaccination misinformation, and politicization of mask wearing and social distancing. Nevertheless, increasing environmental trauma, reduced crop production, increased demand for water, and competition for resources will likely intensify global strife. We can take a lesson in this from a 1960s study using rats and electric currents (Azrin et al., 1967). Azrin et al. (1967) put lab rats on an electrified grid, then turned it on. Over time, the rats began to attack one another and the cage. The lesson herein is that when pressure and threats build, stress increases, increasing interpersonal violence. I have witnessed this behavior during my time counseling survivors of domestic violence. As personal and financial stress increases, perpetrators blame and abuse their partners. A more recent example of this comes from San Francisco. Since the COVID-19 pandemic's arrival in the US, the Bay-area Asian community has experienced a surge in violence, with some attackers blaming Asian Americans for COVID-19 (Liu & Hatzipanagos, 2021). While the January 6 attack on the US capitol was not specifically about race or environmental denial, rioters attacked in support of a sitting president who had labeled COVID-19 and global warming a Chinese hoax, among other mistruths, to rile the mob against the legislative branch of the US government. Bill Gates' sober rationality is much-needed thinking, if humankind is to effectively address the very serious challenges currently facing it.

Bill Gates is scarcely the first person to sound the warning siren regarding environmental destruction and depletion of the earth's bio-resources. He is, however, perhaps the most significant individual to speak out and write about looming eco-destruction. His billionaire status as Microsoft Empire co-founder, and his lofty position in the software industry, provide Bill Gates a natural point position in the environmentalism movement. Gates is unapologetic regarding his capitalistic bent, viewing profit as the best way to promote environmental sustainability to corporations (Gates, 2021). Regardless of how one views Bill Gates—and current perceptions run the gamut from saint to Satan—a more pragmatic view lies in his benefit to the environmental movement. Unquestionably, he has poured billions of dollars into research on sustainable endeavors (Gates, 2021). He also acknowledges his immense privilege and the ironies of his jetting around the globe to promote sustainability. The point I am making herein is that sustainable living, food production, alternate fuel vehicles, smaller housing, and a corporate mindset on environmental sustainability via profit, etc. are part of the problem *and* solution to the global environmental crisis. The difference between eventual extinction and salvation lies in our ability to create a sustainable lifestyle.

Volunteer Simplicity

In the late 1990s, a popular book on volunteer simplicity was *Your Money or Your Life: Transforming Your Relationship with Money and Achieving Financial Independence* (Dominguez & Robin, 1999). The authors offered a nine-step program focusing on mindfulness and frugal financial habits as opposed to strict denialism. The book emphasized decluttering yourself of unnecessary possessions, thoughtful, intentional purchasing, and sound investing. The book has sold well over one million copies, influencing many people. The surviving author, Vicki Robin, released a second edition, *Your Money or Your Life: 9 Steps to Transforming Your Relationship with Money and Achieving Financial Independence* (2018). A large part of the new edition focuses on how millennials can avoid the financial burden of huge college and mortgage debt, and engage in volunteer sustainability and environmental stewardship. Admittedly, as an educator, counselor, and writer, I am no economic expert. What does seem to make Robin's and Dominguez's books different is the focus *not* on creating millionaires, but instead on helping average people achieve financial independence through thoughtful versus impulsive purchasing. For example, instead of imagining that new pair of $300 shoes will make you happy, they suggest you examine what those shoes will actually help you achieve (occupationally, socially, shoe durability, etc.) versus the cost to buy them. Some examples, such as purchasing a quality bicycle for regular exercise and pleasure, could be a wise investment, as regular use assists in better health and a better-quality bike likely is more durable. The authors, with decades in communal, simple living, encourage an essentialism-type lifestyle where fewer possessions generally are better (Robin & Dominguez, 2018). Or, as one expression I recently heard goes, "You always save 100% on that un-needed item you didn't purchase."

The authors do acknowledge that impoverished, fixed-income persons with dependent children have fewer choices than middle-class people holding better-paying jobs. Such is the reason for my preference of essentialism as opposed to minimalism. Working in rural and remote agencies in the US, and volunteering overseas, often in remote and extremely remote regions, has educated me on poverty's devastating impact on education, health care, and length and quality of life. What I appreciate about Robin and Dominguez's book is the focus on a simpler, realistic, sustainable lifestyle. A large part of the US debt burden lies in the fact that many, particularly college students, have little experience with money management, witnessed by their racking up huge credit card debt. Large debt on a high-interest credit card, added to crushing college and graduate school debt, can lead to a lifetime of economic hardship. Furthermore, such sizable debt puts enormous emotional strain on people and their relationships, leading to serious health and mental distress (Zhang & Kim, 2019). Something I noticed in counseling individuals and couples was that a significant part of the distress in their lives and marriages and partnerships was that of financial stress. Specifically, a large part of discord in many couples' relationships involved one party being financially frugal while the other was not. I counseled a couple where one partner had had three bankruptcies, leaving the other tasked with the crushing burden of paying the bills. You can imagine the stress and relationship discord created in such a household. The difficulty perhaps lies in how to achieve financial viability in a consumer culture constantly bombarding us with advertisements emphasizing that buying the right cars, clothes, cosmetics, and beer will enhance the quality of our lives. It's amazing when one considers that advertising is all about viewer manipulation; it's even more depressing is that it works so well.

Sustainability then, involves a process of basic CBT. That is, asking, "What's the evidence this purchase will bring me fulfillment?" Perhaps, then, delaying impulse buying to further reflect, and dialoguing about the issue with a trusted friend, could be a second part of thoughtful spending. This essentialist philosophy involves evaluating how much enjoyment a particular purchase provides. This second involves extended thought and dialogue over a longer period after a significant purchase. For example, consider a couple living in a winter environment who wish to purchase a treadmill to exercise during cold months. They might ask the "What's the evidence?" question and, after talking it over, purchase a quality machine without selecting the most expensive model. Then, over 3–6 months, they engage in further dialogue over how well the purchase is working out (i.e., "How much/little enjoyment and health benefits are we getting?"). Other questions might involve the cost of the treadmill versus a gymnasium membership. This example, nevertheless, illustrates conscious purchasing as evidenced in Robin and Dominguez's book (2018). The lesson therein is not, "Buy nothing and subject yourself to a life of monastic abnegation," but rather "purchase consciously, intentionally, and with sober forethought." Such conscious spending practices habituated over a long period of time likely will result in accumulating less clutter, lowering one's debt, reducing anxiety and depression caused by excessive debt (Robin & Dominguez, 2018; Zhang & Kim, 2019), and likely provides a viable method to create a more sustainable lifestyle (Robin & Dominguez, 2018). For any mental health professional, understanding the role financial exigency plays on client mental distress is significant, as it can trigger much emotional distress and related health concerns (Zhang & Kim, 2019). My anecdotal experience providing counseling over some 25 years is that financial strain has been a significant part of many client's mental health struggles. While money issues may not be the root cause of anxiety, depression, addiction, and so forth, financial stress exacerbates mental health concerns. I have listed ten questions below for consideration before making purchases.

10 Questions to Consider Prior to Making a Purchase:

1) How critical is this item for my home, work, and life? (Could I get by without it?)
2) If you walked away, or went offline and delayed this purchase for a couple of days, what are the chances you would still purchase it?
3) How many hours did you work to purchase this item? (If 100 hours, is this item really worth that worktime?)
4) If this purchase really is worth it to you, could you buy it cheaper at another store or on a different website?
5) Do you have the money to pay cash for this item? (Limit interest-bearing credit card debt.)
6) Are you able to pay off your credit card debt each month? If "No," remember this is why the average American owes over $6,000 dollars in credit card debt. (www.valuepenguin.com/average-credit-card-debt)

7) How long, in years or months, would I be using this item? (Will you use that new purse or pair of shoes for five years?)
8) If I make this discretionary purchase, will I have enough money to pay my bills (mortgage/rent, utilities, insurance, etc.) and buy food for my household?
9) How would this item improve your quality of life?
10) If you believe this item is important, what could you give away in order not to increase clutter?

I offer the previous questions not to squeeze the joy from purchasing necessities and those affordable ones that do bring us enjoyment. (I just bought a new treadmill to replace the old one that died!) Like Robin and Dominguez's book (2018), the important practice to habituate is conscious buying of essential items. Exactly what is essential beyond food, housing, heat, water, and so forth is debatable, requiring forethought and planning. Parker Palmer describes the *clearness committee*, an established clarifying process in his spiritual community (Quaker or Friends). A clearness committee is a process for discernment often used when a member seeks to reach clarity on a significant decision or concern (Palmer, 2000). The clearness committee consists of a small, trusted group who refrain from giving advice but ask honest, open, probing questions to assist the member seeking guidance in reaching a decision on significant issues like changing careers, marriage, or moving overseas. Regarding purchasing, a clearness committee might ask probing questions like, "How might this purchase add fulfillment to your life? How does this desired item fit with your needs and values? What is the likelihood you will still be using this item in one year? What makes this item so important to you?"

The clearness committee's role is not to shame anyone looking to make purchasing decisions, or any other. The function of the committee is to assist in clarifying precisely *why* they desire a particular spouse/item/job/status/etc., and *how* or *what* makes this spouse/item/job/status/etc. so important to their well-being. I am not suggesting we all run out and gather a committee to assist us in clarifying all purchases. Rather, my intent is for each person to develop a clarifying process for conscious purchasing, as my experience is that self-reflection can help us refrain from impulse buying that creates unnecessary debt, needless clutter, and anxiety from crushing debt. I do recommend readers do their homework on large-ticket items (homes, automobiles, colleges, etc.), and put the same diligence into small purchases, as small items really add up over time. Instead of a committee, review questions like the ten previously suggested, and select one or two trusted, sober-minded people for large purchases.

Capitalism and Simplicity

Without question, we live in a proudly capitalistic, consumer-oriented society, as evidenced in big-box stores, internet stalwarts like Amazon, and ads on television and social media. There is little debate capitalism is here to stay in western society and in much of the eastern world (witness Japan, Taiwan, South Korea, etc.). Capitalism encourages spending, something exemplified by the billions of dollars of advertising manufacturing and retail conglomerates use to convince us our lives would be exponentially better through purchasing their product. A significant motivation in writing this book targeting mental health professionals is that we are in a position to assist clients and patients in making conscious choices in their lives, including creating more manageable, sustainable, emotionally secure, less anxious lives. Too many clients in my long career have bought into consumerism at great financial and emotional cost. The emphasis for this chapter, and this book, is to reinforce conscious consumerism. Conscious consumerism has implications for our actions, sustainable living being most significant. Sustainable living includes the homes we choose, vehicles we drive, food we eat, and other related ways of reducing our carbon and personal debt footprint. Essential living with less focus on consumerism is a method of simplifying our lives through living more consciously. By living more consciously, we likely cultivate more meaningful, purpose-centered lives with less debt.

Regarding the simplicity Ryan Nicodemus and Joshua Fields Milburn advocated in the film on minimalism and in their podcasts, minimalism, or essentialism, is a philosophy of life worthy of consideration. Essentialism is all about conscious living, including purchasing only what is necessary, and in turn, living within our means in smaller, more environmentally sustainable housing, utilizing wind and solar energy if possible. Josh and Ryan have interviewed people from many occupations, lifestyles, and with various levels of education and experience. While their guests have chosen to downsize to live more simply and sustainably, some live in communal housing sharing meals, automobiles, childcare, and other expenses; others live in small houses far apart from neighbors. Bryce Langston profiles people throughout the world who have moved into small homes and tiny apartments. While most small home dwellers are single, or partnered with two children or less, others have had as many as five. All have in common having sacrificed a "more is better" consumerism lifestyle for a scaled-down, more sustainable life. Some have achieved simplicity in rural areas, others in large cities (e.g., New York, Tokyo, Sydney, etc.). Many have relocated far from their origins, while others have remained in their same hometown. Essentialism, therefore, certainly is not a one-size-fits-all type of philosophy. What all do appear to be saying in various ways is that they found more fulfillment, purpose, and meaning in their essentialist lifestyle.

Conclusion

This focus of this chapter is to initiate thoughtful conversation within the therapeutic community (and beyond) regarding creating simpler, more sustainable living, as my belief is such is congruent with improved mental health and helps preserve our biosphere. Such conversations go well beyond debate regarding curricula, ethics, therapeutic approach, and general practice. My belief, however, based upon climate science, consumer debt, and a carnivorous, capitalistic, consumption-oriented western world is that we must begin to incorporate sustainable conversations within our professions. Substantial debt increases anxiety and depression (Zhang & Kim, 2019). Industrialization has created mechanisms threatening our species' survival should we fail to make radical change (Gates, 2021). While many in the mental health profession likely already feel overwhelmed given their current responsibilities, we must find time for education and conversations regarding essential and sustainable living.

In the vein of the preceding paragraph and this chapter. I have offered the following questions for consideration. Naturally, answers will vary as much as people's circumstances.

1) How could you realistically begin to live a more sustainable life?
2) What do you consider most essential in your life?
3) Regarding the previous question, how does your current lifestyle match your answer to question number 2?
4) In considering your possessions (e.g., home, vehicles, furniture, clothes, etc.), how much is really essential?
5) Should you continue in your current lifestyle, will your life become more or less fulfilling?
6) If you were to develop your life's vision, what would that vision involve? (e.g., type of home, location, career or careers, family, retirement, etc.)
7) How much fulfillment do you derive from your current lifestyle?
8) If your answer to the previous question is unsatisfactory, how might you begin to create more meaning and purpose in your life?
9) Complete this sentence fragment: "What I would most want to change in my life is . . ."
10) What do you consider most important regarding the remainder of your life?

Resources for Consideration

Living Big in a Tiny House. Bryce Langston, New Zealander highlights small and tiny houses and apartments around the world. www.youtube.com/channel/UCoNTMWgGuXtGPLv9UeJZwBw

The Minimalists Podcast. Joshua Fields Milburn and Ryan Nicodemus. There are weekly podcasts. www.theminimalists.com/podcast/

Minimalism: A Documentary about Important Things. Directed by Matt D'Avella (2016). www.netflix.com/title/80114460

How to Avoid a Climate Disaster: The Solutions we Have and the BREAKTHROUGHS WE NEED. (2021). By Bill Gates. Knopf.

Your Money or Your Life: 9 Steps to Transforming Your Relationship with Money and Achieving Financial Independence. (2018). By Vicki Robin and Joe Dominguez. Random House.

Lessons Learned

I had been living in Oregon for a decade when I met John (pseudonym). John was an addictions counselor whom I met at some social gathering. We had struck up a conversation about simple living, whereupon he mentioned living a small retrofitted garage. Before the evening ended, he invited me to visit his home, with the promise of good beer or wine. As these offers sometimes represent polite etiquette rather than a real invitation, I gave the nebulous offer little thought. Weeks later, we had an impromptu meeting at a local coffee shop, whereupon we sat down together for a chat.

It was summer and we both were on our lunch breaks from the agencies employing us. Over Kenyan roast coffee (or another exotic blend), we resumed our conversation on simple living, particularly how we saw it manifest in our lives. I lived in a communal house with two suitcases of clothes, a meditation bench, and a 15-year-old car as the sum total of my worldly possessions. Comparatively, his lifestyle seemed cluttered, albeit only when compared to those in my camp. As we were preparing to return to work, he offered a more concrete invitation. "How about dinner at my house this Friday?" Somewhat surprised, given a relationship forged on just two conversations, I accepted.

John lived just west of town some ten miles or so from me. John's house had originally been conceived as the garage, with the original owner intending to build on it. For whatever reasons, the larger addition never materialized. Although my memory is sketchy, I would estimate his home was around 400 square feet or so. John, my senior by a decade or so, had never married nor had children. He had purchased the house and acre of land at a very reasonable price, and being handy, had built new cabinets and added a covered patio for the summer and fall months. Stepping into his home, John's minimalist values were evident: his futon doubled as his bed; he had one second-hand easy chair, with dining table and chairs purchased at a garage sale, and a wall adorned with photographs of the many international locations he had visited. His only entertainment was a stereo turntable he had owned since undergraduate days. His 1970s VW Bug was his transportation, when not tooling about on his aged ten-speed bicycle.

Over dinner, the menu of which I cannot recall, we sipped on a couple of his homemade beers and discussed our lives and future life plans. He hoped to immigrate to New Zealand where he had visited some years previously. He wanted to find a small co-housing community or build a small house with the same dimensions of his current home. During our conversation, I grew more curious about him. He was an articulate, educated man (with a master's in Counseling), well-traveled, having visited some 30 countries, and being blond and fit, many would consider him handsome. After protracted talk of places we wanted to visit and live, I inquired, "How did you manage to land here?"

He explained he had grown up in northern California with educated, affluent parents. Moving to Oregon for graduate school, he found it more to his liking, with a much smaller population and more affordable costs than California. He had read Duane Elgin's popular book *Volunteer Simplicity* (1981). Eschewing all except essential possessions, John lived by a simple maxim: "If I don't need it to live, I don't need it." His "not needing it" philosophy included purchasing only secondhand clothes, furniture, vehicles, cooking supplies, and anything else. He had never cohabitated nor married, finding solo life more congruent with his lifestyle. He had no desire to father children and continue his line. "I like helping kids, not raising them," he added. His passion was international travel. Given an early edition of the *Lonely Planet* series, he became infected with the travel bug. Traveling frugally, he stayed at backpacker hostels, tiny motels, bed & breakfast homes, and occasionally with hospitable locals. He stretched money by preparing his own food and working odd jobs for pay or meals. No question about it, John had perfected the art of affordable living and traveling.

Beers empty, he made coffee (naturally) and we moved to his postage-size patio with a view of the Coast Range. He commented about chronicling his life story with me revealing nothing personal. Saying little about myself is no accident. Long ago, I learned others wanted to talk and me to listen. I generally am the listener, close friends and family excepted. The invitation extended, however, I disclosed struggling with the direction of my life. I had been attending a monastery for a few years with the intent of moving in after completing my doctorate. However, the desire for international travel, something always beyond my grasp, burned strong. I recall his reply clearly: "*A monastery! Are you out of your fucking mind?*" We laughed, then, refocusing on my desire for global travel, he inquired what countries or locations I would like to visit.

During childhood, our grandparents raised my four siblings and me. They were financially impoverished people adept at surviving on meager wages. Owning no motor vehicle, my travel came courtesy of the *National Geographic* subscription my Texas relatives gifted us annually. To escape the Ozarks' merciless summer heat and humidity, I would retreat to our cool, dirt-floor basement to read the latest *Geographic* edition. I yearned to visit distant countries and cultures, with a particular interest in the southern hemisphere, especially Australia and New Zealand. In fact, a cover story on the Australian Outback fascinated me, especially given the odd creatures and distant location.

I spoke of my desire to visit Australia and New Zealand. As he had visited Australia, New Zealand, Fiji, and several South Pacific islands, his descriptive tales whetted my appetite. He offered his counsel, expressing that I seemed more animated when discussing travel than becoming a monk. Without judgment, he encouraged me to examine my dreams. "Look, you can save a lot of money living like me. Carry as little debt as possible and if you marry or partner, make sure she likes to travel." We continued our conversation on essential living, visiting exotic lands, most being very far away, and the possible direction of my life. Finally, with darkness descending, I thanked him for his hospitality and drove home.

Life has taught me many lessons, some being difficult and painful ones, as it does to all. Entering counseling as part of the monastic discernment process, I would not become a monk and live in a monastery. My vocation continued in counseling and higher education, later marrying an international traveler extraordinaire, conjointly traveling overseas, while singularly volunteering in the Australian Outback.

The lessons learned over 60-plus years are legion. Volunteer simplicity, as in the popular book, and exemplified by John among others, differs significantly from the socioeconomic demilitarized zone where all too many impoverished people remain incarcerated. The privilege of choice, successful and not, has been my most transforming lesson. Global excursions have taken me to remote locations of ineffable beauty, but also to places of debilitating poverty and desperation. These extremes represent the bookends of my journeys, simultaneously uplifting while haunting my thoughts. My most important lesson is that we must find ways to live more simply so that others may simply live. This means near carbon zero so that island countries like Tuvalu, whose existence currently is threatened by global warming's rising waters, do not destroy a people and culture. It means sharing resources so that the South African shantytowns with open sewers have needed infrastructure for improvement. Sustainability means purchasing less plastic so that ocean species are no longer threatened by this plague, and fishing cultures the world over can continue their cultural ways. Finally, as we all share this biosphere, we must all, counselors, psychologists, social workers, marriage and family therapists, and psychiatrists, among others, find methods of encouraging global stewardship, as environmental sustainability is conducive to optimal mental health. If these noble professions unite in advocating sustainable living, this could provide robust support for visionary ideas espoused by Bill Gates and others. My suggestion is for all mental health professions to infuse environmental sustainability within their ethical codes, graduate training programs, research journals, and in conference workshops. Such sustainable inclusion has occurred within the mental health professions, but not to the extent required for significant change. Absent radical change in reducing our carbon footprint, our very existence lies imperiled. In Peter Weir's epic film *The Last Wave* (1977), cataclysmic natural forces destroy an earth polluted through over-industrialization and unsustainable living. Although a film, Weir's version of the end of known civilization appears prescient, given the upheaval of global warming, glacial melt and rising seas, destructive wildfires, acid rain, holes in the ozone layer, and pollution of lands and waterways. Like the rats on the electrified grid, global warming and industrial toxicity have the potential to create massive chaos resulting in severe anxiety, depression, addiction, and violence. Thus, sustainable living now resides well within the mental health profession's scope of responsibility and practice.

Chapter 8

Life Happens

Changing Our Attitude and Transforming Our Life

My grandparents and teachers taught that attitude, far more than talent, was a better predictor of future success. Unquestionably, belief in such statements is easier in the abstract, particularly when life seems to be proceeding in a harmonious manner. As it happens, however, life throws us a curve and the rains of failure, disappointment, and grief pour down upon us. Hopeful slogans can seem a cruel joke, leaving us wondering how we could have been so naïve. Now, confession time: pardoning the malapropism, I am a hopeless optimist. This is not to say I am any type of Pollyanna in my views, nor toxic in my optimism. Depression has caused me significant distress during points in my life. However, my Black Dog (depression) bites with far less force than in my younger days. I credit both my counseling experiences and a more adaptive attitude. Principally, I am more optimistic, utilizing daily gratitudes, meditation, exercise, and a stronger support system. The first and most important of these necessary ingredients is attitude.

One of the first questions to address is the problem of suffering. From biblical Job, to Tevye in *Fiddler on the Roof*, to Harold Kushner in his uber-popular, thoughtful book *When Bad Things Happen to Good People* (1981), to a broken-hearted teenager, questioning the equity of our misfortune is a natural part of this crucible of life. Philosophers, theologians, and counselors and therapists have grappled with this ageless question. It will surprise nobody that this text fails to adequately answer this ubiquitous question. Viktor Frankl wrote there must be meaning in suffering, as it is an ineradicable part of life and death, and without suffering and death human life cannot be complete (Frankl, 2006).

What I find most intriguing about Frankl's statement is his outright acceptance of suffering. Frankl was a psychiatrist who treated mental anguish, and survived possibly the worst example of human-created suffering recorded history has known. As previously mentioned in this text, his family, including wife and children, were among the 6 million murdered in the Holocaust. Incredibly, he emerged from this human-created hell with an even stronger belief in the power of attitude and meaning. He opined that all may be taken from a person, save the freedom to choose one's attitude in any given set of circumstances

DOI:10.4324/9781003168324-8

(2006). Any mental health professional can speak volumes regarding the value of attitude in successful therapeutic outcomes. Like the powerful construct of optimism, or its opposite, pessimism, attitude is a robust predictor of therapeutic success (Beck, 1979).

One of the most useful theoretical models regarding attitude and positive change likely is the Stages of Change Model (Prochaska et al., 1992). Prochaska et al.'s model primarily addresses the field of addictions, but holds lessons well beyond. This five-stage model is as follows:

1) Precontemplation: The individual has no concept of a needed change, despite ample evidence to the contrary (e.g., legal issues, job loss, health concerns, etc.).
2) Contemplation: After much difficulty, the individual begins to consider change necessary.
3) Preparation: The individual begins making small changes. For example, if they are alcohol dependent, they begin looking up treatment resources and moderating substance use.
4) Action: The individual goes forth for treatment and begins changing use of their drug, maintaining this for three to six months.
5) Maintenance: Individual maintains sobriety for more than six months.

(Prochaska et al., 1992)

Sometimes called the sixth stage, relapse is also common to this change model (Prochaska et al., 1992). Although relapse in addiction treatment is common, many people do successfully recover from addiction and other self-defeating behaviors and cognitions. Without question, attitude is heavily front-end loaded into this model, as without attitudinal change, behavioral change is impossible. Having treated clients in the grip of mental health and addictive disorders, attitude has been a tipping point in all cases of successful treatment. I cannot think of a single client whose emotional and mental well-being improved absent positive attitudinal change. William Miller and his colleague Scott Tonigan have developed the Stages of Change Readiness and Treatment Model (SOCRATES, 1996) to evaluate attitudes towards changing drug use. SOCRATES consists of a 19-item scale on Personal Drinking Questionnaire and a 19-item scale on Personal Drug Use Questionnaire, and is scored on the constructs of Recognition (of an alcohol or drug problem), Ambivalence (unaware or unsure of problem), and Taking Steps (making changes).

Attitude as a healthy psychological construct certainly is nothing new. Frankl (1986, 2006), Ellis and Doyle (1988), Beck (1979), and Seligman (2002) are other notable theorists and clinicians who have infused attitudinal change into psychotherapy. Anyone having studied the variations of cognitive therapy (e.g., CBT, REBT, DBT, etc.) understands the role of reframing negative thoughts into healthier, more adaptive ones. When thoughts become healthier, healthier behavior usually follows (Beck, 1979; Ellis & Doyle, 1988). My anecdotal experience as a clinician mirrors the work of Ellis, Beck, and others. The common challenge is getting clients to entertain the possibility that positive change is indeed possible, given many having experienced significant trauma, addiction, and disappointment. In public mental health agencies, a significant percentage of clientele likely is lower income (Medicaid eligible), and often bring numerous accompanying barriers to therapy (addiction, unemployment, domestic violence, less education, etc.). Although cognitive therapy is well-validated (Beck, 1979; Ellis & Doyle, 1988; Seligman, 2002), clients with multiple barriers and a history of disappointment often have a difficult time envisioning positive change, given their painful experience. Yet, low-income populations are precisely those most in need of a belief in change. Having been fortunate enough to escape poverty's strong gravitational pull, I understand well the difficulty in believing change is possible. Building a strong, respectful relationship with clients is a critical phase of promoting cognitive and behavioral change (Miller & Tonigan, 1996). When I consider it, promoting cognitive and behavioral change in my own life is challenging as well. Therapists must be persistent, even resilient, in modeling and encouraging clients to entertain that positive change can occur.

Focusing on the Good Things

Within this text, I have mentioned gratitude numerous times. Over 30 years ago, my former advisor encouraged me to habituate acknowledging three gratitudes daily. This simple practice helps ground me into a positive frame of mind and is particularly helpful on challenging days when everything seems to be going awry. No doubt, gratitude come easy when our personal, financial, health, and occupational fortunes remain favorable. When the winds of change shift, however, and fortunes plummet, daily gratitudes can seem far less relevant. Yet, when we are struggling, acknowledging daily gratitudes is of critical importance to our functioning. Cultivating an attitude of gratitude correlates with higher self-esteem, healthier relationships, and a stronger sense of resilience (Seligman et al., 2005).

Seligman, as part of his Positive Psychology movement, sought operationalize approaches to happiness and well-being (Seligman et al., 2005; Seligman, 2002). He created the Three Good Things Exercise designed to highlight the positives in one's life. When Seligman and his colleagues tested the Three Good Things, they found regular practice seemed to boost happiness levels (Seligman et al., 2005). The longer the participants performed the exercise, the higher their happiness levels. At a six-month follow up, happiness levels increased by 9% (Seligman et al., 2005). These results certainly are promising, although more study is required. Furthermore, the discipline of daily practice is critical, just as habituating positive thoughts takes daily practice. In fact, my advisor, a monk of 50 years, explained gratitude acknowledgement would take a lifetime of practice for optimal results. Essentially, mental fitness is akin to physical fitness, meaning there is no point where one can say, "Okay, I'm fit. No more exercise needed." With this in mind, let us consider Seligman's Three Good Things exercise.

Three Good Things in Life Exercise

1) Each night prior to falling asleep, think of three good things that occurred that day. Do not concern yourself with whether they were big or small things; just think of three positive things. Perhaps you met an old friend, work went well, or you had your favorite meal at dinner.
2) Write down these Three Good Things. Writing notes with pen or pencil as opposed to keyboarding seems to help with memory recall (Mueller & Oppenheimer, 2014), so writing down the Three Good Things with a pen is very important.
3) After writing them down, reflect on what brought about these positive events and why they occurred. Write down the "Why things went well" part. (For example, "My presentation went well because I worked hard and was supported by my colleagues.")
4.) Do this Three Good Things exercise for one week and notice what positive changes have occurred regarding your mood or outlook. Then, habituate the exercise by committing to it for one month, then six months. (I encourage the practice throughout a lifetime.)

Adapted from Seligman (2006)

According to Seligman (2006), the reason this exercise likely works is because regular focus and practice on positive assets and experiences begins to improve one's outlook. Another researcher found similar results as Seligman when researching subjects focusing on positive assets (Lai, 2017). I have been encouraging a similar Three Daily Gratitudes in my self-care trainings and to my graduate students. Looking further into Seligman's research, I cannot help but see strong correlations with Frankl's Logotherapy. After all, Seligman and his colleagues are promoting related constructs to meaning (i.e., happiness and well-being) and a Three Good Things practice seems to correlate with Frankl's meaning in life model. Both Frankl and Seligman focused on developing intrapersonal and interpersonal prosocial assets. Personal and intrapersonal strengths likely correlate strongly with meaning and purpose in life.

By focusing on the positive in life, I risk accusations of ignoring the *bad things* in life. To address this potential misconception, I would point out Frankl's horrific experience during his incarceration in three death camps and the brutal murder of virtually his entire family. One could well imagine him coming out of that hellish experience traumatized, bitter, and holding a pessimistic view of humanity. Ironically, Frankl emerged from bondage buoyed with an indefatigable optimism and designed a therapeutic approach focused on transcendent meaning. To cite another significant figure, His Holiness, the 14th Dalai Lama and his Tibetan Buddhist followers had their land confiscated by Mao Zedong's forces in 1949. He and his followers have lived in exile in northern India for over 70 years since. Like Frankl, one could well imagine the Dalai Lama being a bitter, angry man. Yet, psychiatrist and author Howard Cutler describes the Dalai Lama as a happy man well known for laughing and making others around him laugh (The Dalai Lama & Cutler, 2020). Cutler reports that if you ask the Dalai Lama if he is happy, he will answer that happiness is the purpose of life (The Dalai Lama & Cutler, 2020).

Frankl and the Dalai Lama represent two intriguing examples of persons having suffered massive losses, yet somehow retaining a very positive outlook. Had either or both of these notable people become embittered, revenge-oriented, and spewing anger, it would have seemed understandable. Perhaps the operative question becomes, how do people who have experienced exceptional tragedy maintain a hopeful, meaningful attitude towards life? For Frankl, meaning emanated from three possible sources: love, purposeful work, and courage in the face of difficulty (2006). The Dalai Lama's approach to happiness springs from learning, reasoning, and disciplining the mind. Through self-discipline, we undergo a transformation of our attitude, outlook, and approach to living (The Dalai Lama & Cutler, 2020). While these two stalwarts of love and purposeful living differ somewhat in how meaning is manifest, clearly there is much overlap in their focus on cultivating a life of meaning and purpose.

Many years ago I counseled a client I will call Bill. Bill's life had come crashing down on him. He had lost his job due to his employer's downsizing, his wife had divorced him, and in the divorce, he lost the home he loved, and now saw his children only on alternate weekends. As often happens in divorce, many former friends scattered, and he found himself isolated and depressed. He became so desperate that with no other discernable options available, he decided to give counseling a go. (His explanation!) When he presented for his intake session, he appeared moody and unkempt, common for someone in grief. We made it through the intake questionnaire with his primarily single-word answers. Finally, we completed the intake, including assessments for depression and suicide. He was not suicidal, though understandably, he was quite depressed. However, he gave off vibes of anger, something I viewed as hopeful, as anger suggests the person has not abandoned hope. I decided to probe into that anger. "So, how are you doing with all these changes in your life?" He blew up at me: "How the fuck do you think I'm doing?!" I let several seconds elapse before inquiring how it felt to express open anger. He gave me a quizzical look, and then smiled. "I feel relieved. No one asks me anything, they just give me fake smiles." He apologized for snapping at me, but I explained he likely had been internalizing his emotions and becoming even more depressed. He agreed this was precisely what he had been doing, and it felt terrible. I asked what he wanted to do with his anger. He replied that he wanted to scream. Recalling a colleague who used primal screams in therapy, I encouraged, "Scream away." "But we're in a church!" he replied, face looking anxious. (It was a pastoral counseling center within a church.) I suggested God could handle honest anger, and furthermore my office's location at the far end of the building meant he could scream without fear of being overheard. Evidently satisfied, he commenced yelling out the F-word and other choice adjectives for the better part of a minute. (A *long* time to listen to high-volume profanity!) Finally ceasing his roar, he wiped his brow with a tissue and commenced crying.

He sobbed for a good couple of minutes then sat upright. I asked if the screaming and cry had helped. He admitted it had, comparing it to opening a window and releasing a bad odor. Consulting the intake, I inquired regarding his goals for counseling. He shook his head and replied, "I just want to feel better." When then discussed what "feeling better" would look like in his life. After a protracted conversation that took us to the end of the hour, he stated, "I want to learn to be happy again." Before he left, I assigned him the homework of finding one thing—behavior or thought—that would provide some happiness or fulfillment. He agreed to the homework assignment and left.

Several days later, Bill arrived for his follow up session looking rested and better groomed. I inquired about his week and the assigned homework. He smiled, stating he had cheated. I asked about his *dishonesty* and he confessed to having completed *two* happiness actions. Encouraging him to elaborate on his heinous act of rebellion, he chuckled, explaining that when he was younger, he was a cycling enthusiast. For whatever reasons, after marriage, he ceased his hobby and put on additional weight. Realizing he missed the enjoyment cycling provided, he purchased a touring bicycle and began riding daily. As we had been using scaling questions, he reported his happiness score had increased from a three to a six or seven. "What's the other thing you did?" I inquired. He explained having applied for a job at a small company advertising for an accountant (his field). Narrowly beating the application deadline, the company immediately called him for an interview. In fact, he had just come from that interview, which he reported went very well. I acknowledged this was indeed good news. Thinking his gains possibly were too soon and a set-up for disappointment, preparation for success and failure were prudent. Seemingly reading my thoughts, he offered, "Oh, I turned them down. The interview taught me I no longer want to be an accountant. The job was making me miserable. My ex-wife used say how I seemed to hate the work. She was right, you know." There was a pause. "So, what else might you do?" I asked, hoping he had not made a decision made based purely on emotion. He smiled his widest smile. "I am going to be a teacher. There won't be as much money in it and kids can be difficult, but it's what I have thought of doing for a long time. Since my undergraduate days, really."

He expressed getting caught up in making lots of money, working very long hours and putting his family a distant second, eventually his ending his marriage. During college, he had been interested in teaching, but his father, a successful businessman, discouraged him, saying, "You won't get rich." "I don't give a shit about rich anymore. I do care about work that matters and I want a relationship with my kids." I congratulated him on finding his inner calling and asked if he wanted to continue counseling. He disclosed the simple homework assignment of finding one happy thing had spurred him to consider what brought him actual happiness. Finding the corporate world unfulfilling, in fact killing his spirit, he decided to pursue his original desire to teach and mentor middle-school students. As he stood and shook my hand he replied, "I think I will occasionally assign happiness-type homework and not just math problems. Thank you for helping me reprioritize my life. I will return if needed."

I had done very little in our mere two sessions, other than be present and empathetic to his pain. My sense is that he simply needed to hit the reset button on his life. There is nothing at all wrong with being an accountant, as it is important work. The issue was he no longer found the work fulfilling, and while he had made a high salary, he was miserable. A thoughtful person, he realized having missed the simple pleasure of cycling through the region's miles of bike trails. He further realized his life was calling, and he elected to heed that calling and retrain as a teacher. His divorce, job loss, and our sessions involving primal therapy and the homework assignment had awakened him from slumber. Bill O'Hanlon's simple book, *Do One Thing Different: Ten Simple Ways to Change Your Life* (2013) had provided me insight for counseling people such as Bill. Keeping homework simple is important, having found clients more likely to follow through, and second, shifting his focus from frustration to pursuits that brought him fulfillment. This has often been part of my approach, although Bill found success much quicker than most clients. Importantly, Bill actually *knew* what fed his soul, and it was not a high-paying corporate job. Not everyone discerns as quickly or chooses as wisely as Bill, as we shall see in the following example.

It was summer and I was working in a large human services agency where my job title, roles, and responsibilities seemed to change almost daily. Initially hired as a Vocational and Employment Counselor, I also staffed the agency's alternative school assisting adults studying for a GED, taught job club, provided 1-to-1 career assessment and counseling, and counseled clients in crisis—with the latter occurring often, given that our clients struggled with a variety of vocational, relationship, and self-medication issues. I recall a particularly promising client in our alternative school, whom I will refer to as Maria. Maria was a divorced, mid-30-something, Latina woman with two children. She had recently left an abusive relationship, achieved sobriety, earned her GED and was preparing to start classes at the local community college with plans of becoming a registered nurse. Despite having dropped out of high school due to pregnancy, she was quite an intelligent and enthusiastic learner. She was taking a psychology class at the community college and using our career center to look for work. I became acquainted with Maria when she requested help writing her resume. She was seeking a job at a nursing care facility, given flexible hours fit with her school schedule and provided time with her younger daughter, a high school senior. A motivated learner, she crafted a well-written resume, and her interview performance could have been a training video. She possessed a strong work ethic, stable employment history, excellent writing skills, and was bilingual and likable. Quickly hired at a senior center, she had a job, health benefits, and weekend work that fit her school schedule. Her case manager and I referred to her as our star. No doubt, Maria's future was bright. "I love my life now!" she had exclaimed. I expected she would continue to achieve, given her intelligence, drive, and winning personality.

Several months later, when back at my doctoral studies and working at the university counseling center, I was meeting with a friend at a local coffee shop when I happened to glance out the window at a disturbing scene. Two people, an adult male and female, were having a loud screaming match. Both appeared under the influence of something (likely alcohol). A police office had responded and arrested both people. As the woman turned towards the coffee shop window, our eyes met and I realized it was Maria. Her face quickly transformed from hostility to sadness. Then the officer put her into the police car, whisking her to jail.

Stunned at her reversal in fortune, I could not imagine what had happened to this intelligent, focused, purpose-driven woman. During the academic year, as I was not employed at the agency, federal privacy laws would prevent me from finding out until the holiday break when the agency hired me. Maria had become involved with another student at the community college. This man was "bad news," as her former case manager related, having served prison time for drugs and domestic abuse. Maria became involved with him, relapsed on drugs, and dropped out of college, culminating in the arrest to which I had a front-row seat.

I do not know Maria's whole story, nor do I judge her for whatever decisions she made. When thinking of her, the most common emotion that arises is sadness. She had battled abuse, achieved sobriety, earned a GED, and was admitted to a nursing program. Somehow, while on this promising pathway, she had a terrible wreck. If I could sketch the face of hopelessness, it would resemble Maria's when our eyes met and she recognized me through the coffee shop window. I certainly have observed other client's sad relapses, but cannot recall any quite like Maria's, given her exceptional progress. I hold out hope she once again righted her life, regained sobriety, found a healthier relationship, and got her life back on track. My hopes, however, do not always translate into realities, and such is the challenging nature of therapeutic work. We pour heart and soul into our clients, hoping the gains they achieve sprout legs once therapy ends. Many former clients continue on their healthy trajectory; others become ensnared in old temptations and patterns, spiraling downward until perhaps able to crawl out of that dark void.

What Does Matter in Life?

I have focused this chapter on people making life transformations. What is transformational for one person, however, can be drudgery for another. While I believe Frankl and the Dalai Lama, for example, are both correct that meaning and happiness are most important in life, how a person infuses meaning and happiness into their life is much more individualistic. Bill, the divorced, recently unemployed accountant discovered his meaning came from his children, cycling, and a dormant yearning to be a teacher. Naturally enough, however, someone else could find fulfillment in friendship, volunteer work, journaling, and yes, even being a CPA. The more important issue likely lies in one's finding their *own* path towards personal meaning, fulfillment, and happiness.

There are numerous assessments to measure happiness, such as the Subjective Happiness Scale (SHS; Lyubomirsky & Lepper, 1999), The Authentic Happiness Test (Seligman, n.d.), the Meaning in Life Questionnaire (MLQ; Steger et al., 2006), and the Purpose in Life Test (PIL; Crumbaugh & Maholick, 1964), to say nothing of numerous career interest and aptitude assessments. These aforementioned assessments can be helpful and important for our personal and occupational lives, yet they cannot provide us the most important ingredient for success: namely, a healthy attitude (Frankl, 1986, 2006). Interestingly, while writing this book, a column in *Counseling Today* was timely. The column (Pressman, 2021, March) mentioned Carl McDaniel's career counseling model being Career = Work (W) + Leisure (L) (McDaniel, 1984). One of the interesting ingredients McDaniel emphasized was the role of fun in work and in life. My former client Bill, for example, had given up a cycling hobby that had brought him immense pleasure. In reclaiming his life, he climbed aboard his new bicycle and began pedaling through his grief.

Admittedly, if treating depression, anxiety, grief, addiction, and any other mental health issue were as simple as exercise, a viable hobby, and a new career, the role of the counselor/therapist would be one of easy money. Many of my former clients maintained active fitness routines, hobbies, and rewarding careers, yet struggled with PTSD, sobriety, depression, and the like. The important point, however, is that in all cases, such clients reported that hobbies (journaling, reading, bird watching, etc.) along with some type of body movement (e.g., cycling, yoga, dancing, etc.) did help in managing their mental health concerns. Furthermore, McDaniel spoke as much to the importance of leisure as he did to a meaningful career. In fact, he seemed to suggest that we work to live, as opposed to living to work (1984). Those of us who are able to work to live, and not vice versa, truly are fortunate indeed. Many, naturally, have fewer options due to lack of education, training, injury, dependents, chronically depressed regions, etc.

Questions to Entertain Regarding Career and Life:

1) What do you find most fulfilling in your life? Alternatively, if life is not currently fulfilling, "What *was* most fulfilling in life?"
2) What do you find most fulfilling in your career? What has been least fulfilling?
3) What is your favorite hobby? What do you find enjoyable or fulfilling about that hobby?
4) What could you do to enhance your sense of career fulfillment?
5) Complete this sentence fragment: "My life would become more meaningful if I changed . . ."
6) What is the most important lesson you have learned in your career?
7) If given the chance, would you choose the same career? Explain.
8) If you are a professional counselor or therapist (or any professional), what advice would you give to those considering your chosen career?
9) Regarding McDaniel's Career = Work (W) + Life (L) (1984), how balanced and healthy is your work-to-life ratio? If you believe it is unbalanced, how might you balance it?
10) Regarding general feelings of happiness, in general, how would you rate your current happiness level on a scale of 1–10, with 10 being high? How might you raise that score one point?

Lessons Learned

My heart pounded against my ribcage like a jackhammer on pavement. My palms were moist and my stomach queasy as if just prior to a big exam. It was January 1981, and I sat in the University Counseling Center lobby awaiting the first counseling appointment of my life. A series of events accumulated over my young lifetime had propelled me towards therapy. I had made the appointment during finals week of the previous term. Recalling Prochaska et al. (1992), I had been mired in precontemplation, denying needing help despite ample evidence to the contrary. This practice worked about as well for me as most, culminating in my academic and personal life crashing into shards. At rock bottom, I surrendered to the reality that my life was unmanageable and my need for professional help.

To say I was struggling would be a gross understatement. I had narrowly avoided flunking out of college, suffered a recent panic attack, misused alcohol, and was depressed. Suicide, fortunately, had not been part of my thought process, but my self-talk was negative and self-defeating. I seemed to have nothing significant for grounding, being socially isolated, with distant family relationships and an unpromising future. Seeking counseling represented a Hail Mary approach towards getting my life on track. As a resident advisor during the previous year and the subsequent summer, I had assisted many students in accessing counseling services while never going forward myself, despite my need likely being greater than those I was helping. Thus, I sat uncomfortably in a wooden chair across from other sad-looking students, all avoiding eye contact.

Finally, a nondescript, balding man in his mid-30s approached, asked my first name, and said kindly, "Follow me." My counselor, whom I will call Carl, had a small though comfortable office. He calmly explained the process, intake interview and subsequent sessions, then inquired if I had any questions. I shook my head, and he commenced the interview, then administered a depression screening assessment. After the better part of an hour, he explained the results. Then he inquired, "Where does your sense of meaning come from?" His question was scarcely abstract. I had stated during the interview that my life seemed without purpose or meaning. My memory is of simply shaking my head. His reply was to smile and suggest that perhaps part of our treatment plan was for me to develop a purpose and rediscover the meaning in my life. As I was about to exit his office, he made what was to me an unbelievable statement. "I can see you being very successful in the future," he offered, looking sincere. Dumbfounded at his overly optimistic view of me, I thanked him and left puzzled. No one had ever said anything so praising of me, and consequently, I took his statement as a charitable act designed to elicit some degree of self-confidence.

I told no one in my social circle about being in counseling. My discretion was less about shame and more a desire for basic privacy. Much later, I would disclose to a friend my having gone to counseling, and was surprised he had as well. The following week, I began my first session feeling slightly more relaxed. Carl probed my background, inquiring about my family of origin. I explained my five siblings, primarily raised by our grandparents, of my mother institutionalized with bipolar disorder, and that my relationship was strongest with my grandparents and my younger brother. He inquired about my motivation for attending college. I explained initially having planned to become a high school science teacher, majoring in chemistry, but reality had settled in (anemic grades). He asked if academics were my primary reason for seeking counseling. I considered his question in depth, as I was on academic life support, but knew my concerns went far beyond scholarly deficits. Frankly, I was very depressed, and pessimistic regarding my future.

During this session, I recall he asked, "If you were living a meaningful life, what would that look like?" That very question would set the tone for an entire semester of therapy. After the session, it dawned on me that I had never really considered how to create a meaningful life. Given the shambles of my life at that point, contemplating, and certainly creating meaning in my life, seemed the highest priority, above even needed academic rehabilitation. Later, sitting in the library, I pondered how therapy sessions might proceed. After all, who teaches one how to create meaning in life? I could not recall my school counselor teaching us how to create meaning. Certainly, no high school or college class I had taken had grappled with anything resembling meaning. My closest approximation was in our rural church, but their answers seemed too formulaic and unrealistic. Looking back, it seems my life had devolved into what Frankl called the existential vacuum (1986). This void was like wandering in a vast desert, feeling lonely, disoriented, and afraid. Such was my life.

At some point during our sessions, we began brainstorming. On a small chalkboard, he asked me to list all the things I enjoyed. I wrote down running, walking, reading, traveling, talking with friends, and so forth. He began to inquire about these. Running had remained my constant, as full-time work plus school took up a lot of time. He noted my dearth of social contact and began to assign me to ask someone to coffee once per week. Another time, he assigned me to read a book by my favorite mystery author. Finally, he asked me to write a one-page journal entry on meaning, including answering the question, "If my life were meaningful, what would be different about it?" Hooked, I wrote far more than a one-page response to this weighty question! We then spent an entire session on my journal. Looking back, that question represented the tipping point of my therapeutic turnaround.

With spring semester winding down, we began wrapping up. My depression had lifted, I was doing well in my new major (English), and my life seemed far more meaningful than any time in recent memory. Prior to our final session, Carl requested I journal on how counseling had proved helpful. He had been a patient, skilled clinician adept at establishing trust and promoting my self-reflection on meaning and purpose. His low-key, though persistent, approach helped open a door into a life previously unimagined. During one of our last sessions, he repeated a question from the intake. "So, where does your sense of meaning come from?" We both laughed, as we each knew this question would serve as the psychological bookends in our four months of counseling. I explained that I had learned my sense of meaning emanated from close relationships, being in my body as in my running, rediscovering my dormant academic self, and developing a fulfilling spiritual life. He encouraged me to continue on my journey of self-discovery, and noted my having met all treatment goals. As we shook hands, he asked if I recalled his statement regarding my future success. Saying yes, I inquired what had prompted such optimism, given but a single hour together. After all, I was skating just north of academic probation and was clearly depressed. "Because you seem so determined and so resilient. Good luck, Shannon!"

Then this counselor, who had been so instrumental in my recovery from depression and in plotting a new course in life, walked out of my life forever. 40 years since, meaning and purpose have been my life's primary foci. This is by no means suggesting a meaning-driven life equates with one of ease. There have been many challenging points, other periods of Black Dog depression, moments I felt friendless, and times when it seemed career success resided on a distant shore. The most significant lesson learned from Carl's gentle guidance was that my sense of meaning was the most important part of my selfhood: more important than academics, career, salary, or any other measuring stick society uses. No, I have not become a famous pillar of the counseling profession, gotten rich or famous. What I have become, however, is *myself*. While that may seem like a pedestrian accomplishment in this social media-driven world, where facades and photo optics rule, I consider being myself a paramount achievement in a society that so desperately desires we be someone else.

Chapter 9

Contemplation in an Action-Oriented World

Addressing Our Inner World Phobia

The Spartan bench was unforgiving and my back sore from a long run the previous afternoon. I sat with a dozen or so others in a meditation circle at a monastery in the rural Northwest. Our meditation advisor, whom I will refer to as Brother B, began the meditation with the statement "Be here now," then struck the meditation bowl and silence descended. Although our meditation advisor had tried to prepare me, a novice, I was woefully prepared for meditation. I was antsy, squirming, my mind wandering, anxious about changes in my life, and confused regarding my future beyond doctoral studies. After struggling through three meditation hours in the morning, I ate lightly and took a brief walk through a scenic path in the woods.

Returning to the meditation house, Brother B was waiting for me. He spoke kindly: "Look, this can be difficult at first. Just focus on your breathing. When you feel restless or your mind wanders, focus on the breath." We returned to our sitting and I seamlessly resumed my struggles. Brother B's counsel returned, and I began to focus solely on my breaths. I slowly inhaled through my nose and out my mouth. When my mind wandered, as it frequently did, I refocused on my breath. My improvement was incremental at best, but meditation became more natural as the afternoon wore on. Finally, around 3:00 PM, Brother B wished us a peaceful weekend in dismissal.

This was my first intensive experience with meditation. I regularly attended meditation sessions at the monastery throughout doctoral studies, with weekend retreats mostly focused on contemplation. Over time, meditation habituated into my life, and the thought of *not* meditating daily seems unnatural as forgoing food. While meditation has not cured me of anxiety, occasional depression, or helped me achieve complete emotional regulation, it has helped me manage all these. More particularly, meditation has been an ongoing asset in stilling my over-active mind, shutting down the incessant chatter that reverberates throughout the chambers of my mind. I recall a colleague advising me to "not believe everything one thinks." I would echo such sentiments, and add that breath-focused meditation is a valuable tool in cognitive and emotional regulation. Mark Epstein chronicles this in his instructive book *Thoughts Without a Thinker: Psychotherapy from a Buddhist Perspective* (2013). Epstein, a psychiatrist who

DOI:10.4324/9781003168324-9

has incorporated meditation into both his personal and professional life, views it as psychologically and spiritually healing, and a pathway towards a more fulfilling life. During the time I was reading his book, I was counseling a number of traumatized clients, many of whom were self-medicating with alcohol and other drugs, self-abusing (e.g., cutting, burning, and other self-injuries), with several struggling with suicide ideation. I was feeling very challenged to be of therapeutic assistance and becoming quite stressed. Epstein recommend therapists find time to meditate between sessions, even for one minute. He endorses this practice as a means to prevent carrying treatment issues from one patient's session into the next. He asserts meditation assists therapists in being present to the client before us, providing the means for building a stronger therapeutic alliance. His *be here now* approach impressed me as strikingly close to Brother B's counsel at the monastery.

Interestingly, having read many of the contemplative masters such as Mark Epstein, Pema Chödrön, Thích Nhất Hạnh, the Dalai Lama, Thomas Merton, John Kabit-Zinn, etc., as different as they may be in culture, orientation, spirituality, and practice, all have in common a focus on and reverence of the present moment. Thích Nhất Hạnh (1999) wrote that the present moment provides the opportunity to be fully awake and aware. In one noteworthy anecdote, he gently admonishes his friend for rushing through the after-dinner dishes to get to their teatime. Thích Nhất Hạnh queries his friend with a question: Are you washing the dishes to wash the dishes, or just hurrying through to get to something enjoyable? Full presence suggests menial tasks like washing dishes may be as important as any other moment, provided we are indeed present. Presence is precisely what Epstein cites as his rationale for brief meditation between sessions. What I discovered after habituating between-session meditations was an increased sense of presence to my clients, and just as significant, an ability to remain grounded with whatever issues the client brought, including suicidal ideation. In fact, one client, a survivor of long-term sexual abuse, struggling with maintaining sobriety, who frequently inflicted cuts on her arms, noticed my being present and commented on it. I explained my recent focus on between-session meditation and she was intrigued. We then launched into a discussion of the value of meditation, and she indicated her willingness to try it. "After all, what do I have to lose?" she joked. I suggested when she was tempted to break sobriety, she was to meditate for five minutes and then call her AA sponsor. Furthermore, when she felt like cutting herself, she also was to meditate for five minutes, then call a friend or the help line. Given that relapse is common, I assigned her to use a rubber dime store knife to simulate cutting, so as not to scar herself.

This client, whom I will call Hailey, returned the following week wearing a look of surprise. She reported the meditation had assisted her in maintaining sobriety and in refraining from cutting for an entire week (real success for her!). I inquired as to specifically how meditation had helped. She reported a focus on breathing reduced her anxiety and assisted in quieting her negative thoughts. For full disclosure, she admitted struggling to maintain her focus and retaining cravings for alcohol and superficial cutting. However, she maintained that meditation was key in her maintaining sobriety and decreased self-abuse. She requested we begin each session with a five-minute meditation. As she reported this was helpful, I readily agreed. Having never meditated in session with a client, I was likely more anxious than Hailey. However, the beginning meditation seemed to have strengthened our alliance and reduced her anxiety. She appeared more open to addressing her flashbacks, intrusive thoughts, and self-defeating behavior after the meditation. She began to complete her homework assignments, which was a noted improvement. Encouraged, she began meditating at bedtime, and noticed this aided her sleep. Given her perpetrator, her father, often abused her at bedtime, small wonder she had trouble sleeping. During several months of counseling, her sleep quality score increased from a SUDS scale (1–10, 10 high) from a 2 or 3 to a 7. She reported that quality sleep reduced her anxiety, providing her more energy to face daily demands. Eventually, she graduated from therapy, maintained sobriety, and ceased self-abusing entirely. In my many years counseling clients, she was one of the major successes. I would not say meditation *cured* her, but she credited it in helping improve counseling sessions, her sleep, and in managing her daily anxiety and depression. My observation was the meditation provided necessary grounding, paving the way for her ability to focus on and address significant treatment issues.

There is another aspect to Hailey's treatment I find worthy of further mention and elaboration. She had mentioned her intrusive, negative, toxic thoughts were as demons. Although not raised with any formal religion, she mentioned the story of Jesus healing the demon-possessed man, and wished someone would exorcise hers. Cognitive restructuring and reframing did not seem to work well, and I suspect the reason was her habit of simply pushing away disturbing thoughts with scant success. Zoloft had provided some assistance, although not significantly increased the quality of her life. "I have an inner world phobia," she confessed. I explained this was most understandable given the abuse she had endured, especially as her mother sided with her abuser, her own father. Interestingly, over time as she began to meditate, she stated it helped her separate herself from those disturbing thoughts. "I just view them as floating past on a river. When I get anxious, I focus on my breath." Nearing the conclusion of a year's worth of sessions, I inquired about her "inner world phobia." She smiled expressing "I'm far less phobic now." She did not say she was *not* phobic, but that her fears were significantly less. When asked what helped most in reducing her disturbing thoughts, she unequivocally identified the meditation. She went on to add that only after becoming a daily meditator for a couple of months were standard cognitive interventions such as reframing helpful.

Having spent some 25 years providing counseling, and over 30 years training counselors, and having counselors, psychologists, and social worker friends (among others), many of us in the broader mental health field grapple with our self-talk. Certainly, Albert Ellis and Aaron Beck have put much focus on noticing, catching, and revising negative self-talk to reduce anxiety and depression, and increase therapeutic success (Beck & Haigh, 2014; Ellis, 2008). I have used REBT and CBT techniques and interventions to good success with clients struggling with anxiety, depression, and substance abuse, both in the US and abroad. I have noticed however, that some former clients such as Hailey need additional grounding tools that until relatively recently were absent from the therapeutic playbook.

Mindfulness, as mentioned in a previous chapter, is actually nothing new, and practiced in Buddhist, Hindu, and Catholic monasteries for over 2,000 years. During the late 1970s, when I began college, workbooks on relaxation techniques were popular. When I had my panic attack, the counselor taught me breathing exercises to slow my respiration and still racing irrational thoughts. He was using a workbook the title of which I have forgotten. Only later, during a writing class, did someone teach me meditation, whereupon I realized the calming techniques in meditation bore strikingly resemblance to that my counselor taught. One of the earliest therapeutic approaches to infuse mindfulness likely was Marsha Linehan's Dialectical Behavior Therapy (DBT). Linehan developed DBT to treat post-traumatized women diagnosed with borderline personality disorder (BPD) to address their suicidal and para-suicidal cognitions and behaviors (Linehan, 2015).

DBT stresses four modules of psychological and emotional functioning: Mindfulness, interpersonal effectiveness, distress tolerance and emotional regulation (2015). These four modules consist of three basic coping skills. The first coping skill taught is that of *observation*. Observation is sitting with your thoughts, feelings, sensations, and behavioral responses in a detached manner, as in meditation, like my client Hailey learned to practice. The second is the skill of *describing* the action of labeling your observations while eliminating self-judgment, or using self-compassion. The third skill is becoming a *participant*. Participation is full and active engagement in the present moment. When the client is able to achieve acting in the present, while practicing self-compassion, they become able to choose healthier behaviors over self-medication, self-abuse, verbal lashing out, etc. Essentially, DBT's overarching goal is for the client to become a participant. Moreover, participants develop the ability to balance the emotional mind with the reasonable mind, thus creating what Linehan calls the wise mind (2015). In wise mind, clients are able to recognize and respect their feelings without judgment while responding to them in a rational manner.

Reading Linehan's book recalled for me the meditation and philosophical training at the monastery. Interestingly, Linehan talks of mindfulness, spirituality, present moment awareness, sitting with one's thoughts, feelings, sensations, and abstractly describing what is going on in one's environment, all which can be found in the works of Thích Nhất Hạnh, Thomas Merton, the Dalai Lama, Pema Chödrön, and other notable spiritual teachers. This is not to say that meditation and psychotherapy are the same, as there are notable differences. Counseling has as an end goal the amelioration of emotional suffering, through changes in affect, behavior, and cognition (the ABCs), meditation, while certainly congruent with counseling (Epstein, 2013), and is utilized by many spiritual movements and individuals to heighten awareness so that one may live with a present moment focus. These are abbreviated definitions naturally, as counseling and meditation have numerous forms, techniques and applications. Regardless of the differentiations between counseling and meditation, there remains little question that mindfulness, meditation, and present moment awareness can offer much to enhance counseling effectiveness, at least for many clients and clinicians as well (Epstein, 2013). My own practice has taught me well of the value of meditation in addressing my own anxiety and becoming more effective in providing therapy.

What I especially appreciate about Linehan's approach is her focus on teaching clients to become present to their painful past and disturbing thoughts in a nonjudgmental manner. In DBT, only when a client can observe and describe their thoughts, emotions, and sensations without self-harm can they proceed to becoming a full participant in therapy and in their own life (2015). Thus, when clients get triggered outside therapy, *and they will be triggered*, Linehan's plan is to observe what's occurring (thinking, feeling, in your body, etc.), and then describe to yourself what is happening, using grounding in the present (looking around, clapping hands, smells, what one hears, and even tastes). Furthermore, DBT coaches that triggers are simply normal reactions to abnormal experiences (2015). This nonjudgmental, realistic therapeutic approach removes the blame from clients, refocusing it where it rightly belongs: on perpetrators of violence, trauma, poverty, and other trauma-producing conditions. While Linehan and DBT practitioners understand that traumatized clients will feel the urge to regress and dissociate, self-injure, and consider suicide, the focus remains on being present to one's discomfort *nonjudgmentally*. Having treated numerous women suffering from PTSD and BPD, DBT's focus on mindfulness, distress tolerance, emotional regulation, relationships, and how to sit without judgment with uncomfortable thoughts, feelings, and sensations makes a lot of sense to me, a counselor, decades-long meditation practitioner, and one having grappled with self-judgment.

Contemplation: The Inner Landscape

I can recall a time when contemplation seemed reserved for monks in a monastery or in secluded sectarian retreats. With the onset of mindfulness-based counseling and psychotherapy, however, mindfulness has become mainstream. For several years, I ran a lunchtime meditation at my current university. Every member of the meditation group, from college freshman to octogenarians, were familiar with the term mindfulness. Some even spoke of their need for quiet self-reflection, or contemplation. Having spent an adult lifetime in higher education and mental health settings, this was not always the case. When interviewing for a faculty position as a newly minted PhD, I mentioned an interest in studying the impact of meditation and chanting on depressed and anxious clients, only to be informed this was an inappropriate area of study and shallow scholarship unworthy of a tenure-track professor. Unsurprisingly, I was not offered that job! Fast-forward to the present, and such a stated interest would likely generate enthusiasm, at least in many counseling, social work, and psychology programs.

So, what specifically do we mean by the term *contemplation*? Having scouted through various dictionaries, philosophy, and religious texts, I was unable to find a definition that satisfied my various and sundry whims, so, at the risk of sounding hubristic, I have offered my own definition: Contemplation is the practice of engaging in intentional, nonjudgmental, present-moment, silent, fully aware thought for a prescribed period. Contemplation may or may not involve meditation, and can be done while sitting in a room, walking through a tree-lined path or a park bench in an urban setting. An important part of contemplation is that of intention and of nonjudgment. People from various cultures, occupations, and numerous spiritual pathways, as well as secular persons, have found great value and purpose in meditation. In full disclosure, however, some have not, perhaps for a variety of reasons. While Viktor Frankl is the psychological and spiritual inspiration for this book, he was not a fan of meditation, preferring direct action (1986). With respect for such a great person, psychiatrist, and for having inspired literally millions, including myself, this represents a rare point of disagreement. However, having read Frankl's significant works (2006, 1986), it seems clear he was engaged in a process of contemplation, albeit absent meditation. For more on the value of meditation, I turn then to a famous monk, Thomas Merton. Merton wrote contemplation was the highest expression of one's intellectual life. He goes on to say that meditation helps one achieve full awareness in life and without meditation, one is incomplete (2007).

Throughout this text, I have drawn support from numerous mental health professionals, some distinctly different from one another, and the same is true for notable spiritual leaders. My attempt is to illustrate that while different, counseling and psychotherapy exist to help alleviate emotional and mental suffering, even while offering different pathways. I see the various spiritual teachings offering something similar, even when holding very different theological foundations and radically different practices. To "piggyback" on Merton's contemplation statement, I will turn to his friend, Buddhist monk Thích Nhất Hạnh, to address the value of mindfulness. Hạnh posits mindfulness, which leads to momentary awareness, as the vehicle towards enlightenment. Hạnh uses the example of drinking a glass of water, suggesting when you drink a glass of water, be fully present to drinking that glass of water and not hurrying off to another task, something he cites as an example of enlightening (1995).

Now, having incorporated the value of contemplation and mindfulness from a spiritual perspective, I must in fairness and of necessity reference a mental health professional. While there are numerous possible theorists and practitioners to quote, I recently read an article in *Psychology Today* (online version) that seems to fit nicely within the confines of this chapter.

The author states that, regardless of whether a person engages in contemplation while sitting in contemplative prayer or meditation, moving gently as part of a mind-body practice such as yoga or tai-chi, or using introspection or reflective techniques as part of their work, all are examples of contemplation, and can result in various benefits to health and well-being (Gordon, 2020).

No question, contemplation is of critical importance, not only for life's sake, but so that our lives may be more rewarding and purposeful. As mental health professionals, teachers, doctors, employers, religious leaders, and anyone else, contemplation, and its first cousin mindfulness, are the *value added* ingredients in our lives. In fact, I cannot think of a single client in 25 years for whom contemplation, or silent self-reflection, was not some focus of treatment. My practice has included the bookend ages of primary school children to the elderly. For children, they often had lost something significant: their family torn apart by divorce, innocence lost due to sexual abuse, death of a parent or grandparent, etc. None of these children presented articulating having an existential crisis, but their affect, body language, and poverty of speech said it all. When I would ask them to draw or color, however, their inner world spilled out in copious portions. For illustration, I offer the following example of a child I treated.

During a three-year period, I provided contract counseling to children and adolescents referred by a state agency formerly called Children's Services Division (CSD). Many times, I was preparing a child for a family reunification, treating a child in foster care or in residential treatment, or where the family was unable to pay a private therapist. I recall one child client in particular. An older cousin had sexually abused him, with the abuse discovered when his mother happened to walk in on an episode. I shall refer to this child as Antonio. Antonio's parents were divorced, but thankfully had a good relationship with Antonio, who split time between their houses and extended family. Antonio was seven and deeply troubled. Reading the state-appointed psychologist's assessment of him, Antonio was experiencing significant guilt regarding his abuser. Convicted of sexual abuse and remanded to a residential treatment facility that specialized in sex offender treatment, the cousin's parents had cut off contact with Antonio's family. What bothered Antonio the most, however, was losing contact with his aunt and uncle. Implicitly, and perhaps explicitly, he blamed himself for the family strife. Furthermore, he had not fully understood what was happening between him and his cousin, and could think of no reason for his cousin's legal woes others than him (Antonio) having been the cause. He was thus a very depressed child, while formerly he had been very outgoing and energetic.

His father typically brought him to therapy at the agency. Although not formally an art therapist, I had training in the use of drawing in therapy. At my regular job, a residential psychiatric center north of town, we regularly utilized drawing, painting, dancing, singing, etc. in our work. A colleague who was a registered art therapist gave valuable in-service trainings and individual sessions. After an intake session attended by both parents, we set a meeting schedule. During the first therapy session, we sat on the floor. I again explained my role, rules of therapy and other matters we have covered in the intake, I pulled out the box of crayons, sheets of drawing paper and asked Antonio if would be willing to draw his family. He hesitated momentarily, then took a sheet of paper, selected a crayon, and commenced drawing. His face was a study in complete absorption to the task. As we were just beginning our relationship, I remained silent, sitting a few feet away. After some 20 minutes, he held up his drawing. While his artistic prowess was roughly on the level of mine (stick figures), his use of dark colors (for clouds, people, homes), two homes at opposite sides of the paper, characters separated from one another and no smiles spoke volumes. I asked if he would be willing to tell me about his drawing and the people in it.

Once he became more comfortable, he was quite an articulate child. He explained there was his home and that of his aunt and uncle. People were now sad and unhappy with each other. I inquired about their sadness and he explained something like, "Because I did something wrong." I was not surprised at his drawing, nor his belief that he and his cousin had misbehaved. Then, I asked if he would draw a picture of how the families would look if they were happy. This time, he quickly took a clean sheet of paper and began drawing. He spent roughly the same time as in the first drawing. The second picture, however, contained bright hues. The sun was a vibrant yellow, cerulean-blue sky, Kelly-green grass, people sporting happy faces, and the homes much closer. He explained the drawing was before the "trouble" between the families. When questioned, he stated no one had really explained why what happened was so bad.

After the session, I put Antonio in the playroom while his father and I spoke. I showed his dad the two drawings and explained them. His dad acknowledged that Antonio did not fully comprehend the nature of the abuse. He also related that relations between his sister (the aunt), brother-in-law (the uncle), and he and Antonio's mother were completely severed. I explained that Antonio was both guilt-ridden and suffering from grief in the loss of a relationship with his aunt and uncle. His father stated both he and his former spouse would have a hard time returning Antonio to the house where the abuse occurred. He acknowledged his sister and her spouse were innocent of the abuse, and equally shocked and disturbed. He and his ex-wife, among others, had explicitly told Antonio none of the family tension was his (Antonio's) fault. Regardless, Antonio internalized the dispute. After further discussion, I floated the suggestion that perhaps he, Antonio, and his relatives could meet in a park, at a restaurant, or a neutral location, given Antonio missed them so much. He agreed to consider it.

After talking the matter over with his ex-wife, Antonio's father contacted his relatives and, after several calls (there remained much tension), all parties agreed to meet at a park. After one meeting that both Antonio and his dad agreed went very well, Antonio's affect changed dramatically. His drawings were now full of brightness and the characters were happy. After two more sessions, his depression had totally remitted, and he was once again an energetic, outgoing child, even making a new friend at school. During the final session, I asked Antonio what had been most helpful in our sessions. Without hesitation he offered it was the drawing. He expressed drawing was his way of expressing his happiness and dealing with sadness. His parents, who attended this *graduation* session, both acknowledged drawing seemed very important to their son. "It's like meditation or prayer for some people," his mother noted. Antonio vigorously nodded his head. No surprise then, my recommendation was for Antonio's parents to continue encouraging his drawing. My additional recommendation was for his parents to inquire about his drawings periodically, especially should his mood turn melancholy again.

Regarding Antonio's case, I caution that few of the sexual abuse survivors are so simple to treat. In Antonio's case, the larger issue was a child's grief and unfair self-blame for a family torn asunder. In such cases, family relations are sometimes forever strained and the simple act of drawing (or another intervention) may not address the core issue. In Antonio's case, however, his drawings were a mirror of his inner world of loss and grief. Antonio further understood drawing was his vehicle towards transformation. What he was unable to verbally express, he articulated through the medium of drawing, selecting color representations for his affect, facial expressions for his mood, and separation between the figures for severed relationships. I do not interpret drawings per se; rather, through the client's presentation and interactive questioning, the client (child, adolescent, and even adult) describes the details of their life, issues, joys and hurts, and these details become part of the therapeutic conversation.

As his mother expressed, Antonio's meditation involved putting crayon to paper and creating a window into his thoughts and feelings. Whenever he drew, he was grounding himself with a practice that enabled him to cope with his grief and guilt. Whatever contemplative or expressive practice works, my encouragement is for everyone to find that vehicle and utilize it regularly, if not daily. Habituation of practice provides one the opportunity to discipline the mind, body, and spirit in order that they may address the anxiety, depression, or grief life transitions bring. Contemplation is thus practiced not only monasteries, but anywhere we live, work, eat, walk, etc. Thích Nhất Hạnh wrote taking refuge can be done every day, perhaps several times a day. Refuge can be practicing when not experiencing difficulty, making it easier to return to your refuge when the need is most dire. In other words, don't wait until a crisis occurs to take refuge. Hạnh suggests living mindfully each moment of your life, said practice becomes habituated. Then when a difficult moment arrives, safe refuge comes naturally. Thus, simple acts of mindful walking, breathing, sitting, eating, and drinking coffee can all become practices of taking refuge (1995).

Regarding Hạnh's instructive counsel, Epstein posits meditation as being critical to his focus as a psychiatrist and in remaining vibrant in his personal life (2013). Like Thích Nhất Hạnh and other mindfulness-oriented teachers, Epstein asserts that contemplative traditions can assist clients as well as therapists in providing the strength to heal their inner wounds. Thus, Epstein lays out a path to the meditation-inspired healing that Buddhist Thích Nhất Hạnh described in his books. Essentially, these two contemplative advocates, one psychiatrist, the other a monk, one a westerner, the other from Asia, hold very similar ideas regarding the value of meditation in coping with the capriciousness of life. While meditation has become the practice du jour in western society, I find many remain resistant to simply sitting and just *being* without *doing*. This may represent western residual guilt at not being engaged in something viewed as tangible or constructive. I will address this dynamic in the next section of the chapter.

Beings, not Doings

While attending a state conference many years ago, I was engaged in a discussion with a fellow therapist. I had risen early and driven several hours from home to a resort located in the mountains of central Oregon. I had been running a community mental health clinic and seeing six to ten clients per week, among my administrative duties. I was excited about seeing friends and colleagues, as well as learning something to assist me clinically or administratively. While catching up with a colleague during an in-between session break, the topic of meditation emerged. My colleague was a clinical director in the Portland area and involved in a meditation group. She found it helpful in managing the demands overseeing a large clinic entails. I shared my meditation practice and how it had helped me survive in my job and was an active cog in my coping strategy. We agreed that most people we knew were overly busy between occupational and domestic responsibilities (e.g., marriage-partnership, raising children, extended family, etc.). Yet, so many stressed people viewed meditation as wasted time. She shared a book she had just read. It went by the catchy title, *Don't Just Do Something, Sit There: A Mindfulness Retreat with Sylvia Boorstein* (1996). I was unfamiliar with the book. However, upon returning home, I discovered the library had purchased a copy.

The book was an affirmation of meditation's value for busy people. Boorstein, who has several children and grandchildren, a busy practice teaching and leading meditations, and coincidentally is married to a psychiatrist, understands the multiple demands well. She suggests a three-day retreat plan in order to assess priorities prior to beginning an active meditation routine. Ever the realist, she advocates that even brief meditation periods could help people with full lives achieve emotional balance. Boorstein credits her meditation practice for keeping her emotionally fit and grounded despite her busy lifestyle. I strongly encourage readers reframe idle moments as opportunities to unplug from their screens and sit in quiet contemplation, with slow breathing in through the nose and slowly exhaling via the mouth (or nose). A simple five-to-ten-minute meditation practice can help one manage stress, depression, and the ongoing demands life presents (Boorstein, 1996; Epstein, 2013; Hahn, 1999).

Interestingly, one of my clients during this mid-1990s period was a working mother of five children. She was also a registered nurse at the local hospital and religious education teacher in her church, who somehow found time to volunteer for various and sundry causes. She made an appointment after an in-service I gave at the hospital where she worked. My presentation had focused on self-care for busy professionals. She was *definitely* one of those busy professionals I had in mind when the hospital administrator requested a presentation on self-care. I shall refer to her as Rosario. Rosario was a Latina and Catholic whose faith was very important in her life. She voiced having never been to counseling, previously believing she should turn to a priest when troubled. Her stated reasons for coming to counseling was her "life being out of control" and her priest's suggestion she seek professional counseling. After attending my in-service, she decided to approach me.

When she arrived for her intake, she seemed composed. While she was a petite woman (just north of five feet), she had a persona that made her seem much larger. When she spoke, it was in a confident voice. I was not surprised when she disclosed being head nurse of her shift. During the intake, however, I noticed a crack in her professional facade. The computerized *Mini-SCID* suggested Panic Disorder, information consistent with my interview of her, and unsurprising given the vast list of her occupational and personal responsibilities. As Rosario had spent a couple of years working in an in-patient psychiatric ward, she had experience with mental health issues. She acknowledged feeling overwhelmed due to the multiple responsibilities of being a mother to five kids, professional responsibilities, her marriage, and volunteerism. She acknowledged her spouse, also a medical professional, was a traditional Latino man and delegated childcare responsibilities to her. She confessed to being on the brink of an emotional breakdown and went to see her priest who recommended our clinic.

As we unpacked her life, I asked, "What changes would you like to make in your life?" She mentioned more assistance with children, a reduced role at work, and finding some way to "power down" from life demands. With session time winding down, I suggested some de-stressing exercises, purposefully not mentioning meditation, given the conservative nature of the area. As she was quite religious and liked saying a daily Rosary, I assigned her to include mindful breathing while saying a Rosary. I further suggested she spend at least ten minutes on a Rosary, primarily focusing on her breathing and the Rosary's words when her mind wandered. I encouraged her to say this daily, perhaps just prior to bedtime, so as to aid in sleep. She agreed to the exercise and left seemingly willing to make an effort.

The following session she appeared noticeably more upbeat. She reported the slow, deep breathing had given her prayer greater meaning. She acknowledged intentional breathing left her feeling more present, relaxed, and aided in sleep. She agreed to continue marrying the breath and focusing to her daily Rosary. We also addressed her other needs regarding childcare and fashioned a plan for her to speak with her spouse regarding childcare assistance. She decided to relinquish her role as shift supervisor to focus on direct care, as making schedules and dealing with upper administration was becoming overly taxing. She seemed to have addressed her anxiety, but something nagged at me, something I could not firmly grasp. Finally, when inquiring if I was missing something, she smiled, stating she was aware I had tricked her into meditating. However, she had researched the matter and discovered meditation had a long history in Catholicism. Realizing there was no inherent conflict between meditation and her faith, she asked if I could recommend any additional resources on contemplation. I explained the style we had used in the monastery, mentioning resources from Thomas Merton and Thích Nhất Hạnh. She agreed to begin silent meditation at the onset of her day while her children were still asleep. Requesting one more follow-up session, she left.

The following week, she again appeared relaxed. She had meditated each morning for the past week and reported continued positive results in assisting her to relax. Furthermore, after much discussion, her spouse had agreed to hire childcare help, and in two weeks, she would be a regular floor nurse, with a colleague taking over as head nurse. "I feel lighter than in years!" she offered, face beaming. I noted the important changes in her life, such as help at home and no administrative duties at work. She acknowledged these changes were very important, but acknowledged meditation, with and without the Rosary, had been the most helpful change in her life. "For the first time in my adult life I have time that is mine," she expressed. She had even spoken to the hospital social worker about starting a meditation group during the lunch hour. She completed counseling buoyed by reducing her responsibilities and crafting quality time for contemplation: that is, just *sitting* there and not *doing*, something previously unthinkable for her.

No question, changes that make our lives more manageable, such as those Rosario made, can enhance the quality of our lives. Unfortunately, far too many people in this world lack the luxury of reducing their responsibilities due to economic, social, and cultural realities. Meditation certainly is no miracle cure for the ills of poverty, abuse, trauma, and neglect. It has been my experience, however, that habituated contemplative practices such as meditation in its various forms (sitting, walking, chanting, singing, etc.) can be as positive an addition as exercise and a healthy diet. Rosario is but one of a long list of former clients I have assigned some type of centering work (often referring to such as "relaxation techniques"), with most disclosing moderate to significant success in reducing anxiety.

Contemplative Exercises for Consideration

Recognizing some readers have incorporated mindfulness practices like meditation into their lives, I offer several examples of contemplative practices. Naturally, what some find rewarding and meaningful, others will not. What is most important lies in discovering what practice works for you. What works best is most likely being what you enjoy, habituate, and continue practicing. Some of the most helpful moments are simply *be here now* periods of breathing, walking, and mindfully drinking your tea or coffee, feeling no urge to rush to begin another task.

RAIN Exercise

Meditation teachers often speak of practicing self-compassion. The acronym RAIN is a helpful mindfulness exercise (Brach, 2019). RAIN, or Recognize, Allow, Investigate, and Nurture, can assist practitioners to gain awareness, clarity, and acceptance of present-moment reality. RAIN has four simple steps:

1) *Recognize* and notice what thoughts, feelings, and sensations are occurring in your mind and body.
2) *Allow* those thoughts, feelings, and sensations to exist without judgment or need to fix a problem.
3) *Investigate* the matter. What messages are these thoughts, feelings, and sensations sending? For example, where in your body is this message located? What is that body part asking for? What is this message trying to teach you?
4) *Nurture* yourself. How can you best take care of yourself mentally, physically, and spiritually?

Mindful Minute Meditation

As Epstein recommends in his book (2013), try to carve out at least one minute of meditation between seeing clients, patients, or ongoing responsibilities. I have taken Epstein's advice and found it helpful in separating the previous client's concerns from that of the current client. More succinctly, it b Hạnh ecame my *be here now* focusing. Just slowly breathe through the nose, then slowly exhale through the mouth for 60 seconds. Should your mind wander to the just-concluded session, upcoming session, or something else, focus your attention on the inhalation and exhalation of your breath.

Sitting Meditation With Mantra

While the monastic meditation group I attended taught silent meditation with a sole focus on the breath, some find the use of a mantra helpful for focusing. While there are variations, I find it easiest to repeat a meaningful phrase. For example, while using the slow, deep breathing and exhaling, I have used phrases (called mantras) like "I am enough," or "I am whole." Trauma survivors may find a mantra such as "I am safe," or "I survived and thrived," or some such statement to reinforce their resilience and progress. Meditating for just five to ten minutes a day can help you de-stress and manage anxiety (Creswell et al., 2019; Madhav et al., 2014).

Walking Meditation

Some find walking in nature to be more helpful than sitting in silence. Retreats at a monastery taught me the value of both sitting and walking meditation. Like sitting meditation, tailor walking meditation to meet your needs. I prefer long meditation walks (30–60 minutes), so I do them on weekends. Some find using a mantra during a walking meditation beneficial, while others prefer to focus on the senses: the feet's contact with the earth, sights, sounds, and smells. Whether walking solo or in a group, the general rule is to observe silence, just as in sitting meditations.

Mindful and Contemplative Coffee or Tea drinking

Many years ago, while a visiting scholar at a university in Western Australia, I frequented a particular coffee shop. I developed a friendship with another professor who also practiced daily meditation. Taking a lesson from Thích Nhất Hạnh (1999), he suggested we spend a silent, mindful, yet emotionally present coffee hour together. Mindful coffee or tea consumption means being present to one's consumption, consciously savoring each sip and the smell, taste, temperature, and feel of the beverage in your mouth. It means a *be here now* approach whereby extraneous demands are viewed just floating past in our minds. (Clearly, pick a time when you have *time*.) Take slow, deep breaths and exhale slowly. Perhaps you may even silently acknowledge two or three gratitudes. Most importantly, *drink your tea or coffee to drink your tea or coffee* and not to hurry to another task. If engaging in this practice with a companion, simply be present with your partner via eye contact, touch, expressions and such without verbal communication.

I encouraged readers to experiment with different forms of meditation. The most important form of meditation is the one that feels most natural to you. Most people are unlikely to sit in silence for an hour. So, find brief, mindful minutes (say, one to ten minutes) and work on being here now, focusing on your breath, and simply allowing deadlines, anxieties, and other matters to float past like leaves on a river. This type of mindset will take practice, but habituation usually is imperative in establishing a meditation practice.

The One Person Empty Chair Dialogue

Although the Empty Chair Technique has long been associated with Gestalt Therapy, Jacob Moreno, founder of Psychodrama Therapy (2013) was the originator. Psychodrama has had broad applications in residential and outpatient therapy, as well as in creativity exercises. I have used the Empty Chair Technique in therapy and on myself. Regarding the latter, I sometimes set an empty chair and engage in a dialogue with my younger self, current self, future self, etc. I have had some clients speak with their chronic pain, trauma, addiction, healed self, wise self, etc. Set up a time where you are alone, and spend 15 minutes or so with this exercise, changing chairs when transitioning from younger self to current self, or current self to future self, for example. I have found this exercise therapeutic, interesting, and insightful, particularly when alone and thousands of miles from home.

Lessons Learned

In fall 2016, I was on sabbatical. I spent the sabbatical as a visiting scholar in Australia. This was my second teaching sabbatical in Australia, this time in the capital city of Canberra. When the term was over, my spouse joined me, and we spent a month visiting various locations throughout Australia. One of our sojourns was a guided trip through the vast, rugged, desert of central Australia. Although I have spent considerable time providing volunteer training, consulting, coaching, and even counseling services throughout the Australia's Northern Territory, I had yet to visit the iconic natural geologic natural wonders of Uluru and Kata Tjuta in the dead center of the continent, nor Kings Canyon, some four hours or so away. After a few days on the southern coast of New

South Wales, we flew to Alice Springs in the dead center of the continent to commence our journey.

I had been feeling out of sorts, to borrow a phrase from my grandmother. I was unhappy about the recent US elections. Closer to home, I sat perched on the crossroads of my life, unsure of what direction to take, with none of the options seeming appealing. Professionally, my life seemed to be on track, as I had just completed a new book, my sabbatical teaching had gone well, our counseling program had a healthy enrollment and had just achieved national accreditation (i.e., CACREP), and I was married to my best friend. On the surface of my life, there was so much to be grateful for that I *should* (apologies to Albert Ellis) have felt pleased. Underneath it all, however, I was floundering. Given my apparent successes, I briefly considered that perhaps prosperity simply was difficult for me. From a formative childhood, adolescence and through my mid-30s, financial impoverishment brought with it numerous challenges. By my mid-50s, however, I had achieved tenure in a well-paying job, had ample money for travel, retirement, and a home that was tidy, safe, and comfortable. Further complicating matters, I harbored guilt in feeling unfulfilled when I knew that I *should* (that word again) be grateful. My situation was reminiscent of a client I had treated for anxiety years earlier. After a few sessions of cognitive reframing and challenging his fears in session and his following through with daily reframing homework, his anxiety dropped to near zero. The following week he returned, stating he realized after a lifetime of anxiety, he found himself anxious that he was no longer feeling anxious! As anxiety had been his constant companion, perhaps life without anxiety was unfulfilling.

Our tour guide and driver was a late 20-something Australian man who had been guiding since his university days. He had a mature presence, having spent considerable time among Indigenous people in central and Western Australia. He confided to me a plan to build an off-grid small house just outside Alice Springs and teach in an outdoor education program (his degree and background). As per usual, my spouse and I were the oldest people on the excursion with our fellow travelers an assortment of early-20s-to-mid-30s, mostly males, another American, a Brit, a Kiwi (New Zealander), and a few Aussies.

Everyone was social and jumped enthusiastically into introductions with the usual name, place, occupation, partner status (all but self and spouse single), and so forth. Announcing my occupation typically leaves me feeling anxious, as others either misunderstand ("Oh, so you're going to psychoanalyze us!"), seek some type of assistance ("Uh listen, I have a *friend* . . ."), and in rare instances hostility, often based on misunderstandings. This travel group, however, unconditionally welcomed us with no articulated expectations. Introductions over, we commenced the dusty, beautiful, desolate, hot, seven-hour drive to Uluru and Kata Tjuta National Park.

We took the one sealed (paved) road towards Uluru through the colorful West MacDonnell Range. Central Australia has its own iconic beauty, as the rising sun brings the ancient, broken West MacDonnells to a flowing cinnamon-like fluorescence, and a mesmerizing experience. Beyond appreciating the natural beauty and socializing with our fellow travelers, I had ample time to self-reflect on my current dissatisfying situation. Looking back on it, my Black Dog had returned, courtesy of my silent whistle of discontent. For persons having never grappled with depression, it is difficult to explain just why you cannot simply *snap out of it*. I was quite good at treating depressed clients, likely because I understood them so well. The most challenging part of depression, for me anyway, lies in hosting and keeping up that weighty facade for extended periods throughout the day. Given that I would be surrounded all day, for an intense three and a half days, the very thought was exhausting. What gave me hope, however, was being in the Outback, a region that has fascinated me since reading a *National Geographic* article during elementary school. There is something regenerative this very rugged, remote, unique, seemingly endless landscape holds for me. The Outback is a harsh beauty, with risks and dangers afoot, appreciated through the lens of respect for her beauty and capricious moods: extreme heat, cold, even freezing nights, deadly snakes, dingoes, and certainly her resilient Indigenous peoples, perhaps the world's oldest culture.

With apologies to John Kabit-Zinn, living in the present moment with compassion and wisdom had eluded me of late. My daily meditation practiced had lapsed, and my morning gratitudes seemed perfunctory, much like those mindlessly mouthing a creed without any thought to what they are saying. In essence, I was going through the motions of gratitudes and meditation to get to something else, precisely Thích Nhất Hạnh warned about (1999). Having led numerous meditation and mindfulness trainings, I felt like a complete fraud, expecting and deserving of being unmasked any moment. Looking back, meditation, both sitting and walking, in addition to sincerely acknowledging my gratitudes, likely would have improved my mood. Like an addict relapsing back into pre-contemplation, denial had set in, leaving me stumbling aimlessly about.

Finally, after several hot, arid hours on that narrow strip of bitumen, the world's largest and most iconic monolith emerged into view like some great vessel cresting the ocean. We watched in rapt fascination as that great, red hue of sandstone, over 1100 feet high (863 meters), with a circumference of nearly six miles, swallowed up our view. This world has much higher, loftier natural landmarks, but there is indeed something magical about Uluru, its shape, girth, undulating folds, crevices, changing hues, and how it just seems to swell up from that vast, crimson sea of sand, especially in early morning and at twilight. The Anangu people have inhabited the area around Uluru for over 30,000 years, the site sacred to them as Jerusalem to Jews, Christians, and Muslims. After a quick trip to Kata Tjuta (many heads) in the same national park, we tucked into our shaded campsite for relief from the merciless summer sun (seasons reversed in the southern hemisphere).

My mood still edgy, I did what I always do when feeling gloomy, and worked out. Too hot for jogging, I went through my push-ups and other isometrics, then my yoga routine, and more centered for the first time in months, sat and spent half an hour in a walking meditation with my spouse. Focusing on my breath with that mesmerizing view of Uluru, slightly lighter in the late afternoon sun, cleared my mental detritus. Walking completed, we sat, staring at Uluru in rapt silence for another hour. Our guide then informed us we would drive to a prime viewing spot for snacks and Champagne. We boarded the bus, slaloming through the thick, red, sand as we journeyed to the viewing spot. We parked and gathered at a high point looking directly at Central Australia's most magical sight. The silence of the people gathered about was reminiscent of pilgrims in a holy place, appropriate for where we stood. Over the next hour, tones of crimson and purple, gave way to a bluish-violet just before the curtain of darkness dropped, ending the amazing display of color.

Buoyed by Uluru's magic back at camp, we had a meal ("a feed") of barbecue Kangaroo washed down with South Australian cabernet. Then, early to bed for the 4:00 AM wake up. The desert is such a contradiction in conditions: unmercifully hot in daytime, near freezing in the dark hours of morning. Bundled up, we sipped coffee and ate a snack on the short drive back to Uluru. Disembarking, our guide led us to the holy rock as the sun began its gradual ascent. Our guide announced we would hold a meditation at the Uluru's base for those interested, which was everyone. We sat in silence, in the dead center of the world's oldest continent, on this 500-million-year-old work of arkose sandstone, in one of the most sacred, remote sites in the southern hemisphere. Something within me shifted, triggering memories of a lonely, impoverished childhood, lost in the shuffle of all male siblings, taking the *National Geographic* into my grandparent's dirt-floor basement where I shared a bed with my younger brother, and reading of and viewing glossy pictures of this amazing, harsh, remote place, seemingly distant as Mars, wishing so dearly to experience it. Fast-forwarding nearly 50 years later, I touched this amazing rock, unable to articulate the transcendence of that moment. Silent tears streaked my face as my depression began lifting in time with the rising sun. Relativity emerged and time slowed until our guide gently tapped me on my forearm, informing me it was time for our interpretive hike around Uluru.

Life provides ongoing growth opportunities and many, many lessons in our rugged trek. One need not travel 10,000 miles to find a sacred place, as the sacred and profane coexist everywhere. As Oglala Sioux shaman Black Elk said in *Black Elk Speaks* (2008), the center of the universe can be anywhere one stands, if the attitude is right. It is accurate to report I had much work to do to climb out of depression, including daily gratitudes, meditation, revising my self-talk, and other proven exercises. None of these practices are complicated; in fact, all are quite simple. The difficulty comes in doing them every day and knowing I will need to continue this practice every day for the remainder of my life. As previously noted, just as with physical fitness, emotional fitness has no stopping point whereby we can say, "Okay, I'm done." The habituation and discipline of continuing, especially on days when we lack desire, is the larger challenge. I have succeeded on this challenge of discipline, while also failing a legion of times.

During lunch I sat on the red base floor for another meditation. An Indigenous man came over, silently studied me, nodded, and then sat down beside me in the lotus position. Finally, my attitude was right, after having been so terribly wrong.

Chapter 10

Rewriting Our Stories

Learned Happiness Through Daily Practice

Recently I watched a film to relax and temporarily take my mind off academic responsibilities and COVID. The film, a noir mystery, had a very famous actor and several other well-known ones. The lead character is a private detective hired by a wealthy man to spy on his wife, whom he believes is cheating on him. Soon thereafter, the lead character "Jake," played by Jack Nicholson, a cynic known to be loose on ethics and morals, has a conversation with a friend's servant, an Asian character named Khan. During the conversation, Khan inquires if Jake is successful. Jake replies he has no complaints. Khan then asks somewhat abstractedly if he (Jake) is happy, to which the hardboiled PI shrugs answering something like, "Who can answer that question?" To which Khan replies, anyone who is happy.

Interestingly, happiness is a much bandied-about term in US society. My experience is people have only a vague understanding of that term's actual meaning. That said, ask someone, "Are you happy?" and should their eyes light up, face break into a smile and answer an enthusiastic, "Yes!" a definition is perfunctory. My background as professor, however, dictates a more academic answer. *Miriam-Webster* defines happiness as "A state of well-being and joy" (n.d.). Martin Seligman has authored a popular book titled *Authentic Happiness: Using the New Positive Psychology to Realize Your Potential for Lasting Fulfillment* (2002). His book and assessment, *The Authentic Happiness Inventory* (n.d.) are noteworthy examples of an attempt to chronicle, teach and quantify the state of happiness in people's lives. According to Seligman, people experience happiness in three ways: (1) Pleasure and gratification, (2) embodiment of strength and virtues, and (3) meaning and purpose. (2002). Seligman posits these in a progressive path, from happiness of pleasure/gratification to strength and virtues and finally to meaning/purpose, the latter being a more mature, intrinsic type of happiness. His *Authentic Happiness Inventory* assesses 24 signature strengths. He splits the test into five headings: Wisdom (e.g., love of learning, judgment, etc.), Courage (e.g., bravery, perseverance, etc.), Humanity and Love (e.g., justice, kindness, etc.), Temperance (e.g., self-control, etc.), and Transcendence (e.g., hope, optimism, faith, etc.). Clearly, the state of happiness is composed of many ingredients, with some strengths likely being more sustainable. For example,

DOI:10.4324/9781003168324-10

Seligman's courage, wisdom, and transcendence sections of his *Authentic Happiness Inventory* suggest far greater depth than one typically considers. Seligman's strengths thus provide a foundation for greater personal fulfillment, as opposed to the transient state of happiness.

As a longtime counselor and professor of counselor education, and one interested in meaning and purpose, happiness is clearly a related and desired construct in the mental health field. Practically everyone who sought my counseling services informed me they were unhappy. In my long counseling work, regardless of culture, I have heard the same expression in a variety of ways: "I am not happy" or "I am not as happy as I used to be." The initial session provided a sense of which clients were likely to make progress and end therapy feeling happier. One item on the *Beck Depression Inventory-II* (Beck et al., 1996) focuses specifically on the item of pessimism. As per Beck's research (Beck & Haigh, 2014), pessimism inversely correlates with positive therapeutic outcomes. Regarding the BDI-II, many clients have endorsed doubting their situation (depression) will improve. With such clients, I knew my work definitely would be arduous. Another set of clients endorsed feeling sad, but believed they would improve, and thus their outlook was far brighter. In the former belief, there is little incentive to work if one truly believes things cannot improve (check for suicidality!). In the latter statement, there is plenty of incentive to work the treatment plan, as such clients expect their mood will improve. This is the old self-fulling prophecy at work. For clinicians and educators like myself, promoting a belief in transcendence is essential for therapeutic success. Basically, I want clients to revise the deterministic story they have been telling themselves. Essentially, it is the 3-Cs process: (1) *Catch the negative self-talk*: "I will never feel better." (2) *Challenge the negative self-talk* with a "What's the evidence for never being happy again?": "Well, I have been happy before and likely will be again. So, the evidence does not support my never being happy again," and (3) *Change it*: "I will work the treatment plan in and out of session and will feel better." This type of approach is standard CBT-REBT and has demonstrated strong efficacy (Beck & Haigh, 2014; Ellis & Ellis, 2011). Now, while mental health professionals likely are aware of the 3-Cs' efficacy, such effective strategies may disappear during challenging moments, such as another driver road raging at us, our supervisor's criticism, or when presented with a major disappointment. Sometimes, we must step back from the brink of despair, practice mindful breathing, acknowledge gratitudes, and make use of the 3-Cs exercise or another helpful intervention.

My experience with happiness, both as a counselor and in my own personal experience, is that happiness seems both an *intrinsic* and *extrinsic* job, or a being and a doing. Intrinsically, happiness likely begins with our belief regarding personal happiness. Beliefs such as "I am happy" or "I am unhappy" are reinforced through our self-talk and consequently through our actions. Intrinsic well-being remains closely related to our internal dialogue (Ellis, 2008). That is, messages of shame, telling ourselves what failures we are, or how unattractive, dumb, worthless, and so forth, reinforce an unhealthy belief in ourselves (Beck, 1963; Ellis,

2008). Whether we refer to such as irrational beliefs (Ellis, 2008) or negative schemas (Beck, 1963, 1979), over time, this habituated negative self-denigration becomes automatic, leaving us feeling depressed, anxious, and perhaps even suicidal (Ellis & Doyle, 1988). Fortunately, the converse of negative self-talk also is true. That is, when we tell ourselves realistic or rational stories, we tend to feel happier and well-adjusted (Ellis, 2008). Unfortunately, my professional experience is that negative self-talk is insidious and very resistant to efficacious interventions such as the 3-Cs or healthy behavioral adaptations such as healthy risk taking (e.g., asking someone of interest to have coffee with you).

Given the potentially self-destructive nature of the negative stories we tell ourselves, disputing and rewriting our self-talk, and making simple behavioral changes (e.g., asking someone to meet our needs and continuing to seek this even after a failure) become critical tasks in helping us live healthy, peaceful, productive lives. While this likely sounds rather elementary to any seasoned mental health professional, consider the number of stressed, depressed, anxious mental health professionals you may have known. I have known unhealthy colleagues who likely needed a mental health break from their clinical duties given their impairment. Everyone, especially mental health professionals, need active self-care plans. Effective self-care requires external physical activities such as yoga, jogging, walking, cycling, and swimming, etc., as well as *internal* practice like healthy self-talk, meditation with positive mantras (e.g., "I am enough," "I am whole," "I am loved," etc.), and self-fulfilling hobbies such as journaling, singing, playing a musical instrument, among other pursuits. Naturally, we all need healthy support systems composed of family and friends (*healthy* family members and friends!). The following exercises are specific examples of retraining our minds to think we are capable, successful (not perfect) people.

Acknowledging Strengths

For this exercise, bracket off your inner critic and focus on your strengths. Give yourself full permission to be forthcoming in your answers. Use a notebook or journal to answer these questions.

1) What are three key strengths you possess? These strengths help you persevere during challenging times.
2) Think of difficult times when you persisted despite pressing challenges. How did you keep moving forward to reach success?
3) Most people are more courageous than they give themselves credit for being. Briefly describe a time when you demonstrated courage in the face of adversity.
4) Regarding the previous item on courage, what did you learn about your courageous self?
5) Everyone is creative, albeit in different ways. Describe your creative self and the ways you express creativity.

6) Consider a significant accomplishment you have achieved in your life. Describe this accomplishment and how you achieved that success.
7) Now, considering the previous question, what did you learn from that success? How will this knowledge help you achieve future goals?
8) Consider ways in which you have demonstrated emotional strength. Perhaps your emotional strength was evident during grief, disappointment, a relationship ending, job loss, etc. How has overcoming these difficulties enhanced your emotional strength?
9) Consider your compassionate self. Think of a time when you demonstrated compassion to someone in need. How did you feel during that time? What did you learn from that experience?
10) Many people suffer from a persistent inner critic. What helps you silence that inner critic? How might you become more successful at silencing your inner critic?

Now consider the following happiness and fulfillment enriching exercises.

Happiness and Fulfillment

Happiness and fulfillment provide life satisfaction, increase well-being against anxiety and depression, and possibly lengthen our lives (Seligman, 2002, 2006). Using a journal or notepaper, answer the following questions.

1) What brings you happiness and fulfillment? (e.g., family, close friends, spiritual beliefs, etc.)
2) What might you do to feel happier and more fulfilled?
3) When you are happiest and most fulfilled, what is occurring during those times?
4) Sadness, grief, anger, etc. are natural emotional states. When you experience such emotions, what is your process in moving out of these towards a happier state of being?
5) What thoughts and behaviors might increase your sense of happiness and personal fulfillment?

Meditation on Happiness

Meditation is a few thousand years old and practiced by many religions and spiritual movements, as well as the mental health profession. The following is a brief meditation (say, one to ten minutes depending on time and need). Find a quiet place for this meditation (office, the beach, a park, place of worship, etc.). Make your sitting as comfortable as possible. Breathe slowly and deeply in through your nose, then exhale slowly through your mouth. Repeat this rhythmic breathing through your meditation. While you are breathing slowly, deeply, and rhythmically, silently tell yourself something like "I am enough,"

"I am whole," "I am loved." When your mind wanders, simply focus on your breath and the saying. Notice any tension in your body and focus on releasing it. Repeat this meditation three times per week for one to ten minutes.

Happiness Gratitudes

Gratitudes represent our acknowledgement of being thankful. Whether secular or spiritual, they provide a focus and format for verbally and silently giving thanks. For this exercise, acknowledge three reasons for being happy. These reasons can be major (birth of a child) or ordinary (a sunny day, the rain, a beautiful sunset, etc.).

Examples:

1) I am grateful for my health.
2) I am grateful for spouse/partner/children/special friend.
3) I am grateful for the promise this day brings.

Micro Writing and Revising: Writing Your Personal and Occupational Story for Increased Happiness

Writing can be a therapeutic endeavor (Parker-Pope, 2015). In a journal, write a short story about your life. Describe your family, upbringing, values, education, work history, and anything else relevant up to the present. Include in the story your level of happiness and personal and occupational fulfillment. Review your personal story for any editing or changes. Next, write a brief paragraph describing how you might increase your happiness and sense of personal and occupational fulfillment. Perhaps use a brief measuring stick such as a scaling question. "On a scale of 1–10, with 10 high, my happiness and fulfillment score is___." How might you raise your score by one point? Write down your plan to raise your score. If you do not know how to raise your score currently, give the matter some thought and then write down ideas that later emerge.

Drawing My Life

This exercise is a series of drawings to help provide you with pictorial images for your current life. Drawing can be beneficial for our mood and well-being (Drake, 2019). Thus, the focus is on drawing happiness and fulfillment. Use a notebook or journal so you can save and review the drawings and to assess changes in your life. Use any drawing instruments you choose, whether crayons, colored pencils, magic markers, etc.

Picture 1: Draw your current world: Draw a picture of you in your life. Include family members, work colleagues, friends, hobbies, and anything you deem meaningful. Take your time with this drawing.

Picture 2: After completing drawing 1, then draw your life as you would like to create it. Give yourself license to draw it any way you would want. Turn off your inner critic, as this is your moment to create something fulfilling.

Now, compare and contrast pictures 1 and 2. What differences exist between the two drawings? Regarding the positive changes in picture 2, how might you begin to create this more fulfilling world?

Picture 3: Give yourself some extended time after drawing pictures 1 and 2—say, one to two months. Then, draw your life as it has become. How is this picture different from pictures 1 and 2? What has led up to the changes? How happy are you with these changes? How might you maintain these positive changes?

Purpose in Life and Emotional Wellbeing

Consider the following questions. I encourage you to write them down in a journal, as this likely makes a stronger impact. (Drake, 2019).

1) What do you consider your life purpose being about? If you do not know, give the matter some extended thought and then write about it. Perhaps discuss the matter with a couple of people you trust.
2) Consider your family and close friends. How much fulfillment do these relationships bring you?
3) Consider your job/occupation. How much fulfillment does it bring you?
4) What is your favorite hobby? What makes that endeavor so fulfilling?
5) This chapter recounts a movie character asking another if he is happy. So, are you generally happy? If not, how could you begin to create a happier, more fulfilling life?
6) What is one significant change you would like to make in your life? Now, how might you begin to make that change?

The *Why* of Happiness and Fulfillment

In the first chapter, I mentioned Nietzsche's famous quote regarding the person with a *why* being able to endure almost any *how*. This iconic statement certainly applies to the state of happiness, and perhaps for some the trait of happiness and fulfillment. Like the theme of this text, Nietzsche's *why* correlates well with Frankl's belief meaning in life is the primary motivating force. No doubt, a person may find their life meaningful, yet be struggling with chronic depression, anxiety, grief, trauma, etc. This latter person may find the concept of happiness, much less fulfillment, simply out of reach. As a counselor, I have witnessed this phenomenon often. Many former clients with diagnoses such as major depression, bipolar disorder, and various types of anxiety found their lives meaningful and at times quite happy. This statement may seem incredible to some, so I will unpack it in the following paragraph.

Early in my career, I worked at a large agency. One memorable client whom I will call "Heidi" came for counseling. Heidi was a mid-30s single parent of two children. She had struggled with depression since late adolescence. Her brief marriage was unhappy but produced two children, with whom she reported a strong relationship. Her comment regarding her kids was "they are my world." Nevertheless, she stated a desire to feel better and live more fully. She had some assets, having returned to the local community college to complete her associate's in business, and was an academically gifted student. She worked part-time as a bank teller and reported that while this role was not fulfilling, she got along with her colleagues. When I inquired what she sought from counseling, she replied "I want to be happier." Her response was scarcely noteworthy, as virtually every client I have counseled has stated such in some manner. While acknowledging her struggles with depression, I inquired what reasons she had for feeling happy. She explained her children brought her the most joy and meaning. She went on to express that outside of being a good student, the other talent she possessed was parenting. Even when depressed she explained that playing with her kids, reading to them, or interacting with them helped lift her heavy moods, grounding her with a sense of meaning and purpose.

In collaborating with Heidi, we created a typical treatment plan to address her depression, utilizing CBT strategies of the 3-Cs of negative thought replacement (catch that negative thought, challenge it, change it). For physical activity, we added a 20-minute walking routine three times per week, continuing with her medication (she was under care of a psychiatrist), and for her to reach out weekly to a friend for a social engagement. I added that she continue close daily interactions with her children, knowing her motivation was such she would easily meet this treatment goal. She appeared satisfied with the plan, then inquired, "So what are my chances of feeling happier?" Interestingly, while virtually all former clients have indicated a desire to be happier, few have inquired regarding their chances to attain happiness. Consulting with my inner counselor (my gut), I turned the question back to her: "What do you believe your chances of being happier are?" She smiled, shrugged, and then explained she thought they were "pretty good." She went on to express optimism in her relationship with her children and recalled that when she regularly exercised she felt better, even during the long, gray winters. She went on to mention, however, needing something else to help achieve a happier state. Unfortunately, she had not identified this missing element, just that *it* was lacking in her life. We ended the session with a plan to identify and add this element to her life.

Heidi was a motivated client and made significant progress. Her scores on the Beck Depression Inventory-II dropped by a third after a few sessions, and she reported walking 30 minutes three times a week with her neighbor, exceeding her assignment. Her kids were doing well and involved in summer programs they enjoyed. Thus, she reported life being generally better. However, she continued to express something was missing from her life. Neither of us could identify this missing piece, but like mental archeologists, we jointly resolved to continue our search to uncover her personal Rosetta Stone. I staffed her case with a more experienced therapist, but she could think of nothing to add. Besides, as my colleague said, the client was showing clear improvement in her mood and evidencing positive behavioral change. "What else is there?" she inquired.

A couple of sessions later, she arrived looking noticeably upbeat. While she had previously evidenced significant mood improvement, and as a motivated, educated client, positive change is common. In this session however, she practically radiated joy. Noting her disposition, my comment was she seemed quite happy. She agreed wholeheartedly and mentioned having had an epiphany regarding the missing element in her life. Most interested, I encouraged her to please enlighten me, being most curious. Evidently, while walking with her neighbor, it occurred to her she had lived her life for others: her parents, children, ex-spouse, etc. "But I've never really asked myself, 'what are my needs?'" We explored the issue for the remainder of the session and agreed to continue addressing this theme. The following session she determined what she most enjoyed was being with children. She particularly liked reading to her kids, helping them with homework, and playing soccer or other games with them. She went on to express that the business world, while financially lucrative, was not a fulfilling career for her. She had recently begun exploring different career possibilities and decided she would pursue becoming an elementary teacher. She reported feeling excited about a career for the first time in her life. Encouraging her interest, I suggested she interview a couple of elementary teachers for more information regarding the pros and challenges of the job. Interestingly, the neighbor she walked with was herself a teacher, and the two had already spoken at length on the pros and cons. To garner more feedback, she agreed to solicit information from two additional teachers.

The next session turned out to be our final. Heidi had met all treatment goals, with her Beck Depression Inventory-II depression rate cut by more than 50%, which I attributed jointly to her motivation and discovering a fulfilling career path. Expressing she had never been happier with a major decision (other than having kids), she thanked me profusely, which I found both satisfying and embarrassing. After all, she had done the real hard work. Although she placed her highest value on raising healthy children, she had no real personal direction for her own professional fulfillment. For the first time in her life, she had a career direction she was excited about, and which she believed would be personally fulfilling. She had found the *why* that was previously lacking in her professional life. She admitted her negative self-talk would return at moments, but explained the 3-Cs exercise plus her new occupational purpose would help silence her inner critic. Given her intelligence, work ethic, resilience and a clear purpose, I have no doubt Heidi became a very good teacher.

Heidi's example illustrates self-efficacy's value to those in treatment for depression, anxiety, self-doubt, or those who simply have not found a constructive, purposeful career. Heidi clearly valued a career where she could work helping to educate and model healthy behavior. My read on her after several sessions was she would likely make a very good teacher. No doubt, healthy self-talk, regular exercise, strong family relations, a good psychiatrist, and a helpful counselor/therapist can help reduce and mitigate even major depression (Ellis, 2008; Beck & Haigh, 2014). The missing component, however, was her finding meaningful, purpose-driven work, something she lacked in her current job. Her job as a bank teller was not bad, and she liked her coworkers. However, the world of finance did not fill that existential void in her life. What seemed so compelling was she *knew* something was missing, even though she did not know what that missing piece was. I did encourage her to continue taking her medication and to use the college counseling services for support, as she likely would need periodic assistance to manage her depression. Career changes, especially when retraining, can bring on much stress, and thus the need for occasional therapeutic check-ins.

Admittedly, Heidi is scarcely the most challenging client I have counseled, having counseled ex-convicts, men who battered their partners, addicts, sex offenders, and chronically mentally ill people, among former clients. However, she was one of the clearest examples of someone who realized she had a missing element in her life. In fact, most of my clients who improved, regardless of the issue, articulated that discovery of something personally meaningful was the tipping point towards healing. In most cases, an attitudinal change followed meaning much like that in Heidi's case. Parker Palmer writes eloquently regarding the value of discovering personal meaning in one's life (Palmer, 2000). Incidentally, depression temporarily disabled Parker Palmer, and he writes of lessons learned during that time. His depression began to remit when he discovered his purpose in life, education (Palmer, 2007). I do not mean to imply that becoming a teacher, professor, therapist, or plumber is the magic elixir for curing depression. What I am suggesting is that living a meaningful, purpose-driven life almost certainly provides emotional buoyancy, and likely would assist in reducing depression (I speak from personal experience). Parker Palmer writes and speaks movingly of how discerning his true vocation helped him manage depression and provided him a clear purpose, a *why* if you have it.

Perhaps a crucial question we all must ponder and engage with is, "What is the *why* that motivates and provides me the reason to persevere during difficult times?" Viktor Frankl found his why in the form of small meanings in that hell-like existence of the Nazi death camps. In fact, Frankl maintained finding meaning was the reason he and others were able to keep their slender hopes alive (2006). In my years providing counseling, the clients who made significant improvement discovered their *why*. Frankl posited his Logotherapy as a meaning-oriented approach to psychotherapy, but I suspect the hidden variable lay in helping his patients discern a *why* in their lives. Aaron Beck (1963, 1979) and Martin Seligman (2006) each posit optimism as the best defense against depression and suicide. Discovering a *why* is likely is a large part of developing and instilling that optimism. Thus, a necessary function to habituate in our lives likely lies in the developing and maintaining a *why* in our professional and personal lives. Discussing Nietzsche's *why* can be interesting in the abstract, but identify and exploring that *why* likely becomes important in making it operational. Consider the following questions regarding your why:

Exercises for Exploring the *Why* in Our Lives

1) What is the *why* in your life?
2) If you do not know your *why*, how might you begin to explore or create it?
3) If you know your *why*, how does your *why* improve your quality of life?
4) If you were to have an empty chair-type discussion with your *why*, what might you say to your *why*? What might your *why* say to you? (Consider having this unorthodox discussion.)
5) If you are of mature age, how has your *why* changed over your lifetime?

Considering the *why* of life and the reason it is so important for well-being, the uplifting story of Oseola McCarty, an African-American laundress in rural Mississippi, comes to mind. Forced to quit school in the sixth grade to earn money for her family, she never married, had children, nor even learned to drive. A minimalist before popularization, she had few possessions, purchased only food and second-hand clothing, while managing to save over $150,000. As the money was more than she would ever use on herself, she donated her savings to finance scholarships for African-American students at the University of Southern Mississippi (USM). She explained Mississippi's racist policies would have kept her from attending college. That barred door to opportunity forged her desire to assist younger African Americans in realizing an education she was denied (Bragg, 1995). Oseola further explained she wanted to prevent her people from low-wage, otherwise dead-end occupations and viewed education as the most likely means towards social mobility. *The New York Times* article on her life goes on to reveal she cut the toes out of her shoes when they were uncomfortable and taped her Bible together, eschewing spending money on new shoes or a new holy book in order to invest the maximum amount of money for her chosen cause.

As a fellow southerner from impoverished roots—albeit a white one—I can well imagine this impoverished, black woman in southern Mississippi living her life along the lowest, downwardly mobile strata of society. Oseola, however, had her vehicle for transcending rural poverty, ignorance, hatred, racism, and the ever-present danger of assault and death at the hands of a fearful, angry, white majority should she cross that invisible, yet ever-present racial DMZ. This emotionally resilient, determined, deeply spiritual, can-do woman constructed a long life of personal and educational transformation. Each day she calculated how much money could go into her budding scholarship fund. In 1988, just three years after her announced gift, USM awarded her an honorary doctorate degree. She received scores of additional awards, including an honorary doctorate from Harvard University. While she could scarcely have imagined the outpouring of such honors, what she *could* envision was that each day, her life was a testament to the power of belief, perhaps the strongest example of a *why* in daily action. Nothing, not poverty, hatred, oppression, minimal education, nor a life of menial labor, would keep this determined woman from her sacred task. Each day while washing soiled clothes, she reminded herself she was making an investment to help others achieve their dreams. Oseola McCarty had a *why* that transcended any *how* extreme poverty and Jim Crow hatred could erect. I can think of few people who managed to transform their lives as completely as Oseola McCarty.

Final Thoughts

Much work goes into authoring a life of meaning, purpose, and happiness. Frankl (1986), Palmer (2000) and Seligman (2002) have written volumes regarding these important and closely inter-related traits and states. My own experience, mirrored by research in cognitive therapy, is that our self-talk is that canary in the mine (more appropriately, in the *mind*) that helps us assess and track our sense of meaning and purpose (Beck, 1963; Ellis & Doyle, 1988). More simply, everyone needs to discover Nietzsche's *why* in their life, keep it close at hand through reminders (e.g., posted on the refrigerator, on your social media sites, in your journal, etc.), and to call it up during times of challenge and doubt. Use exercises like those mentioned in this chapter and in this book (and other books and resources) to explore the meaning, purpose, and happiness in your life and to discern your *why* in life. Few of us will encounter the severe challenges and restrictions Oseola McCarty overcame, but *some* people do. While it is easy for a middle-class, white, educated, privileged university professor to scribe on important matters like meaning, purpose, happiness and that all-important *why* in life, such exploration is much harder in the world of experience. My experiences and wanderings throughout life have taught me the difficulty of practice *over* preaching very, very well.

Resources

Subjective Happiness Scale

Another resource to measure happiness is the Subjective Happiness Scale (SHS) by Lyubomirsky and Lepper (1999). The SBS is a four-item scale of global self-happiness. Two of the SHS items ask respondents to characterize themselves using both absolute ratings and ratings relative to peers. The other two ratings offer brief descriptions of happy and unhappy individuals and ask respondents the extent to which each characterization describes them.

http://sonjalyubomirsky.com/subjective-happiness-scale-shs/

Lessons Learned

After completing a six-hour workshop, I was looking forward to a cup of coffee and some much-needed R&R. However, the principal informed me one of the middle school teachers desired to speak with me. I was volunteering in Arnhem Land, an uber-remote location in the northeast region of Australia's remote-enough Northern Territory. My reason for being 10,000 miles from home was a sabbatical as a visiting scholar at the University of Canberra. As my sabbatical involved teaching two graduate courses while working on a book, sabbatical was a contradiction in terms (my fault!). I had planned to spend my spring break (in September, opposite seasons down-under) on the south coast, relaxing at a colleague's cabin. However, a colleague at a remote school, where I had provided workshops, consultation, and co-counseling with children three years earlier, contacted me inquiring if I would spend my break week providing training for them. Despite looking forward to a relaxing week at the coast, I agreed to make the long trip to the remote northeast, albeit with a measure of disappointment.

This particular school possibly was the most remote of all remote Northern Territory public and Catholic schools I have volunteered at. The Australian Department of Education classifies the school as *very remote*. During the wet season (November to April) when floodwaters rise significantly, the only way to reach the community and school is by small commuter plane. Because the community and school lie on the Arafura Sea in the Tropic of Capricorn, hurricanes are a constant threat. The school library, a real gem of a resource, also doubles as a hurricane shelter, with thick walls and heavy shutters. The buildings are well cared for and the classrooms modern. The football field, for Australian Football League or AFL, is well loved, as "footy" is a passion in remote, Indigenous communities. This community had already produced several professional AFL players, despite having a small population.

The reason the school counsellor and principal had invited me was the community having Australia's highest child trauma rate. My stated role was to provide training on managing traumatized students in the classroom without further traumatizing them. As often occurs, this would be only a small part of my role during my "break" week. As per request, I presented two three-hour mandatory workshops titled *Teaching Children with Behavioral Challenges*. Despite being mandated to attend, the teachers proved an enthusiastic gathering. Most were under age 30, with a smattering of longtime veterans. One veteran had taught at the school nearly 30 years. Due to the high level of trauma, severe isolation, dearth of social outlets, and the persistent social and health challenges in remote Indigenous communities, the attrition rate for new remote schoolteachers runs to over 50% within two years. As such, the Territorial government offers a high salary, free housing, and numerous additional incentives to stem the tide of attrition. Many teachers begin their careers in these *bush schools*, although few remain for a career. One veteran bush teacher joked, "We're the three M's here, mate: Missionaries out to save the world, Misfits with nowhere else, and Misanthropes who can't get along with others."

My workshop led to follow-up workshops on recognizing suicidal behavior in students, self-care for teachers, and the like. In fact, each day I gave workshops, provided coaching for teachers, visited classrooms, and assisted the school counsellor with the most high-risk students. Despite the very busy schedule, I enjoyed the work. Exhausted by Wednesday, I was eager to return to my relatively light teaching and writing schedule back in Canberra, where I also could access coffee shops and jog the many bike lanes the Australian Capital Territory offered.

Raising myself wearily from the couch in the teacher's lounge, carrying my battered thermal mug of coffee, I followed in the principal's wake like some somnambulist. I was introduced to a late 20-something teacher I recognized from my just-completed afternoon workshop. I shall call her Sarah. Sarah had an earnest look about her. She had taken copious notes and asked several questions during my workshops. Unfailingly polite, she naturally apologized for interrupting well-earned rest. She explained that she was a first-year teacher who had returned to university upon discerning teaching would be her passion. A New Zealand native ("Kiwi"), from a rural community on the South Island, she took a remote job to "help the Indigenous children." She then added, in a confessional tone, the pay was good and hiring in desirable suburbs of Auckland, Christchurch, and Melbourne bad. Nodding sympathetically, I inquired how I might be helpful. At this point, she burst into tears.

I sat for a moment in respectful silence while she collected herself. She explained being naive and "totally clueless" about the abysmal health and living conditions Indigenous Australians face in remote communities. Indigenous Australians in remote communities live in third-world conditions surrounded by a very successful, western nation that finds it convenient to ignore them. The long-term, dominant Australian Terra Nullius (meaning no land ownership prior to European arrival) policy of refusing to recognize native title to lands owned for at least 40,000 years only ended in 1992 (Jozuka, 2016). Thus, Indigenous Australians, perhaps the world's oldest culture, were strangers in their own land, leading to a sense of rootlessness, hopelessness, self-medicating with alcohol and other drugs, and consequently one of the world's highest suicide rates (Jozuka, 2016). She expressed roughly 70% of her students were severely traumatized. She described her classes being like combat zones, defiant children acting out, fighting, and even cursing at her. "I just can't keep doing this!" she exclaimed. Having visited many remote Indigenous school classrooms, I had witnessed extreme behavior, likely much due to trauma and being triggered. An unrealistic national curriculum, including teaching European history, and a lecture teaching format, all a poor fit for Indigenous children, are common culprits. Essentially, young, idealistic teachers like Sarah are set up for failure, much like Indigenous schoolchildren who cannot relate to the curriculum and passive teaching approach.

After composing herself, she asked, "Can you help me?" Frankly, I felt much empathy for this obviously underprepared, overwhelmed, naive young teacher. Having visited many well-managed classrooms throughout the Territory, I knew success was most often about the ability to build a relationship with the students. Going with my inner counselor, I asked how much time she spent asking the students about their lives, engaging them on the playground in pick-up footy, or some other game. Was she introducing herself to their parents, aunties, and uncles? She shook her head and replied she did not understand the *blackfella* Australians (term Indigenous Australians use to refer to themselves, not derogatory) as they were unlike the Māori back in New Zealand. Sarah stated she was not sure she could return after break, which would commence Thursday afternoon, tomorrow. This gave me an opening: "Okay, what would you need in order to return after the break?" For the first time, she looked thoughtful. She replied she did not know. Before conversation ended, I suggested she consider the question and then inquired whether she had made friends with colleagues. She reported not being close to anyone but had found a veteran female teacher helpful. I suggested she speak with that person and for us to check in the following day after my final presentation.

I recall little of the following day, other than I gave two presentations and met with a couple of teachers for one-to-one coaching sessions. At the end of the day, when the children had gone home, Sarah found me in the teacher's lounge having coffee. She suggested we walk over to the coast, a mere five minutes' stroll. She appeared less stressed, though still sported the eyeball-spinning, overwhelmed look. Sitting on a pair of rocks, we watched the Indigenous women casting their traditional handmade nets fishing for Barramundi or "Barra." Sarah disclosed having spoken to the veteran teacher and found her counsel thoughtful and somewhat helpful. I inquired about the helpful part, and she explained her colleague had acknowledged having a very difficult first year experience herself. Her colleague admitted she had seriously considered quitting as well. Sarah had inquired what had changed and kept her at the school for over 20 years. Her colleague answered, "You have to find a sense of purpose in the challenge of educating and reaching the students." Inquiring what her colleague meant by "reaching," she admitted having done little beyond the standard curriculum, an unmitigated disaster for her. I asked, "How might you develop that sense of purpose and reach the kids?" "I just don't know," she answered. My opinion was she would have to discover her purpose, or indeed she would not last. Sarah nodded in assent, look of utter concern returning.

Friday was the last day of an extremely busy "break" week for me. Mercifully, I was free of presentations and spent an hour in conversation with the principal encouraging more trauma training for all staff. She was supportive but realistic regarding the tight training budget, and pointed out that few mental health professionals dispensed their expertise pro bono, a mild joke at my expense. The fact that remote Indigenous lands have such an alarming rate of trauma and suicide, yet had little monies for training, spoke volumes about commonwealth and territorial priorities (something I have witnessed in the US). Being the final day of the term, with practically all staff flying out that afternoon, the jubilant mood was akin to expectant students anticipating vacation. There was even real brewed coffee, not the yucky instant variety, numerous baked goods, and other culinary delights. The principal acknowledged the staff, including me, inciting a round of applause, leaving me feeling appreciated and a tad embarrassed. I spoke with a number of teachers and other staff, met a friendly AFL coach who had recently married one of the teachers, and had a nice yarn with an Indigenous teacher about her country (her tribe and land). At liberty until my flight, I took a long relaxing walk along the water accompanied by an Indigenous teacher, who soberly cautioned me not to stray too close to the "salty" (Saltwater Crocodile) waters. I visited the famous cultural center, examining expensive Indigenous art, much being shipped to art galleries and private owners throughout the world.

After catching up on correspondence that afternoon while killing time before my afternoon flight, I returned to the teacher's lounge for another coffee and snack. I sat down as Sarah walked in looking much lighter than anytime the past week. She poured a coffee and sat across from me. Noting she appeared more upbeat, she smiled and nodded. "I may have found my purpose!" she announced. Interested, I asked her to elaborate. She reported Skyping her parents for a reality check, spending time journaling, and finally praying had helped. Referencing her elder colleague's comment on purpose, she offered that perhaps her purpose lay in learning how to reach these culturally different learners. "It's clear the teaching style taught in my university for whitefella Aussies and Kiwis just doesn't work with the Indigenous children," she admitted. She went on to express the successful teachers, those who remained and found their work fulfilling, had adapted to a more active learning approach, often blending culturally appropriate stories, terms, songs, dances, and dreamtime spirituality (Indigenous origin mythology). "I have to emulate them if I am going to make it."

We spent an hour talking about our joys, challenges, and struggles. I explained my various and sundry academic foibles, including nearly quitting college and completing my doctoral degree by the narrowest of margins, which surprised her. "What kept you going forward?" she asked. Providing a brief overview of my grandparents who had raised my siblings and me, and Nietzsche's famous quote, my answer was succinct: "I had a *why*." She nodded. "That's what I have to do. I have to find my *why*."

Virtually the entire school gathered at the small airport terminal, a small cinder-block structure with just room enough for two staff selling tickets. The 30-minute flight to Darwin was festive, with teachers frolicking at the prospect of three weeks of freedom. I sat beside a young teacher, originally from Melbourne, who had attended one of my workshops and we spoke of students, mental health, and then lighter topics of weekend plans. We landed in Darwin, and after goodbyes, I spent a restful night in the airport Hilton, lodging a far cry from my accommodations at the school. The following morning, I flew to Canberra via Adelaide. On the long flight south, I reflected on my very full spring break week. Emotionally and physically spent, I had a coffee and thought of Sarah, hoping she would discern her *why* and be of some help to her amazing, yet very challenging students, who can raise your spirits while breaking your heart all in the same moment. I looked out the small plane window at the red terrain from some 40,000 feet as we cruised above the world's oldest continent, observing the vast ridges of broken, arid mountains which once were peaks high as the Andes. There was something mesmerizing about the lonely, Mars-hued landscape far below. I thought of many related themes: well-intentioned people like Sarah; Indigenous Australians, inconvenient and invisible, despite over 40,000 years on the continent; my seven-year-old self, propped up on my bed in my grandparents' dirt-floor basement, reading that *National Geographic* cover story of the Australian Outback; my grandparents who always believed in me, their least promising grandchild.

The ping of the plane's PA system announcing food and beverage service interrupted my meditations. As the perky flight attendant handed over my food tray, that inner voice whispered inside the caverns of my mind, *find your* why, *find your* why.

Chapter 11

Love

Transformation and Challenges of Relationships

"What is love?" the professor inquired, his expressive face animated in anticipation of the class' response. The class, Psychology and Religion, was a graduate course taught by a stalwart of the Oregon State University Philosophy department. The professor, erudite and simultaneously folksy, would become one of my all-time favorite faculty. I enjoyed the course so much I developed and taught a version of it at a different university several years later. Our class was an assortment of undergraduate seniors and sundry graduate students. This particular class, we were discussing a reading from William James' seminal opus *The Varieties of Religious Experience* (1902). James declared that religious experiences fell into the category of ineffable understanding. That is, one may have such experiences, yet be unable to articulate the profundity of said experiences. Despite the inability to adequately describe or quantify spiritual encounters, James expressed that they fundamentally changed the lives of the persons who had these mystical experiences.

The professor's question on love was met with furrowed brows, shaking of heads, and awkward body language along those sporting curious looks. After all, everyone knows what love is, *right*? He suggested we consider the word, love, as being a universally common cross-cultural experience. "Now, someone give us a complete definition of the term." Several brave souls (not myself!) ventured into that realm where angels might hesitate attempting a definition. One stern-looking fellow even suggested a mathematical proof to explain love. No one, not even the erstwhile Euclid protégé, managed an answer that proved satisfactory. The professor smiled, and explained some experiences, such as in James' prophetic book, simply had no clear definition. Our student offered the best answer, suggesting love was a gestalt-type term: you can list reasons for why you love someone, but you always know there is more you cannot explain. Essentially, the whole of love exceeds the sum of its parts. Thus, in writing this chapter, I did what all post-modern scholars do and consulted the internet, the Oracle of our time. *Merriam-Webster's* site broke love into romantic love, sexual love, maternal love, affection for old friends, etc. Numerous other sites offered various and sundry definitions,

DOI:10.4324/9781003168324-11

sometimes with significant variation. Yet, all had in common the notion of love being deep affection for someone other than oneself. (Narcissistic love excepted.) There was one noteworthy website devoted to love addressed in the following paragraph.

Having experience in couples and family therapy, I went to The Gottman Institute's site (www.gottman.com). From his book *Principia Amortis: The New Science of Love*, John Gottman describes three phases of love. He admits love is a very complex experience with many variations. Gottman discusses what he calls choice points where love may progress to a deeper place, or where deterioration, disengagement, and break-ups occur. The three phases of love are:

1) Phase 1: Falling in love: Characterized by physical symptoms (e.g., increased heartrate, flushing, trembling, etc.), excitement, fantasizing, intrusive thinking, and fear of rejection. This phase is typically brief and based more on the lover's own projections.
2) Phase 2: Building trust: The critical question in Phase 2 of love is, "Will I be able to trust you?" Gottman posits trust, or lack thereof, as the basis for all secure or insecure attachments (2015). Success involves both partners discovering they trust one another and moving to Stage 3. The converse, however, involves couples unable to trust one another with arguments, sadness, and usually break-ups ensuing. It is noteworthy to mention that while trusting couples argue, their arguing is constructive (e.g., no name calling, violence, etc.), versus destructive arguing involving name calling, and even physical or sexual violence. Gottman lists his acronym ATTUNE for this phase:

   A = Awareness of one's partner's pain.
   T = Tolerance and understanding for a partner's different viewpoint.
   T = Turning toward one's partner's needs.
   U = Attempting to understand your partner.
   N = Non-defensive listening.
   E = Empathy towards one's partner.

3) Phase 3: Building commitment and loyalty: This last phase involves establishing commitment, nurturing, and cherishing the relationship with their partner. Phase 3 is about making love last for the long term, or slowly nurturing a betrayal and simmering resentment.

(The Gottman Institute, nd)

When I step back and consider the couples I have counseled, most of the breakdown seemed to have been in Phase 2, with the exception of young undergraduate romances. I would boil my experiences down to two important issues: trust and empathy.

Trust

In Gottman's theory, healthy couples encourage their partner's friendship circle, trusting each other. They reinforce their commitment through loyalty towards each other and prioritizing their relationship (Gottman, 2015). In such healthy relationships, partners are not jealous of their beloved's platonic relationships. For couples lacking solid trust, however, relationships outside of the partnership are viewed with suspicion, hostility, and even verbal or physically abusive behavior. Any experienced therapist can recount far too many stories of abused clients and relationships, and providing mandated counseling to abusers. In two settings, I co-facilitated batterer's intervention groups for men convicted of intimate partner violence. While the men varied in age, education, and culture, the commonality was believing they had a right to use violence in relationships. Naturally, there was little trust nor empathy towards their partner. Most, though not all of these men, had grown up in violent homes whereby a male adult abused his female partner. Considering Bandura's social learning theory (1977), the men in the batterer's intervention groups had father figures modeling domestic violence against their mothers. In their warped sense of relationships, intimate partner violence was *normal.* In fact, one of the first agenda items in batterer's intervention treatment is a discussion of why intimate partner violence is not normal, healthy, or legal. From experience, this foundational construct is a difficult sell to men who, having spent a lifetime being mentored in violence and who themselves may have been victimized during formative years by a violent male, believe they have a right to exact such violence on their partner and often their children.

Being completely vaccinated against COVID, I have returned to grocery shopping. Recently, while in the checkout line, I had time to scan the covers of several magazines and tabloid newspapers. Most of the messages dealt with relationships, including one tabloid with a story on a woman married to an alien. Perusing a publication devoted to celebrities, one young actress dating a fellow actor exclaimed she had found the man of her dreams. The statement, based on a one-month relationship, essentially Gottman's Phase 1, represents a brief, although often intense, period. With no judgment intended towards anyone in this dreamy, energizing phase, those of mature age realize it is a transient period ended by baser realities of differing opinions, values, and priorities. Having said this, we can learn a lot from such *immature* periods. I have counseled many late adolescent and young adults in residential living and college counseling centers looking distraught over the ending of "such a perfect relationship." In fairness, I recall being that distraught person myself. Thus, as love is a universal constant across all cultures, a deeper dive into the subject is required, especially for therapists. After all, given all the romance novels, films, songs, and childhood tales (e.g., *Cinderella, Beauty and the Beast, Rapunzel,* etc.) filling the senses with romanticized, idealized, unrealistic versions of love and relationships, the helping professions are the occupation to assist individuals and couples in discovering meaning in their loving relationships. The following example in the next paragraph illustrates the role of a therapist in relationship recovery and rebuilding.

A tall fellow with a mesomorph frame came stumbling into the counseling center, forlorn look evident on his face. I had witnessed the look often enough to hypothesize he was victim of a romantic breakup. Sure enough, barely had he sat down when he began spilling out his tale of personal woe before I could begin the intake. So upset was he, I deferred the intake to later in the session, given his need for emotional first aid. Evidently, his girlfriend of two years had dumped him just before he was preparing to propose marriage. He described never having been to counseling, and previously viewed it with suspicion. He was a college baseball player hoping to make the cut for the minor leagues and play a few years before coaching. Unpacking his young life, he was a good academic student with a detailed life plan: graduate from college, get married, play two or three years of minor league baseball, have kids, break into the coaching ranks, etc. All had evidently been going according to plan until the previous evening, when his romantic partner abruptly ended their relationship. While he denied any suicidal ideation, he admitted to feeling depressed, even lost regarding the change in his personal life.

Any reader of mature years will recognize this as a typical case of a young person's developmental struggles with the ending of romantic relationship. Most, if not all, readers can relate to feeling devastated in the aftermath of a breakup, an almost universal experience. In time, however, we move through this painful transition with emotional support from friends, perhaps counseling, and finally, when ready, meet someone new. In the immediate aftermath of an ending, however, the bereft party needs support sorting through their romantic post-mortem. I shall refer to my former baseball-playing client as Bill.

Bill was a personable, intelligent, optimistic person. He described himself as good at making friends, getting along with most people, and generally a happy person. He had dated only briefly during high school, as he was very busy playing baseball and studying. During his sophomore year of college, he met his girlfriend through a teammate, and had dated steady for two years. He planned to propose in the upcoming months, and even began looking at engagement rings. Much to his shock and dismay, however, his girlfriend shattered his illusions. At the end of the session, we set a follow-up appointment. My given homework assignment was reaching out to his mom, with whom he was close, a friend, and that he begin revising his depressed self-talk from "my life is ruined" to "I will learn from this difficult time." Although he was skeptical of this last assignment, I encouraged him to gently reframe his self-talk with the suggested saying.

Over several weeks, he evinced progress, albeit struggling with the grief accompanying the end of a relationship. The most instructive moment occurred in a later session. Bill was planning to buy a new stereo system, and had conducted extensive research on a quality system. I was impressed by the information he had compiled, with two dozen factors to consider. Realizing the teachable moment, I praised his diligence, and then inquired perhaps we might apply equal effort in choosing a partner. I asked, "What qualities would you desire in a spouse or life partner? I'll write them on the erasable board." Bill, who researched over 20 factors for the new stereo, could not cite even a handful of qualities for a spouse! Pausing to let the message sink in, I added, "Seems your stereo system research is more extensive than that for a future spouse." He shook his head and replied something like, "My priorities have been all messed up." This particular session represented our breakthrough. He realized that, having worked diligently on his sport, studies, and career, he had taken his romance for granted. Perhaps unsurprisingly, most of his friends were like him. "Like, we know to work on school and baseball, but just expect love to fall into place, I guess."

In my long career as a counseling faculty member and professional counselor, I have met many like Bill, with most well past their early 20s. Bill's statement, "like we just expect love to fall in place, I guess," is emblematic of my observation regarding relationships. Witness the multibillion-dollar wedding and wedding planning profession. Once an engaged colleague showed me her copy of a well-known bridal magazine, with professionally coiffed models in white lace, and honeymoon vacations to best locations one might dream of going (provided unlimited funds). The reality is, weddings are brief, and with the US divorce rate hovering around 50%, one has to question all the emphasis and money spent on a one-day event when a marriage or unmarried partnership is expected to last a lifetime. Now, the US divorce rate has hit a 50-year low (Wang, 2020), and a majority of married US couples (58%) say the pandemic has brought them closer (American Family Survey, 2020). College-educated and economically better-off couples are more likely to stay married, but working-class and impoverished Americans face more stress (likely higher unemployment, lower-paying jobs, live in more economically depressed areas, etc.) and have higher divorce rates (Wang, 2020). Many poorer Americans cite unemployment and underemployment as reasons for remaining single, or perhaps as cohabitating couples who do not marry. The interesting part for me is the heavy emphasis on an expensive wedding, with scant attention paid to life after the honeymoon. Western society loves a celebration, but is decidedly unenthusiastic regarding the less glamourous minutiae of making relationships work.

What Makes for a Happy Marriage or Partnership?

Whether married or not, straight or LGBTQ, the issue in loving relationships remains the quality of the marriage or partnership. Couples of lower socioeconomic standing face more stress due to impoverishment: lower earnings, higher unemployment rates, more pregnancies and dependents, less educational achievement, etc. Of course, romantic, sexual love is only one type of loving relationship. There is the love between parents and children, grandchildren and extended family, to say nothing of extremely close friendships, or "family of choice," as some have called close friendships. Our focus will stay with couples for the moment, as couples are so prominent in our lives.

Perusing The Gottman Institute, over 50 years of their research suggests healthy relationships condense to three basics:

1) Treating your partner as you would a good friend.
2) Managing conflicts in a gentle and positive manner.
3) Working to repair the relationship after conflict.

(Navarra, 2015)

Now, my guess is that any healthy relationship will have at least some ratio of Gottman's trio. There also are numerous marital and relationship assessments, such as the *Marital Satisfaction Inventory* (Snyder, 1997), *Triangular Love Scale* (Sternberg, 1998), *The Couples Precounseling Inventory-Revised* (Stuart & Jacobson, 1987) and many, many more, of course. My anecdotal experience has been that Gottman has been accurate, having counseled couples reporting some variation of Gottman's three basics. I have utilized a number of relationship satisfaction assessments, although I have found a subjective exercise far more revealing and helpful.

While working in a residential psychiatric center, one of my colleagues was an art therapist. I learned the value and efficacy of using creative arts approaches in counseling, most especially art, whether drawing, coloring painting, collage, etc. During my time counseling clients in addictions, I made extensive use of art and other creative endeavors, including drama therapy. At some point I incorporated drawing into couples work. After an intake, I placed couples on opposite sides of the room, providing sketch sheets, numerous crayons and magic markers and suggested they draw their relationship. On the first drawing, I would ask them to draw their relationship as they viewed it currently. Then, some 20 minutes later, I would request they draw their relationship as they would like it to be. Completing both drawings usually left 10–15 minutes in the session, at which point I requested each partner explain their drawings. Few counseling interventions I have witnessed have been as impactful as this conjoint drawing exercise. The efficacy of this drawing exercise likely lies in providing a vehicle for each partner to create and describe their relationship on paper prior to presentation. In a later session, I assign the partners to co-create a drawing of a functional future relationship. Sometimes, the final drawing illustrated the couple going separate directions, with the relationship ending.

Many couples were unable to create a conjoint relationship drawing with them remaining together. Some created a drawing that had them divorcing (or ending the relationship) yet illustrating co-parenting (two homes, visitation, occasional meals with everyone, etc.) and for a select few, a potential post-couple friendship. Interestingly, all these couples found the drawing process helpful either in creating a more fulfilling partnership, or in assisting them in splitting up without tearing themselves and their children apart emotionally. While arguments persist among some, healthy marital/couple endings can be beneficial for all involved.

The Four Horsemen of the Relationship Apocalypse

The four horsemen of the relationship apocalypse are critical indicators of a relationship headed for severe conflict and likely a divorce or other ending. John Gottman (1994a) maintains that his four-horseman model can predict divorce/ending with a greater than 90% accuracy rate. Gottman's four horsemen are criticism, contempt, defensiveness, and stonewalling. The following exchange illustrated the Gottman's four horseman:

CRITICISM: "You're such an idiot for missing the turn!"
CONTEMPT: "You are such a lousy partner! You cannot do anything right!"
DEFENSIVENESS: "I can't do anything right with you. I might as well just not offer my opinion."
STONEWALLING: One partner silently ruminates in response to the other's behavior.

Regarding these four horsemen, Gottman (1994a, 1994b) suggests what he terms the *gentle start-up*. This involves the use of I-statements, something very common in couples counseling. For example, regarding contempt, perhaps the most challenging of the horsemen according to Gottman (2015), a reframe to the statement, "You are such an idiot for missing the turn!" might be, "I am frustrated we are likely to be late to this important social event." For defensiveness statements such as "I can't do anything right with you," the gentle start-up might be "I am sorry for forgetting our anniversary. I now have it on my phone as a reminder." Basically, Gottman uses a well-validated reframe from CBT to address his four horsemen of relationship doom.

Recalling my years counseling couples, Gottman's research and simple intervention seems very accurate. In fact, my experience is that many interventions are simple (e.g., reframing self-talk for example), work well, and are easy to incorporate into daily life. The more problematic issue lies in the reality that using, say, reframing negative self-talk, requires the necessity of ongoing habituation. Like staying physically fit, there is no stopping point to it. Like personal fitness, relationship health requires gentle reminders (and much else!) for the remainder of the relationship. Another factor in relationship unraveling is that many people are not taught how to make relationships last. Witness how the divorce rate, while having fallen to a 50-year low, remains high (Wang, 2020). Given Bandura's social modeling theory (1977), a large percentage of people have witnessed modeling on how to fail in marriage or partnerships. This statement is not intended to blame people for divorce, as marriage certainly qualifies as an inexact science, particularly in such a dynamic era. Furthermore, considering all the women who have experienced intimate partner violence, divorce is a sad necessity in society and stigmatization of divorce is not a healthy nor helpful answer.

Therefore, regarding love and relationships, what are some qualities of healthy relationships? As one who likes to keep things simple, I return to John and Julie Gottman's research. John Gottman has been researching couples since 1972, involving over 3,000 couples (Navarra, 2015). While it is helpful to understand the four-horsemen model that threatens relationships, it is even more important to realize the components of a healthy relationship. The Gottman's key findings really come down to three essential elements:

1) Are you and your partner good friends (or best friends)?
2) Managing conflicts in gentle and proactive ways.
3) Developing the ability to repair and work through conflict.

(Navarra, 2015)

Gottman goes on to illustrate how partners treat one another when they are *not* fighting is predictive of their ability to manage conflict and repair residual damage occurring in the relationship. There is little question that partners who manage conflict well are likely to enjoy a more harmonious, fulfilling, lasting relationship (Navarra, 2015). Keeping in mind the three essential elements previously cited, consider the following questions regarding creating and maintaining relationships (romantic, familial, close friendships, etc.).

Relationship Enhancement Questions:

1) On a scale of 1–10, with 10 being high, how satisfying is your marriage/partnership?
2) Regarding the score you assigned to the previous question, how might you raise your score just one point?
3) Regarding friendship, would you describe your spouse/partner as your best friend? Why or why not?
4) How effective are you and your spouse/partner at managing conflict in gentle and proactive ways?
5) How might you and your spouse/partner improve your conflict management skills?
6) The Gottmans speak of gentle start-ups (use of I-statements). When you and your spouse/partner have conflict, how often do you employ I-statements ("I am hurt when . . ." "I get upset when . . ." "I feel disappointed at . . ." etc.)?
7) If you could make one change in your marriage/partnership, what change would you make? Would you be/are you able to address this desired change with your spouse/partner?

8) If someone were to solicit your advice on creating a healthy, loving relationship, what advice might you give?
9) Regarding the previous question on advice you would give regarding creating a healthy relationship, how well has that advice worked for you in relationships?
10) What is the most important lesson you have learned in your marriage/partnership?

Considering the Gottman's research and the previous reflective questions, I revert to this book's major influence: psychiatrist and Logotherapy originator Viktor Frankl. While Frankl focused primarily on meaning in life, he also wrote of love, and the crushing loss of his beloved wife, children, and virtually his entire family in the Holocaust. As Nazi guards mustered Frankl and his fellow prisoners out into an icy night's formation and armed guards patrolled, attack dogs snapping all about, gazing upward at the stars, he somehow was reminded of his late wife. He wrote poignantly of the experience, mentioning for the first time in his life seeing ultimate truth as rhapsodized in song by poets and philosophers. That truth was love representing the ultimate and highest goal to which people can aspire. He goes on to mention that salvation of humanity comes only through love (2006).

There is little doubt that Frankl's writings are transcendent in nature. Frankl posits love as a means of transcendence even unto and beyond death's veil. Perhaps what seems most remarkable is Frankl's transcendent thoughts of love within a compound founded and fueled on hate. The extreme conditions Frankl and his fellow inmates endured leave one pondering how he could look into the jagged teeth of camp hell and find any semblance of meaning or love; it suggests an emotional resilience difficult to fathom. Yet, he not only managed to find meaning and love, but emphasizes these as the primary reasons he could maintain his humanity and keep hope alive in a seemingly hopeless situation.

The Holocaust raises a long stream of questions regarding human nature that goes well beyond the scope and purpose of this text. The salient feature of Frankl's writing on love and meaning is his insistence on love being our most powerful emotion, referring to love as the "ultimate and highest goal" (p. 57). As interesting, inspiring, and engaging as his evocative book is, this section leaves me wondering if I have missed that proverbial bus in my mental health and academic career. In our graduate counseling, counseling/clinical psychology, social work, etc. courses, how often have do we speak of love in the manner of Frankl? Having taught a graduate counseling theory course for over two decades, I cannot recall ever running across any theoretical approach positing love as the ultimate goal. Yet, here is one of the most famous psychiatrists writing of love in terms one would expect of poets, philosophers, and theologians. The medical and therapeutic community came to embrace Freud's Oedipal

Complex as valid (at least *much* of them), yet how many would make the same allowance for Frankl's view of love? Psychoanalytic theory has certainly carved its niche in the psychotherapeutic world, and without question, it is a far more intriguing theory than, say, Cognitive Behavior Therapy, if less efficacious in research (Society of Clinical Psychology, n.d.). For this chapter, the overarching question might well be, "Do you believe love is the highest goal in your life?" If so, "What is the evidence that you (or we) have made love the highest goal in your practice/training/life?" My experience as student, longtime clinician, and professor is that the evidence does not support love being the highest therapeutic goal. Certainly, I have written treatment goals addressing how to create a healthy relationship or marriage, yet not in the manner in which Frankl spoke. Therapists and researchers naturally focus on therapeutic efficacy, standardized assessments, and research emotions, beliefs, and behaviors related to love, while remaining quite distinct from transcendent love. Thus, you will find little in the mental health literature mirroring Frankl's beliefs regarding love. However, a perusal of literature, poetry, and music will illustrate human fascination with love in all its formats: love won, lost, and unrequited. Love, and loss of love, is a major reason music, poetry, fiction, and film are such popular genres. The following section illustrates one of my therapeutic encounters with love as the theme.

Love Conquers All: Sometimes

Many years ago, I was counseling a 30-something woman whom I will refer to as Jane. Jane had never been married nor even had a serious relationship. She was well educated, held an advanced degree, and had a good-paying job. Jane was an African American and very religious. She presented to counseling expressing feeling sad. After an intake interview and assessment, which suggested moderate depression, we commenced therapy. She denied suicidal thoughts or gestures, expressing her "relationship with God helping her through her pain." Inquiring how I might be helpful, she replied, "I want to find someone to share my life." Her statement was by no means novel to me, so I suggested we explore the topic. She sat back in her chair and crossed her arms. "There's a problem," she offered. "See, I'm gay." LGBTQ issues are certainly common in the therapeutic encounter, so I inquired as to the problem. She explained that, as her evangelical church viewed homosexuality as a sin, she was stuck. As a pastoral counselor, an LGBTQ-religious conflict was something occasionally encountered. I suggested we examine how she might get her relationship needs met while at the same time satisfying her spiritual beliefs.

Jane reported discovering early in life that she was attracted to girls and not boys. She recounted going on a few dates with men during undergraduate years, but not exploring her love of women for religious reasons. She admitting feeling torn between her desire to find a life partner and the spiritual life she found otherwise fulfilling. During our sessions, I suggested online and community resources (Pride Center, the Metropolitan Church, local support groups, etc.) which she was aware of but had not explored. She spoke about her mother, a single parent, and the church community that had provided emotional, social, and spiritual support. She did not wish to leave her church, yet if she desired to find a suitable female partner, she would almost certainly need to do this. She was also concerned about her mother's reaction, as she had not come out to her. "This is why I'm stuck," I recall her saying.

We had hit a therapeutic impasse: Jane wanted to keep her religious faith, and yet doing so meant she was unable to fulfill her romantic desire for partnership. After dancing around this conflict for a couple of sessions, with no discernable progress made, I considered referring her. While lost in my meditation on how to proceed, an idea occurred. Given that her faith was so important to her, I thought we perhaps needed a conversation with a higher power. When Jane returned for the next session, I explained the empty chair technique and its various uses. She seemed interested, but wondered how it might help. I suggested that as a Christian who prayed and read the Bible daily, perhaps she might bring Jesus into the room to address the faith-love conflict. Studying me for a long moment, her gaze suggested that I might be *off kilter*, as my grandmother used to say. After more discussion and explanation of the empty chair process, she agreed to try it. I moved another chair directly across from her, stated Jesus occupied the chair, and encouraged Jane speak to Him. She hesitated, and then somewhat to my surprise, began crying profusely. Not wanting to disturb the moment, I covertly slid the tissue box her direction and remained silent. She cried for some time before speaking.

She expressed having felt so much emotional support from "You, my savior," especially as an African-American woman in a white, male-dominated world. She thanked the empty chair for answered prayer, encouragement, support, and hope. Then, she began to talk of love and loneliness, of wanting to find someone to share her life. She inquired, as God created her gay, and if God did not make mistakes, why was being gay a sin? After some period, she became silent. I suggested she move to the opposite chair and speak as Jesus might. I must confess that although raised in a religious home, albeit a tolerant one, and with formal religious education, I felt well beyond my depth! Interestingly, as she began to speak in the Jesus role, she opened up. She (or *He*?) spoke of the Bible verse regarding faith, hope, and love, yet love, not faith, being the strongest and most important (*1 Corinthians*, 1973). So, perhaps there was no real conflict in her loving another woman, provided she actually *loved* the woman. She further reasoned that her church did not observe the dietary or numerous other Judaic laws in the Book of Leviticus, the same biblical book prohibiting same-sex love (note, Leviticus only references *male* homosexuality). If, say, eating pork, prohibited in Leviticus, was now okay, she questioned, what made her type of love wrong? Finally, speaking in Jesus' seat, she said, "it was supposed to be about love and not judgment." Jane began to cry again, but this time they were the tears of relief and joy.

This became our last session. Jane had found the answer she needed and would seek community support from the Pride Center. Some challenges remained, such as was what decision to make regarding changing her faith community. She still had no timetable for coming out to her mother, something the Pride Center could assist with. Nevertheless, she disclosed believing her faith and her sexual orientation were now compatible. I confess that setting up an empty chair intervention involving such a prominent historical, religious, and potentially polarizing figure like Jesus was both daunting and risked potentially alienating Jane. I made the decision to take the risk, being stuck therapeutically, and because both her religious faith and her sexual orientation appeared co-equal to her future well-being. My decision was not made lightly, but I came to it after much reflection, meditation, and by tuning into my inner counselor. The client came to view love as transcendent over a dogma that left her feeling alienated, lonely, and ashamed. More significantly, voicing her prophet of faith's statement of love being stronger than faith provided a satisfactory answer, ending her emotional-religious stalemate. She could now explore her sexuality and simultaneously embrace her religious faith. This exercise certainly represented a risk, as a different client with a similar issue may have come to a very different answer than Jane. Anyone in the therapeutic field understands counseling is an inexact science. In this situation, and with this particular client, the leap of faith worked.

Making Quality Time Count

Perhaps some of the most important work mental health professionals, the clergy, medical professionals, etc. can provide is offering real presence to the client, patient, student, or parishioner before us. Quality time certainly is a valuable commodity in therapists', physicians', clergy members', or teachers' work. My own doctor has remarked numerous times his biggest frustration is how time-compressed he is with patients. Many of my former students, now in practice, have shared similar sentiments regarding time crunches. No question, there is seldom if ever enough time for helping professionals with their clients and those they supervise. Given that we all feel time-compressed, the issue then becomes using time judiciously. Quality time best refers to being fully present with whomever we are in professional or personal contact with. In thinking of quality time, I naturally revert to a story involving one of my former graduate school professors.

The chair of our Department of Counseling program was very good at evidencing presence with students and colleagues. I recall waiting to speak with him late one afternoon during what clearly had been a hectic day. I arrived a few minutes early, and sat waiting outside his office. During that respite prior to our meeting, a couple of faculty drifted in and out, there were a couple of phone calls, and one distraught student arrived in tears (I suggested she meet with the chair ahead of me). After an extended period, the student emerged puffy-eyed but more emotionally regulated. Finally, and rather late, I entered the chair's office reluctantly, not in trepidation, as he was a personable, kind individual. Rather, I was concerned he might be exhausted. That in mind, I was prepared to suggest we reschedule. His office certainly bore the telltale signs of chaos: papers strewn across his desk, notes taped to his phone, piles of books and papers stacked haphazardly about, and nary a cleared place to sit. The chair sat with tie askew, shirtsleeves rolled to his elbows, and his reading glasses dangling from his neck like a sacred object. Yet he smiled, saying, "I have been looking forward to our meeting." This he said in a tone that indicated sincerity. Deciding this was a good time to talk, I cleared a chair and sat down.

Interestingly, I cannot recall the subject of our meeting (likely my never-ending dissertation), but I do recall how present he was. Leaning back in his chair, one leg crossed over the other, thoughtful look across his face, and appropriate eye contact all indicated I was his most important focus. Even when the phone rang, he let it go to voice mail and continued with me. Despite competing demands, he had modeled genuine presence. I have met with faculty who appeared distracted during office hours, and having been a longtime professor and clinical supervisor in treatment centers, there is *much* distraction. I resolved, however, no matter what was going on around me, I would work to be as present as the chair. He had a reputation as a very good listener among his colleagues, students, and staff.

This excerpt from my graduate school days reminds me of a workshop I attended several years ago at the American Counseling Association's national conference. The workshop presenter related advice given by famed psychologist Carl Rogers when asked by a graduate student, "What can we do if all we have only 20 minutes with a client?" According to the colleague, Rogers answered the graduate student expressing, "Then give them the best 20 minutes you can." Regarding Rogers' salient advice and the behavior modeled by the former department chair, an important factor in any relationship, marriage or partnership, close friendship, family, professional, etc. is to model genuine presence. In an earlier chapter, I wrote of Indigenous Australian poet, artist, and retired teacher and principal Miriam-Rose Baumann's concept of *dadirri* (pronounced da-da), or deep listening. Dadirri is all about developing presence. "We cannot hurry the river," she says in a video on her website (Baumann, n.d.). Too often, we as helping professionals in the workplace, and in our own professional lives, try and *hurry the river*, so to speak, failing to give our best quality time due to all our distractions. People as different as Miriam-Rose Baumann, Carl Rogers, and my former department chair all were address the need for quiet, respectful, and sincere presence in relationships. If this chapter could be summed up in a brief sentence, it might be, *presence is the primary ingredient in all healthy relationships*. Presence embodies respect, healthy boundaries, genuineness, and yes, even love. Perhaps we must then reflect upon just how present we are with our loved ones, friends, colleagues, students, and the people who serve our food and clean our offices.

Further Relationship Exercises for Consideration

Some of the following exercises require pen and paper, one involves speaking with your partner/spouse, while others are informal. These exercises are to help readers explore their relationships. They are *not,* however, a substitute for professional relationship counseling with a qualified therapist.

1) Consider writing a brief essay on your closest loving relationship (500 words maximum). Describe your relationship with regard to affection, respect, and healthy boundaries. What are the notable challenges you have faced in this relationship? What is the most important lesson this relationship has taught you?
2) Consider Frankl's assertion that love is the ultimate and highest goal to which we can aspire (Frankl, 2006). Would you agree with Frankl? Why or why not? If love is not the highest goal, what is the highest goal to which we can aspire? How does your answer influence the way you live your life?
3) Gottman (2015) posits three relationship factors as essential: (1) treating partner/spouse as good friend; (2) managing conflicts in a gentle and positive manner; (3) repairing the relationship after conflict. How well do you and your partner/spouse function regarding Gottman's three essential factors? On the other hand, if reflecting on a past relationship, how well did you and your ex-partner/spouse function?
4) During this chapter, the author had a couple draw their relationship in current, desired, and future outcome if no positive change occurred. Consider drawing your relationship (separately, or with partner). Use crayons, magic markers, colored pencils, etc. Draw the relationship: (1) as you currently view it; (2) as you would like the relationship to become; (3) finally, draw the relationship as it might become in six months to one year if no positive change occurs. Finally, what do you learn from this drawing exercise?
5) The Listening Partnership Dyad: Select a regular day of the week for a Listening Partnership. Each partner would get a specific period to be speak and heard by his or her partner (say, 15–30 minutes). The speaker must use I-statements to own their own feelings, thoughts, and behaviors (e.g.: "I felt hurt when . . .", or "I felt validated when . . .") and not use accusatory or inflammatory language against their partner ("You're the reason I'm unhappy!" or "It's all your fault I'm unhappy!"). The listener's role is simply to be present and not to interrupt their partner or offer advice. The listener is encouraged to use minimal encouragers such as head nods,

appropriate eye contact, and open body language. Many couples begin the partnership session with a "What's new and good in your life?" question for the speaker. At the end of time, the listener asks, "Would you like a *be here now* question?" Be here now-type questions can be any simple type of question to ground the speaker to the present: "Which of your five senses seems most noticeable right now?" Or, "What are you most excited about in the upcoming week?" The questions ideally are simple and easy to answer. When the first speaker's time is done, the couple switch seating places and the previous speaker is now the listener. Some couples take a brief break between sessions (five minutes maximum) to ensure transition. The new speaker must also ask and receive permission to refer to any topic their partner mentioned in their session. Interrupting, arguing, blaming, etc. are inappropriate in the listening partnership. The listening partnership *is not couples counseling*, but rather a time to share thoughts, feelings, concerns, and be heard by the other partner. Partners may hold hands if they wish. As with all exercises in the text, the listening partnership *is not* a substitute for counseling with a qualified therapist.

Lessons Learned

She walked gingerly down the hall in obvious discomfort, and upon entering my office, with deliberation, sat carefully, pained expression visible across her youthful face. She bore the telltale signs of intimate partner violence, with a black eye and yellowish bruises about her face. Louisa (pseudonym) was a mid-30s Latina who had just gotten out of a violent relationship by fleeing to the shelter. Referred by a counselor at the shelter, she came to the clinic reluctantly. Although offered a female counselor, she requested me, as I had spoken to her workplace on anxiety and depression. I did not recall meeting her, but my presentation evidently left her with a positive impression. She expressed not seeking therapy previously as her family and culture tended to recommend services of the parish priest regarding personal matters. Talking about family business was otherwise something kept "in the family," as she expressed.

After the formal intake, Louisa told her story of growing up with parents who were first-generation citizens, having emigrated from Mexico. Her parents had experienced much racism growing up in a rural mountain western community in the United States. Although a promising student, her parents discouraged higher education, expressing that her husband would take care of her. She admitted this contradicted her upbringing, as her mother was a nurse's aide in a senior center, working full-time while helping raise five children, Louisa being the eldest. As the eldest, she assisted with childcare, cleaning, and meals when her mother was at work. Her father worked as a farm laborer, and later, in a more stable job at a large agribusiness company. She reported her childhood being generally happy and stable, and that her parents were strict but not abusive.

As she became more comfortable in session, she voiced that her parents modeled the father being the absolute head of the household. While she suspected her parents discussed matters behind closed doors, dad made all the decisions, as far as she knew. While she loved and respected her father, she described her relationship with him as distant. Her relationship with her mother was more conflictual, especially around dating and her desire to attend college. She reported being close to her brother who was a year younger, but more distant from her other siblings. Currently, while living only an hour or so from her parents, she visited them infrequently and described her relationship with them as conflictual.

While the conflict with her parents had its roots in childhood, her current relationship was a large part of the troubles between them. She was in her mid-30s and unmarried, when her parents expected her to be married with children. Having helped raise her younger siblings, she was in no hurry to marry and have children of her own, something her parents viewed unfavorably. Finally, she had moved in with a man without first being married. This same man had violently assaulted her. She described wanting her parents' emotional support, but as they approved of neither her boyfriend nor her "living in sin," as she referred to their relationship, she had not informed them of the abuse. When we spoke of treatment goals, she replied, "To find someone who will love me, accept me, and won't abuse me."

Louisa signed a release to speak with the counselor at the shelter. Her counselor stated Louisa seemed dedicated to permanently ending the abusive relationship and had faithfully attended and participated in daily group sessions. Returning for our second session, she looked physically better, the bruises having disappeared and her eyes less black and swollen. She also appeared more at ease, expressing a desire to create a healthy, loving relationship. I inquired regarding her opinion as the ingredients of a healthy relationship. Not surprisingly, a supportive, non-abusive partner was at the top of the list. She desired a man who respected her and would make joint decisions, unlike her parents. Using the dry erase board, we filled the board with a list of some ten or so items. I suggested she copy this list and review it regularly, especially after our counseling had ended. When she met someone special, she could compare how well the relationship matched the conjoint list. She thought this to be a worthwhile idea, and as she always carried a pen and small notepad in her purse, she took both out and quickly copied down the list.

Our session proceeded smoothly, with Louisa presenting on time and clearly motivated for each session. She soon moved from the shelter and into an apartment with a co-worker, making plans to enroll at the local community college majoring in business administration. Always a good student, she planned to transfer to a four-year university and eventually earn a Master's in Business Administration (MBA). Our treatment for PTSD had included self-soothing techniques such as grounding, safe place meditation, and journaling on her healing, along with standard CBT therapy. After some ten sessions, she met all treatment goals, with her anxiety and depression scores dropping over 50%. Her living situation was harmonious, and she had recently visited her parents, who were relieved at her being out of the relationship (she had not disclosed the abuse, however). As she was interested in furthering her education, I held a mock graduation ceremony during our last session, where she recounted what she had learned in counseling and how she would apply that information in future relationships. With her head held upright, she strolled confidently from my office, very different from her original entrance. I was proud of her work and, although I knew better, my hubris soared on the wings of therapeutic success.

I occasionally saw her around our small town and, as she had indicated a desire for me to acknowledge her, said a quick hello each time. She appeared happy and greeted me with a smile, informing me she had started classes and was excited about this new phase in her life. "I keep that list right here in my purse," she proudly exclaimed, tapping her purse. Having counseled far too many survivors of intimate partner violence, most of whom chose to return to their abuser, I generally am realistic regarding relapses. This time, however, I felt confident Louisa would meet her life goals, including a supportive, loving, non-abusive partner, and would graduate from college. In fact, her name appeared on the honor roll the college posted in the local paper. To borrow a poplar cliché, "all's well that ends well." Or so I believed.

Several months later, however, a familiar name showed up on my caseload. Expecting she was returning to update me on her progress, I gave the matter little thought until Louisa returned to my office looking even more battered than her initial session. Stunned, and even more concerned, I was quiet as she spent a couple of minutes crying, expressing that she had recently reunited with her abusive ex-boyfriend. She recounted a familiar tale of a contrite former abuser having learned his lesson. He even promised to come to the clinic for couples therapy and vowed that he would never again strike or verbally belittle her. Louisa expressed these promises lasted about one month before the abuse resumed. This time, however, she required overnight hospitalization. Upon discharge, she returned to the shelter and decided to return to counseling. "I still have my list," she offered weakly.

We spent several more sessions working on recognizing the signs of abusive partners, as well as revisiting our original list regarding ingredients of a healthy relationship. After a couple of difficult session involving her forgiving herself for returning to her abuser, she returned to her former motivated self. During our last session, using the empty chair, I had her speak to her former, abused self, and then for her former, abused self to speak with her. Part of the empty chair conversations were about lessons learned from her family, past relationships, in counseling, and through life experiences. The most important moment came when, speaking as her former self, she encouraged her current self to remember what she had learned about healthy relationships and not to judge herself. After acknowledging the progress she had made, we shook hands and she left my office. This time her walk appeared more measured and thoughtful. For my part, there was no hubris, only the stark reminder that all therapeutic progress made can come unraveled when therapeutic interventions run headfirst into real life. Louisa was frank in acknowledging she had not made allowances for the ease in which she could relapse into an abusive relationship. "Like an addict returning to a drug," she described. She had learned a harsh lesson, but one that might just save her life. As for myself, I experienced my own relapse and learned my own harsh lesson. Pride certainly is the penultimate step preceding a bad tumble. Beware!

Chapter 12

Joy and Grief

"I have always been grateful for the 55 years your grandfather and I had together," my grandmother said, parallel, earnest lines set on her octogenarian brow. I had returned to my rural Ozark hometown from the west coast for a stopover. With a brief window prior to the onset of fall term, and facing a long, daunting solo drive back to Oregon, my hand was literally on the doorknob. "You boys were a gift and have been our joy." We embraced and I jumped into my battered, cramped, four-cylinder VW Bug and sputtered off to commence a journey of more than 2,000 hard-earned miles. The meeting would be one of our last prior to her health failing and her death at age 86. Together with my grandfather, she had raised my four siblings and myself. No question, parenting five boys, close in age, active, and often mischievous, we had been *very* difficult for our grandparents at times. Saddled with five grandsons on a lean income invited serious financial challenges, to say nothing of the emotional investment for two elderly empty nesters. Yet, she clearly wanted to deliver that message prior to my departure. Perhaps, given her age and serious health issues, she sensed time was short. Her use of the word joy and the expression on her face has remained etched in my consciousness since that early September afternoon.

Joy and Its Shadow Sibling Grief

Merriam-Webster defines joy as "the emotion evoked by well-being, success, or good fortune or by the prospect of possessing what one desires" (n.d.). By the venerable *Merriam-Webster*'s definition, my grandmother must have been referring to that desire part of the definition, as given the challenges involved, and the circumstances by which they assumed guardianship, well-being, success, and good fortune went AWOL. Much heartbreak preceded my siblings and me prior to coming under the care of our grandparents. My parents exited the parenting picture for different reasons. My mother was residing at the Kansas State Psychiatric Hospital, where she would spend several years, while my father simply exited the picture. During my first day of first grade, I was the only child whose mother was not present. My grandfather stepped up for official duty, garnering additional questions such as the dreaded, *Where's you*

DOI:10.4324/9781003168324-12

mom? Explaining your mother was indisposed in a psychiatric hospital was a traumatic answer for a young child in rural Arkansas during the mid-1960s. Had I thought of the term joy, such would have had little relevance to the current state of my parents' whereabouts. That first day of school was my initiation into the realm as outlier in society's bell curve mindset. Word of mouth goes viral quickly in a small, cloistered, rural environment, and soon my peers knew my mother's address. To their credit, most were kind to me; only twice do I recall my mother's mental illness raised as an insult. I was one of only two first-grade kids whose parents were divorced, known then as "broken homes." The other boy and his siblings also resided with their grandparents, who owned the small grocery just down the street. He and his grandparents were key allies. They *understood.*

My grandparents, however, always maintained publicly and privately that we were their meaning and happiness, as were all their children and grandchildren. I noticed the occasional cracks in their facade, however. Once I overheard my grandparents whispering anxiously about our desperate financial situation, only the first such hushed talk regarding household economics. Another time, my grandmother called us together to say our mother had had a relapse and would not be returning from the hospital as planned. It was the first time I saw her cry. No, joy was scarcely the operative term I associate with my formative upbringing. The words difficult, impoverished, stressed, lonely, and certainly grief-stricken seem far more applicable. Previously, my siblings and I had been residing with various relatives. Financial constraints, a two-generation gap between our grandparents and ourselves, no vehicle for transportation, and being social outliers all collaborated to ensure our lives were complicated. Our life illustrated the Gordian knot of familial ties, and I have spent many years hence untangling the complexities of my formative years. Occasionally, when visiting my family and hometown, some vestigial issue emerges from the depths of my psyche like some Loch Ness creature long believed extinct, but still trolling the murky waters of the subconscious, occasionally rearing its head. One struggle involved making sense of my grandparents' insistence of life's intrinsic meaning, even in the face of extreme poverty, depression, and death of loved ones. For me, it seemed incomprehensible how they could remain steadfast in their personal philosophy, undergirded by a belief in God, when struggle and pain were all about us.

Thornton Wilder's Pulitzer Prize-winning novel *The Bridge of San Luis Rey* (1927) tells the tale of five interrelated characters who die when a Peruvian bridge collapses beneath them. A Catholic monk witnesses this tragedy and then goes about investigating the lives of the victims, seeking some type of closure and answer to this otherwise senseless tragedy. Brother Juniper, the main character, who was on his way to cross the bridge yet was spared by fortune, goes about interviewing everyone who knew the five victims. Over the course of six years, he compiles a voluminous book to illustrate God's plan for the victims. The book focuses on the victims, and concludes with Brother Juniper proclaiming God's goodness and mercy—whereupon however, a Canonical Council pronounces his work heretical, and Brother Juniper and his book are burned together at the stake. Wilder's book then shifts back to the funerals for the victims of the bridge's collapse. Despite the collective grief, the Abbess of Santa Maria Rosa de las Rosas manages to pull a few of the victims' loved ones together to assist with helping the mentally ill, the deaf, dying, and those in grief. The novel ends with the Abbess' observation that the bridge represents a spiritual link between the living and the dead, with the bridge representing love, the only enduring meaning that survives beyond death.

We might say much with regard to Wilder's popular and well-regarded Pulitzer Prize-winning novel. The book combines western thought on values such as love, religious faith, loss, grief, injustice, death, and finally, transcendence. Was the bridge collapse simply a tragic accident, or was it God's will that five people should die in order to teach others a valuable lesson? Brother Juniper investigates and arrives at the conclusion that as all five had recently resolved a problematic situation in their lives, perhaps fulfilling their life's mission and making this the appropriate time to die. I recall when a promising young colleague of mine died unexpectedly in her sleep, leaving a grieving spouse and three young daughters, one person opined this shocking death was "God's will." Another, who was not religious, proclaimed, "There are no accidents." I suppose what we might extract from such reasoning is that people are pawns for an autocratic supreme force who, in some divine plan, sends people senselessly to their deaths in order that we might all learn some deeper lesson. This would appear to be Wilder's central message conveyed via his Brother Juniper character.

I must confess to finding such reasoning as represented in Wilder's epic novel to be very unsatisfying on moral, theological, and ontological grounds. Pick any tragedy, whether plane crashes, mass shootings, sunken ships, or genocidal atrocities like the Holocaust, and the concept of using people as collateral damage in some cosmic lesson seems downright blasphemous. Consider how many victims of senseless violence and tragic accidents are parents with young children, or are promising youth, grandparents who desire to live long lives engaged with grandchildren, and numerous others with promising lives cut tragically short. In literature and film, where an author or director can manipulate facts and emotions, presenting otherwise senseless tragedies as something heroic and transcendent, readers and viewers can be persuaded to believe such. Real life, however, differs vastly from the pages of popular books or scenes in epic films.

Several years ago, while attending the American Counseling Association's (ACA) annual conference, one of the keynote speakers was Dr. Jeremy Richman, a neuropharmacologist researching drugs for Alzheimer's disease. His elementary-school daughter Avielle was one of the 25 victims of the Sandy Hook Elementary School mass shooting in 2012. I attended his keynote presentation and found myself deeply moved by his tale of grief, anger, and his making meaning from this horrible tragedy by co-founding the Avielle Foundation with his spouse. He spoke eloquently and poignantly of his and his wife's grief, and how creating a foundation in his slain daughter's name helped him reconstruct his life from the ashes of a senseless tragedy. Later that day, during a break, I happened to find myself sharing a table with Dr. Richman. I introduced myself and stated how moved I was by his keynote. He graciously thanked me and then inquired about my work. I explained my academic and professional practice background in trauma treatment, suicide prevention, counseling, publications, and related work. He was most interested in my pastoral work and my thoughts on tragedies such as Sandy Hook Elementary. I referenced Rabbi Harold Kushner's writings, especially his thoughtful book *When Bad Things Happen to Good People* and Viktor Frankl's *Man's Search for Meaning*. He was quite familiar with both books, stating what he had learned from personal tragedy was a need to construct something meaningful from the senseless violence that had killed his daughter and her classmates. I recall his saying he wanted no other parents to have to go through what he, his spouse, and others went through in Connecticut. He expressed frustration and pain at seemingly well-intentioned, yet naive, callous statements such as "God never gives us more than we can handle." We both agreed such well-intended, universally hurtful sentiments left us wishing we were emotionally weaker. He expressed that the foundation he established in his daughter's memory had brought him much fulfillment and even joy in helping others. After we finished our coffee, I thanked him again for sharing his painful, yet uplifting story, and wished him the best with the Avielle Foundation. He shook my hand and thanked me for the talk.

A couple of years later, ironically while at another ACA national conference, I read of Dr. Richman's shocking suicide. Stunned, I recall taking a walk along the length of the convention center to work off the aftereffects of this tragic news. That I had spent time in protracted conversation with Dr. Richman made it even more disorienting. I tried to make sense of his death, discussing it with a colleague and later my spouse, who also was attending the conference. Eventually I arrived back at my usual conclusion regarding tragic circumstances: tragedy may have no good answer or lesson, other than working to prevent future such tragedies. While speaking with a colleague, a traditional religious woman, she expressed Dr. Richman's death was, like his daughter's, tragic. She went on to say, however, that perhaps it was for the best, given his suffering was over. She did not address Dr. Richman's widow's compounded suffering, having now lost a young daughter to murder and a spouse to suicide. My colleague's well-intentioned sentiment represents the type of blasé dismissal I find so painfully disconcerting, particularly when expressed by someone in the mental health community.

Like characters in Wilder's famous novel, colleagues, friends, and others, we all make sense of tragedy in ways that likely have less to do with comforting the bereaved than of creating comfort for ourselves. While a student in the master's degree program at Oregon State University, I took a workshop on grief counseling. The trainer, a local therapist whose name I long ago forgot but whose counsel has remained with me, suggested grief work was far more about the counselor's presence than any sage words or complex intervention. In point of fact, he expressed grieving persons often do not recall your words, save pithy, non-empathetic phrases like "Only the good die young," "This was the will of God," or other well-intentioned, yet callous statements. Rabbi Kushner himself admits in his bestselling book *When Bad Things Happen to Good People* (1981) that he had spent years dispensing formulaic counsel to the bereaved, thinking he was doing good works, only to discover how hollow, insincere, and painful such sentiments felt in receiving them after his young son's death from a terrible illness. Speaking from experience, Kushner articulates people offering such trite statements have little idea of the additional pain they cause the bereaved with such thoughtless comments.

Is There a Satisfying Answer to Grief?

Like many reading this text, I have counseled numerous people grappling with grief and loss issues. My former clients run the gamut from survivors coping with Sudden Infant Death Syndrome (SIDS), a loved one's suicide, sudden, unexpected deaths such as in automobile accidents and heart attacks, cancer or another progressive disease, divorce, estrangement from a loved one, etc. Often I have heard some variation of, "I have been a good person, so why has this [tragedy] happened to me?" In addressing this ubiquitous question, Kushner's counsel is as instructive as any that come to mind. After long pondering unanswerable questions like, *Why is there evil in the world? Why did my father get cancer? Why did my child die?* Kushner arrives at the conclusion there likely is no satisfactory answer available. Perhaps the best we can offer is to learn and grow through tragic experiences. Through that crucible of pain, loss, and despair, the pain, anguish, and the sense of unfairness likely remain (1981).

If we accept Kushner's school of thought, then as therapists, clergy, physicians, parents and loved ones, or in fact anyone else, there is no satisfactory answer to some of life's tragedies. "Shit just happens man," uttered a former client, himself grieving the death of his son. In this case, as in all grieving clients I treated, finding a satisfactory answer to their loved one's death was not part of the treatment plan, nor was closure part of any plan either. Frankly, the best I had to offer of all unsatisfying options was to be present and assist the bereaved client in processing her or his grief. Much of the work involved emoting (e.g., crying, raging, cursing, etc.), unpacking their grief, and facilitating ways to memorialize the deceased, whether it be a scholarship, becoming a counselor or social worker, or running self-help groups to assist others such as themselves. While undertaking a trauma counseling program, I met a woman who was a successful lawyer. Her college-student son had committed suicide several years earlier. She resolved to learn skills to help prevent suicide and provide grieving parents like herself a support group to deal with complicated bereavement. Another colleague, whose 22-year-old son died in a cycling accident, started a foundation with a newsletter in memory of her son. The newsletter has over 1,000 subscribers composed of people living all across the country. "The foundation and newsletter doesn't bring my son back, but keeps his memory alive in a transcendent way," she informed me.

Constructing Meaning from the Meaningless

In all cases of grief I have encountered, as counselor, colleague, friend, through national presenters like Dr. Richman, and reading stories in books, grief stories also involve joy. The joy of a daughter's birth, son's marriage, spouse's graduation from medical school, child's first communion, father's retirement party, etc.—these deep emotional bonds, ties that bind well after death, are strongly intertwined with the oppressive anchor of grief. A former professor of mine, whose daughter died suddenly while at college, told me he had no good answers for why she had died. However, while mentioning that her death never gets easier per se, he did say his grief was getting *lighter* with time. Viktor Frankl, an irrepressible optimist, never denied grieving his spouse, children, and family murdered during the Holocaust. His memorialization was to commence writing *Man's Search for Meaning*, much in the vein that Dr. Jeremy Richman and his spouse founded the Avielle Foundation to memorialize his slain daughter and assist other grieving parents.

Often, many people grieving a senseless death create something constructive, as per Frankl, Jeremy Richman, and countless others. A friend and colleague who was a Holocaust refugee was one of several scholars who collaborated on a poignant book titled *Light from the Ashes: Social Science Careers of Young Holocaust Survivors* (Suedfeld, 2001). In this unusual text, various authors wrote chapters on surviving the Holocaust, fleeing Nazi persecution, living refugees' lives in transition, and finally their road to a scholarly career in psychology and related social sciences. My colleague and friend expressed to me the satisfaction that the hateful Nazi regime was not able to wipe out him and his colleagues. He expressed that writing had been very therapeutic for him and likely his fellow authors in the text. The very title itself, promoting light coming from ashes, is an evocative method of illustrating defiance through survival of people who persevered, becoming professors and clinicians who helped others heal from trauma. The externalization of grief, anger, trauma, and such is an example of a cognitive, behavioral, and emotional adaptation reframing trauma and tragedy as something to process, experience, learn from, and finally to provide transcendent meaning and lessons for a senseless, horrific action. Suedfeld's text, like Frankl's earlier, represents a cathartic opus of putting traumatic memories into publication, perhaps a more extreme example of the benefits of writing to address trauma and grief (Pennebaker, 2004). In grief counseling, assigning clients journal on their grief and loss is a common part of treatment. Former clients have authored journals, poetry, created artwork, and sculpture memorializing their late loved one. There likely is an innate human tendency to create the tangible from inert ashes of grief. (Hence part of the book title, *Light from the Ashes*.)

Years ago, my mother-in-law resided in an apartment complex in the greater Chicago area. For her 75th birthday, family and close friends gave her a birthday party, comprised of 75 reasons we loved her. As my mother-in-law, my spouse, and their family are Jewish, I met a number of relatives and friends, most of whom were Jews. One notable person in attendance was a nonagenarian Holocaust survivor. A spry, engaging person, we spoke of my mother-in-law, our families, travel, and such. As it was August and quite hot, we were dressed in summer wear. At some point, I noticed a blurred set of numbers on her arm, an old tattoo long faded. "They gave it to us in the camps," she added in response to my gaze. Immediately, I felt myself shrink in my chair. This kind, elderly Holocaust survivor squeezed my arm and went on to express her revenge was in creating a new life with a loving spouse (deceased), several children, grandchildren, and many friends such as my mother-in-law. She disclosed each morning upon viewing her blurred number, she says to it, "You did not destroy my life. I lived and defeated you!" She began making this statement every day since liberation from that Nazi death camp where so many of her family and friends had perished. Her defiant statement helped in lifting her from victim to victor, and was instrumental in her rebuilding her life and creating a large family that would carry her memory and genes throughout ongoing generations. "Our attitude is so critical," I recall her saying.

Now, undoubtedly, this elderly Holocaust survivor must have had days full of overwhelming grief where it would have been a challenge for her to believe her words. We do know, however, we tend to believe what we tell ourselves (Ellis & Doyle, 1988). Over time, healthy self-statements such as this Holocaust survivor's "I defeated you!" are likely to make a big difference in lifting our mood and helping us with pro-social behavior. Unfortunately, the converse also is true, as people who tell themselves self-defeating messages will feel more anxious and depressed (Ellis & Doyle, 1988). Certainly, it would be understandable for anyone heavily traumatized to give in to grief, depression, anxiety, or addiction, and consider life to be without meaning or purpose. Here is where I return to Frankl and the 90-year-old Holocaust survivor, in that attitude, and likely social support from family and friends, makes a huge difference. Interestingly, the elderly Holocaust survivor gave every appearance of being a joyful person, laughing loudly and often. Granted, she likely worked *very* hard to achieve that state. Regardless, she was adamant in her belief that an upbeat attitude had helped her overcome perhaps the worst possible trauma anyone could endure. She discovered her meaning and purpose in her survival and family despite those blurred, never-quite-faded numbers across her arm.

Were someone to inquire for the thumbnail sketch of "what's this book about?", my answer would be that meaning in life is critical for both survival and optimal functioning. More accurately, meaning also is important for even less optimal functioning. Many clients in the various locales where I have provided counseling have informed me our sessions were helpful in their maintaining hope, even while admitting they continued to struggle with depression, anxiety, addiction, etc. One offered, "Our talks have helped me to rise from bed every morning and go through my day." This client made only minimal progress in reducing his depression. (He was also under care of a psychiatrist.) Therefore, it is prudent to remember that hope and meaning, while crucial, will not lift all boats equally high, to borrow a well-known cliché. As therapists, physicians, clergy, teachers, supervisors, and anyone else, your best work with a client, patient, parishioner, student, employee, etc. may be only enough to keep that person moving forward, if only incrementally. That your efforts help that person continue living and functioning, however, is significant. As healers of various types, while desiring our charges achieve and not simply endure, endurance sometimes is the best we can offer, at least at that time.

Beauty from Suffering

In their uplifting book, *The Book of Joy: Lasting Happiness in a Changing World* (2016), His Holiness the Dalai Lama and the late Archbishop Desmond Tutu, both Noble Prize Laureates, along with Douglas Abrams, have a chapter titled *Nothing Beautiful Comes Without Some Suffering*. In the chapter, Desmond Tutu writes that when Nelson Mandala went to jail, he was young and intent on revenge. As head of the armed wing of the African National Congress, he spend 27 years imprisoned. Tutu acknowledges many people would see 27 years as a terrible waste. However, Tutu views Mandela's 27-year imprisonment as being necessary for Mandela's development as a leader. He goes on to write that Mandela's suffering in prison helped him become more magnanimous and willing to listen to the opposition. Throughout his imprisonment, Mandela discovered people he regarded as his enemy were also human beings molded by their society, harboring their own hopes and fears. Tutu doubts that, without his 27 years in captivity, Nelson Mandala would have had the compassion and the empathy to put himself in the shoes of the other.

Desmond Tutu's statement regarding his friend and colleague Nelson Mandala seems incredible, perhaps stunning, and possibly callous on a number of levels. First, the very idea that someone could be imprisoned for one-third of his life for challenging a racist society likely raises many hackles (guilty!). However, Tutu goes on to express that imprisonment was a type of incubation, or perhaps more appropriately a meditation, as if those nearly three decades were in a monastery instead of a vile prison. Yet, as a close friend of Mandala,

Tutu has a perspective few anywhere would have. Somehow—how, I cannot fathom—this long imprisonment left Nelson Mandala not brimming with rancor and a desire for vengeance, but rather with a sense of empathy for Afrikaners (white South Africans). A few pages later, the Dalai Lama, when discussing his grief in being exiled from his homeland by the Chinese government, advises we always maintain a joyful mind. Of course, what is a joyful mind, and equally important, how does one cultivate that joyful state, particularly in the face of grief and suffering? In essence, Buddhists believe that joy is our natural state and the ability to express joy can be cultivated as a skill (Dali Lama et al., 2016). To develop joy as a state requires habituating the Buddhist practice of mind training, called *lojong* in Tibetan. Practicing *lojong* requires lessening self-absorption through meditation, including a refrain from grasping at our desires (Dali Lama et al., 2016). In the vernacular, the use of daily gratitudes, meditating on joy and releasing sorrow, embracing grief as well as joy, and ultimately through long practice of keeping that joyful mindset regardless of circumstances. Unquestionably, achieving *lojong* is *very* hard work, perhaps more difficult than anything else in life. We all experience grief as loved ones die or simply decide they no longer love us, disappointments happen, sometimes we fail, make mistakes, and find ourselves in unfulfilling circumstances. These unwanted and unfulfilling states, along with happiness and joy, are ironically a necessary part of composing a happy, fulfilling life, according to these two learned theologians.

Tutu and the Dalai Lama go on to mention that our ability to cultivate joy has not been studied as thoroughly as our ability to achieve happiness. In the late 1970s, for example, psychologist Philip Brickman et al. (1978) published a landmark study that found when lottery winners and those paralyzed in accidents were studied one year after their life-altering event, there was little difference in their respective happiness scores. This and subsequent studies introduced the theory that people have a certain happiness mean that remains steady throughout their life. That is, happiness seemingly does not vary much over our lifetime, excepting temporary periods (e.g., winning the lottery).

Sonja Lyubomirsky's (2007) research on happiness suggests perhaps 50% of happiness is determined by immutable factors such as genetics or temperament. The other 50% of happiness comes through a combination of our circumstances, over which we may have limited control, and our attitudes and actions, over which we have significant control. According to Lyubomirsky, the three factors that appear to have the greatest influence on increasing our happiness are our ability to reframe our situation more positively (CBT self-talk), our ability to express gratitude (daily gratitudes), and our choice to be kind and generous with others. These are the precise types of actions and attitudes Frankl mentions that the Dalai Lama and Tutu write of, and the ones that my mother-in-law's Holocaust survivor friend practiced. Perhaps, then, happiness and joy are more a by-product of healthy self-talk, daily gratitudes, and regular generous and kind actions towards others. None of these practices is difficult to do; rather, the difficulty comes in habituating them for the remainder of our life.

Furthermore, grief, the shadow side of joy, is a state nobody is eager to enter into, as it means someone close has died or distanced from us. Who would describe their grieving process as beautiful? During a graduate course on death and dying, we read Elisabeth Kubler-Ross' seminal book, *On Death & Dying: What the Dying Have to Teach Doctors, Nurses, Clergy & Their Own Families* (2014). While Kubler-Ross' work was groundbreaking and instructional, her stages of grief—denial, anger, bargaining, depression, and acceptance—more accurately represent phases grieving persons move back and forth between, as opposed to a developmental process. The numerous grieving clients I counseled vacillated between these *stages* in various ways, sometimes within moments of one another. I cannot recall any of them mentioning beauty as a descriptor in their grieving process. In sudden deaths like automobile accidents, sudden heart attacks or something unexpected, the shock value is great, leaving many with flashbulb memories of what they were doing when informed their loved one was dead. "I recall having just come from a department meeting," a former client recounted in session. "I had been annoyed at a colleague and was ruminating on that when the call that changed my life came through my phone." Another recalled having to ask the police officer to repeat the news, and still she could not believe it, as her husband had just left an hour ago. When my 37-year-old colleague died of a seizure in her sleep, another friend and colleague called to inform me early Sunday morning. I also had to ask her to repeat the message. Grief news, especially unexpected, tends to be difficult to assimilate into our minds.

What we want is the impossible: namely, to rewind the video to when our loved one was alive and healthy. Unfortunately, we are unable to accomplish that feat. Leonard Cohen, one of my favorite folk singers, has a thoughtful song on healing (Leonard & Cohen, 2012). He sings of splinters of a cross left behind, grief, and sacrifices we gladly would not have endured, but also of mental, physical, and spiritual healing. Healing involves moving towards that needle of pain that we can never permanently avoid despite denial, distortion, and living in the past. We wear the pain of our suffering like some thorny crown, some never totally relinquishing that crown of anguish. We desire to reach that point where Cohen sings of a yielding darkness to a greater light. In this case, he sings about healing the mind, body, and spirit, not just in Kabbalistic fashion, but in a universal manner. Cohen's lines and images are beautiful in a painful sort of way, the type those recently emerged from that darkness of grief can best appreciate. While metaphors tend to be culturally specific, grief is a burden humans carry cross-culturally, individually and collectively, where one may heal but the reminders remain, like those blurred numbers on the Holocaust survivor's arm.

In my professional and personal experience, healing occurs through the continuum of engaging with the pain, then working through the pain and grief to emerge to the other side of that dark tunnel, having learned much and with the relief that the most unpleasant part may be over. Recalling my former professor commenting on his daughter's death, he said, "It doesn't get easier, but it does get lighter." That oppressive weight of grief gets lighter with therapeutic work, social support, help from a higher power for many, and with time. Lori Gottlieb, a grief therapist, writes that healing doesn't mean that the pain goes away. Rather, the pain becomes a sacred part of you that one carry inside themselves forever. She goes one to express that while grieving people come to her hoping she can aid in their finding closure, she views closure as an illusion. (in R.J. Rosen, 2021)

As per Gottlieb's salient counsel, perhaps the best we can offer is to help them acknowledge and honor that grief. Perhaps for some, grief does become a sacred part of their lives, honored at particular points, especially when nearing the anniversary of that loss. My grandmother, who raised my siblings and me, lost her younger son in an automobile accident when he was just 16 years old. As the anniversary of his abrupt and untimely death approached, she would talk about his death, how the mortician let her bring his body home for one last night. Her pain and grief were evident on her face and while she gladly would never have suffered it, there was a memorializing approximating something sacred, and at times, also profane.

Helping Those in Grief

As professionals of all types may read this text, not just mental health professionals, this book represents both theory and practice, the yin and yang of our occupational being and functioning. I recall in a workshop somewhere (cannot recall where), a grief counselor spoke of honoring grief. She mentioned her experience working with bereaved clients was that once they began to embrace that natural sadness, the grief process seem to become less daunting, although not necessarily less painful. Then, her clients began to discover ways to honor the deceased loved one's memory. I have witnessed this myself as former clients have written poetry, songs, established scholarships, and donated time to hospice camps and other worthwhile causes in memory of their beloved. None of my former clients who have used such vehicles to transform their grief ever mentioned their grief was healed through this process. Many have said, however, that the transformative process of memorializing their departed family member or friend provided a sense of meaning and purpose to their grief. Several have confided to me that such memorialization was the most cathartic part of their healing. They likely carry some vestiges of their grief, as is natural, but grief no longer overwhelms them, and perhaps while never achieving closure, grief becomes lighter.

The following exercises represent a few examples to help clients, patients, parishioners, and anyone else honor the memory of a loved one. Some examples involve interventions mentioned previously, but in a grief-healing manner. As grief expression is cultural, some exercises may be more appropriate for particular cultures than for others. As with all examples in this text, these are meant to provide suggestions and to stimulate the reader to consider additional interventions. Furthermore, much grief in life involves the living, as in grieving a divorce, end of a friendship, alienated family member, etc. Grieving is also individual as well as culturally processed, and we must not fall prey to classifying a person's grief into particular categories. Rabbi Kushner, for example, offers wise counsel on this (1981). Be aware and respect the grieving person's culture, while remembering at the same time their suffering remains unique to them.

Note: The exercises below are not a substitute for professional grief therapy, although it is possible to use them in conjunction with therapy.

Writing a Letter to the Deceased Person

There are many variations on this exercise. The simplest is for the bereaved person to write a letter enumerating their love for the deceased, how they are missed, in what ways they helped bring fulfillment to the survivor(s), and how the author of the letter will honor the decedent's memory. Naturally, some people will carry this exercise further and write a series of letters to the deceased. In one case I know of, the author had the decedent write back in a literary empty chair-type exercise. (Note: Some write goodbye letters to the decedent. Others prefer something ongoing.)

A Conversation With the Decedent

Once again, this involves Moreno's empty chair technique. As per usual, use two chairs across from each other, of if preferred, angled in some acceptable manner. The bereaved person can speak to the empty chair as if their departed loved one occupied it. Then, after the bereaved person has spoken, they move to the empty chair and reply as the decedent. Be aware that some cultures do not directly address a departed loved one, nor even speak their name. In such cases, they refer to the departed loved one in an indirect manner. ("Girl who was my daughter," for example.)

Drawing or Painting Your Grief or Drawing or Painting Healing From Grief

This exercise is flexible and dependent on the grieving person's preference. The person in grief can use any drawing or painting instruments to create their drawing or painting. Encourage the person to silence their inner critic and draw or paint whatever they find meaningful regarding their grief process, feelings for the departed (e.g., sorrow, joy, anger, etc.,.) and anything they deem important. The bereaved might also consider a different drawing or painting on the topic some six months or so after the initial was completed. This comparison provides a means of measuring change in the grief process.

Daily Gratitudes

Gratitude may be difficult to entertain when in the throes of grief. However, my personal experience is that daily gratitudes, hard as they might be during the grief process, help in managing grief. We can still be grateful we had the beloved person in our lives, grateful for healing, for lessons learned, for being alive, etc. The recommendation is for the bereaved to acknowledge three gratitudes daily, either by writing them down, saying them aloud, or silently in one's thoughts.

Short Story Memorial

The Short Story Memorial came about when counseling a client who was a writer. The exercise involves writing a 500-word (or of any length; 500 words gives a basic parameter) short story involving the departed person. The story can involve, joy, sadness, anger, humor, and anything the author finds cathartic. The author may also choose to write a different version of the story six months (or so) later.

The Grief Sentence Stem Technique (GSST)

Nearly two decades ago, I created the Sentence Stem Technique (SST) to help counselors and others better understand a client's current mood (the SST is not a projective assessment). The Grief Sentence Stem Technique is not a diagnostic test, but rather, an exercise to help gauge the bereaved person's current mood and provide a means of measuring change in the grief process. The bereaved person simply completes the sentence stems below, either in writing or aloud.

1) My grief . . .
2) What I miss most about the person who is gone is . . .
3) When I feel sad I . . .
4) My greatest hope is . . .
5) The emotion I feel most strongly at this moment is . . .
6) If I could do one thing different right now it would be . . .
7) What most helps me manage the grief is . . .
8) What I tell myself about my loss is . . .
9) What I would want others to understand about my grief is . . .
10) The most significant lesson grief has taught me is . . .

Lessons Learned

"I wonder if I might have a yarn with you?" she asked after I had just finished a full day of trauma training in her school. I had been volunteering in Australia's remote Northern Territory Indigenous schools for over a month, providing trainings and individual coaching on trauma treatment, student behavioral issues, suicide prevention, and related topics. The Territorial government classified this particular school as very remote. The governmental distinction between remote and very remote schools seemed most arbitrary, as mere remote schools were in small communities of a few hundred people, located two or three hours from the next small community of a few hundred people (or less). This particular community was the most far-flung outpost I visited. My colleague Cheryl, a Remote School Counsellor covering eight remote-to-very-remote Indigenous schools, and I had driven five hours down mostly unsealed, washboard roads to arrive at this school, where we would spend the week. My additional duties included classroom presentations on mindful meditation, yoga, self-care, and behavioral observation of target children (those at risk for suicide). I also played sports with the children during recess, met with community elders regarding addictions and other mental health treatment, and provided co-therapy with children and adolescents.

This woman, an Indigenous Assistant Teacher (like a teacher's aide), had attended all my trainings during the past week. I shall refer to her as Sally. As it was Friday, Cheryl and I would be making the five-hour trek back to Katherine after lunch. As Sally had a free period, we sat down in the teacher's lounge with two cups of tepid, instant coffee. Even by the relaxed standards of bush Aussie schools, the ersatz coffee was terrible. Sally painstakingly stirred her coffee for a long moment. Time in the remote, Indigenous Northern Territory had taught me to sit patiently until the Indigenous person was ready to speak. Silence was a cultural method of expressing, "This will take what time it takes." After a cautionary sip, she commenced expressing her reason for asking to meet. Sally informed me that during my PD (Professional Development training) on grief the previous day, she thought the entire time of her grandson who had committed suicide. "He turned to grog (alcohol) and petrol sniffing . . . lost his connection to culture." She looked away for a long moment and then continued. "Lots of sorry business here (grief) with all the suicides and grog death." She went on to express she was often a listening ear for family members and schoolchildren who wanted to talk when sad. She paused again, seemingly studying me, likely wondering how much she could trust me, a whitefella visitor. Finally, after I seemed to pass some unspoken test, she nodded her head and commenced her story.

She spoke of having been a good student and wanting to attend a university with the goal of becoming a certified teacher, but family circumstances interrupted her studies. After returning home to assist her family, she found work as an Assistant Teacher, a job she had continued in for decades. She expressed distress that so many of their young people had died due to grog, drugs, and suicide. "Too much sorry business" (grief). She then switched topics abruptly and began talking of her niece. Sally had never married nor had children, something virtually unheard of in her culture. She had been a very promising student and had graduated from a boarding school in Alice Springs. Commonwealth and Territorial schools have a contentious history among Indigenous people due to the stolen generation (children forcibly taken from family), not allowed to speak their language at school, and the Terra Nullius history denying land rights to Indigenous peoples, despite some 40,000-plus years on the continent. These are just a few reasons Indigenous schoolchildren's nonattendance and attrition can run as high as 70%. This particular school, incidentally, would hold a graduation for the first time in several years.

Sally's niece would be one of the students graduating, and was planning to attend Charles Darwin University in Darwin, roughly eight hours away. The niece would be the first in their family to attend university (college connotes high school in Australia). As the niece was the daughter of Sally's sister, Sally had raised her. "Taught her about dangers of grog, which destroyed her parents, how to prevent pregnancy, and keep from being sexually abused," In fact, the Australian Broadcasting Corporation (ABC) had run a story of how this particular community had one of the highest child sexual assault rates in the entire country. "I tell my kids being strong in culture does not mean respecting those who would hurt you. Tell them to come tell me." She had dealt with community elders who had abused children, despite pushback from community elders wanting to deal with such issues quietly. Such practice typically involved moving the abused child to another community, something Sally correctly viewed as blaming the victim. She had received numerous threats, been assaulted, and had lost friends and family over turning in community sex offenders to law enforcement. My observation was the schoolchildren respected, listened to, and trusted her despite a tough love-type approach. She confessed to having assumed I was "yet another all-too-naive, well-intentioned whitefella." On this note, she would have been correct in many regards, given my brief time volunteering on Indigenous land. However, I had visited her niece's class and her niece spoke well of me. That meeting likely made the difference in Sally's approaching me.

The question still running through my mind was *How I might be helpful?* As if clairvoyant, Sally addressed her reason for asking to meet. "I want to know more about grief resources. Can you suggest some books for me? We can get them through our library loan system." I explained that I could make several recommendations, while admitting most resources focused primarily on whitefella populations. She asked for them anyway. After our talk ended, I compiled a list of recommended books and workbooks, leaving the list with her, had a quick lunch, and then my colleague and I took the long, dusty drive back to Katherine and a much-needed weekend.

Two weeks later, we returned to Sally's school, whereupon she requested another meeting. We met after school and she was far more forthcoming. She had gotten most of the recommended books and perused one of the workbooks, finding it helpful. She spoke poignantly of three siblings' death from alcohol and drugs, and several other relatives who died much in the same manner. She spoke of promising students' lives wrecked from grog, drugs, and trauma. After reading the workbook and another grief book, her opinion was that her mob (culture) were victims of ongoing cultural trauma, resulting in a pervasive sense of hopelessness, leading to self-medication through grog and drugs, often ending in incarceration and suicide. I inquired how she kept herself from giving in to hopelessness and self-medication. She was steadfast in wanting to be a positive role model for her young people, especially her niece. She also mentioned enjoying her role as educator, despite the overwhelming odds stacked against her students. Having visited her class, the students were noticeably more on task than any other I visited. A natural speaker, she frequently led a lesson, providing the young whitefella teacher a needed respite. No question, Sally derived a lot of meaning, purpose and satisfaction from teaching and tutoring her people's youth.

It is difficult to fathom the multigenerational layers of cultural trauma Sally and her people have endured since colonization over 200 years ago. As in the US, Indigenous Australians have endured genocide, their land stolen, their languages outlawed, the British and later Australian government's Terra Nullius policy which denied them rights to their own cultural lands and was eliminated only in the mid-1970s after Indigenous activist Vincent Lingiari's Wave Hill Walk-off (suggest you research him), and outright, belligerent racism throughout the country. That I had *anything* helpful whatsoever to offer Sally regarding self-care seemed ludicrous to me. Sally, however, maintained that my presentation had been a springboard for her feeling more optimistic. Specifically, my suggestion of addressing trauma in the school and at a community level resonated with her philosophy. Her reading of the workbook and a text had led her to research culturally appropriate ways to address trauma and addiction. Impressed by her tenacity and motivation, I encouraged her to build consensus among community elders. "My mob needs a lot of healing," she offered, and stated that if she were younger, she would become a counselor or social worker. She mentioned planning to groom students for these important professions.

I thanked Sally for her support and encouraged her to seek additional, ongoing training in treating and educating traumatized youth. She smiled and thanked me in her language. She continued her regular attendance at my trainings, even bringing in community elders to participate. Driving back from her remote community, the question of who was helping whom was foremost in my thoughts. By admission and her actions, Sally gleaned something from the trainings, most especially igniting her passion to learn and be of service. Focused and determined to create more opportunities for the youth in her culture, Sally was prepared to address any obstacle in her path. The lesson I relearned is the transformative power of knowledge in the hands of someone determined to create positive change. As change takes time, and as the needs in her very remote community were legion, Sally would face many challenges within and beyond her culture. I have no doubt, however, that she made an important impact with many of her students. In a seemingly hopeless circumstance, this resilient, adaptive, woman continued working to find ways to reach children whom most of the country had given up on. Anthropologist Margaret Mead wrote of a small group of committed people being the only force that changes the world. In her isolated community, Sally was a force of one, never giving up hope, never surrendering to despair. To borrow from a previous phrase, she had found her *why*.

References

American Counseling Association (2014). *American Counseling Association code of ethics.* American Counseling Association. Author.

Azrin, N. H., Hutchinson, R. R., & Hake, D. F. (1967). Attack avoidance, and escape reactions to aversive shock. *Journal of Experimental Animal Behavior, 10*(2), 131–148. http://doi.org/10.1901/jeab.1967.10-131

Bandura, A. (1977). *Social learning theory.* Prentice-Hall.

Baumann, M. R. U. (nd). *Dadirri: The deep inner spring inside us* (Official Miriam Rose Ungunmerr-Baumann video). Miriam Rose Ungunmerr-Baumann Foundation. https://video.search.yahoo.com/yhs/search?fr=yhs-trp-001&ei=UTF-8&hsimp=yhs-001&hspart=trp&p=Mirian+Rose+Baumann+dadirri&type=Y143_F163_201897_102620#id=2&vid=6ede9a5a537e55beef2f9c8e103c129f&action=view

Beck, A. T. (1963). Thinking and depression: Idiosyncratic content and cognitive distortions. *Archive of General Psychiatry, 9*, 324–333.

Beck, A. T. (1976). *Cognitive therapy and emotional disorders.* International Universities Press.

Beck, A. T. (1979). *Cognitive therapy and the emotional disorders.* Plume.

Beck, A. T., & Haigh, E. A. P. (2014). Advances in cognitive theory and therapy: The generic cognitive model. *Annual Review of Clinical Psychology, 10*, 1–24. http://doi.org/10.1146/annrev-clinpsy-032913-153734.

Beck, A. T., Steer, R. A., & Brown, G. K. (1996). *The beck depression inventory* (2nd ed.). Pearson.

Beck, A. T., & Weishaar, M. E. (2014). Cognitive therapy. In D. Wedding & R. J. Corsini (Eds.), *Current psychotherapies* (10th ed., pp. 231–264). Brooks/Cole, Cengage Learning.

Becker, J. (nd). *Declutter your closet with a project 333 experiment.* www.becomingminimalist.com.

Blakemore, E. (2019, January 31). Aboriginal Australians. *National Geographic.* www.nationalgeographic.com/culture/article/aboriginal-australians

Bolles, R. N. (2020). *What color is your parachute*? Ten Speed Press.

Boorstein, S. (1996). *Don't just do something, sit there: A mindfulness retreat with Sylvia Boorstein.* Harper One.

Brach, T. (2019, February 7). Feeling overwhelmed? Try RAIN. *Mindful: Healthy mind, healthy life.* www.mindful.org/tara-brach-rain-mindfulness-practice/

Bragg, R. (1995, August 13). All she has, $150,000, is going to a university. *The New York Times*, section 1, p. 1.

Bramble, D., & Lieberman, D. (2019). Endurance running and the evolution of human endurance running capabilities. In K. McGonigal (Ed.), *The joy of movement: How movement helps us find happiness, hope, connection, and courage*. Penguin.

Brickman, P., Coates, D., & Janoff-Bulman, R. (1978). Lottery winner and accident victims: Is happiness relative? *Journal of Personality & Social Psychology, 36*(8), 917–927.

Brown, J., & Wong, J. (2017, June). How gratitude changes you and your brain. *Greater Good Magazine*. www.greatergood.berkeley.edu

Brown, K. V., & Sink, J. (2020, April 24). Trump's comment on disinfectant prompts experts to warn against inhaling bleach to kill coronavirus. *Time*. Retrieved November 20, 2020, from www.time.com

Cambridge Dictionary (nd). *Cambridge dictionary*. Anonymous. www.dictionary.cambridge.org

Childs, S. (2019, August 23). *Failing forward—and why it's ok*. www.forbes.com

Clark, G., & Egan, S. J. (2015). The Socratic method in cognitive behavior therapy: A narrative review. *Cognitive Therapy Resource, 39*, 863–879. http://doi.org/10-1007/s10608-015-9707-3

Corey, G. (2017). *Theory and practice of counseling and psychotherapy* (10th ed.). Cengage.

Creswell, J. D., Lindsay, E. K., Villalba, D. K., & Chinn, B. M. A. (2019). Mindfulness training and physical health: Mechanisms and outcomes. *Psychosomatic Medicine, 81*(3), 224–232. http://doi.org/10-1097/PSY0000000000000675

Crumbaugh, J., & Maholick, L. (1964). An experimental study of existentialism: The psychometric approach to Frankl's concept of noogenic neurosis. *Journal of Clinical Psychology, 20*, 200–207. http://doi.org/10.1002/1097-4679(196404)20:2200

Csikszentmihalyi, M. (1990). *Flow: The psychology of optimal experience*. Harper.

The Dali Lama, & Cutler, H. (2020). *The art of happiness: A handbook for living*. Riverhead Books.

The Dali Lama, Tutu, D., & Abrams, D. (2016). *The book of joy: Lasting happiness in a changing world*. Penguin Random House.

D'Avella, M. (2015). *Minimalism: A documentary about the important things*. D'Avella Productions. Netflix.

Dominguez, J., & Robin, V. (1999). *Your money of your life: Transforming your relationship with money and achieving financial independence*. Penguin Books.

Drake, J. E. (2019). Examining the psychological and psychophysiological benefits of drawing over one month. *Psychology of Aesthetics, Creativity, and the Arts, 13*, 338–347. http://doi.org/10.1037/aca.0000179

Edmondson, A. C. (nd, April 2011). Strategies for learning from failure. From *Harvard Business Review*. https://hbt.org

Elgin, D. (1981). *Volunteer simplicity*. William Morrow & Company.

Ellis, A. E. (1985, August). *Some religious beliefs help produce emotional disturbance and needinvestigating*. Paper presented at the meeting of the American Psychological Association, Los Angeles.

Ellis, A. E. (1999). *How to make yourself happy and remarkably less disturbed*. Impact.

Ellis, A. E. (2000). *How to control your anxiety before it controls you*. Citadel Press.

Ellis, A. E. (2008). Cognitive restructuring of irrational beliefs. In W. O'Donohue & J. E. Fisher (Eds.), *Cognitive behavior therapy: Applying empirically supported techniques in your Practice* (2nd ed., pp. 91–95). Wiley.

Ellis, A. E., & Doyle, K. A. (1988). *How to stubbornly refuse to make yourself miserable aboutanything. (Yes, anything!)*. Citadel.

Ellis, A. E., & Ellis, D. J. (2011). *Rational emotive behavior therapy*. American Psychological Associational.

Epstein, M. (1996). *Thoughts without a thinker*. Basic Books.

Epstein, M. (2013). *Thoughts without a thinker: Psychotherapy from a Buddhist perspective* (rev ed.). Basic Books.

Fixx, J. (1977). *The complete book of running*. Penguin; Random House.

Forester, E. M. (2002/1910). *Howard's end*. Dover.

Frankl, V. E. (1946). *Man's search for meaning*. Beacon Press.

Frankl, V. E. (1969). *The will to meaning*. Random House.

Frankl, V. E. (1986). *The doctor and the soul: From therapy to logotherapy* (3rd ed.). Vintage.

Frankl, V. E. (2006). *Man's search for meaning*. Beacon Press.

Frankland, H. C., Turnbull, A. P., Wehmeyer, M. L., & Blackmountain, L. (2004). An exploration of the self-determination construct and disability as it relates to Dine (Navaho) culture. *Education and Training in Developmental Disabilities*, *39*(3), 191–205.

Freud, S. (1995). Religion is a neurosis. In *Moses and monotheism (SE XXIII)*. Hogarth Press.

Garcia, H., & Miralles, F. (2016). *Ikigi: The Japanese secret to a happy life*. Penguin Books.

Gates, B. (2021). *How to avoid a climate disaster: The solutions we have and the breakthroughs we need*. Knopf.

Glasser, W. (1998). *Choice theory: A new psychology of personal freedom*. HarperCollins Publishers.

Gordon, W. V. (2020, January 12). Why should you contemplate more? The importance of Experiencing your own existence. *Psychology Today*. www.psychologytoday.com.

Gottleib, L. (2021, June 7). In R.J. Rosen's The paradox of grief. Family. *The Atlantic*. www.theatlantic.com/family/archive/2021/06/dear-therapists-guide-grieving/619104/

Gottman, J. M. (1994a). *What predicts divorce: The relationship between marital processes and marital outcomes*. Erlbaum.

Gottman, J. M. (1994b). *Why marriages succeed or fail: And how you can make yours last*. Fireside.

Gottman, J. M. (2015). *Principia amortis: The new science of love*. Routledge.

Hahn, T. N. (1995). *Living Buddha, living Christ*. Riverhead Books.

Hahn, T. N. (1999). *The miracle of mindfulness: An introduction to the practice of meditation*. Beacon Press.

Hanson, R. (2013). *Hardwiring happiness: The new brain science of contentment, calm, and confidence*. Harmony Books.

Heinrich, B. (2002). *Why we run: A natural history*. Ecco Publishing.

Hemingway, E. (1995). *The old man and the sea*. Scribner.

Hesse, H. (1951). *Siddhartha*. New Directions.

James, K. H. (2017). The importance of handwriting experience on the development of the literate Brain. *Current Directions in Psychological Science*, *26*(6). http://doi.org/10.1177/0963721417709821

James, W. (1902). *The varieties of religious experience*. Longmans, Green, & Co.

Jozuka, E. (2016, September 22). Aboriginal Australians are earth's oldest culture: DNA. *CNN News*. https://edition.cnn.com/2016/09/22/asia/indigenous-australians-earths-oldest-civilization/index.html

Kabit-Zinn, J. (2017, January). John-Kabit Zinn: Defining mindfulness. *Mindful: Healthy mind, healthy life*. www.mindful.org

Klinger, K. (1977). *Meaning and void: Inner experiences and the incentives in people's Lives*. University of Minnesota Press.

Kubler-Ross, E. (2014). *On death and dying: What the dying have to teach doctors, nurses, clergy, & their own families* (50th anniversary issue). Scribner.

Kumai, C. (2018). *Kintsugi wellness: The Japanese art of nourishing mind, body, and spirit.* Harper Wave.

Kushner, H. (1981). *When bad things happen to good people.* Avon Books.

Lai, S. T., & O'Carroll, R. F. (2017). The three good things: The effects of gratitude practice on wellbeing: A Randomized controlled trial. *Health Psychology, 26*(1), 10–18.

Langston, B. (nd). *Living big in a tiny house.* www.livingbiginatinyhouse

Leonard, P., & Cohen, L. (2012). Come healing. *Old ideas.* Columbia Records.

Linehan, M. M. (2015). *DBT skills training manual* (2nd ed.). Guilford Press.

Liu, M., & Hatzipanagos, R. (2021, February 25). Nobody came, nobody helped: Fears of anti-Asian violence rattle the community. *The Washington Post.* www.washingtonpost.com.

Lyubomirsky, S. (2007). *The how of happiness: A new approach to getting the life you want.* Penguin Books.

Lyubomirsky, S., & Lepper, H. S. (1999). A measure of subjective happiness: Preliminary reliability and construct validation. *Social Indicators Research, 46*, 137–155. http://doi.org/10.1007/978-94-007-0753-5_2898

Madhav, G., Singh, S., & Sibinga, E. M. S. (2014). Meditation programs for psychological stress and well-being: A systematic review and meta-analysis. *Journal of the American Medical Association, 174*(3), 357–368. http://doi.org/10.1001/jamainternmed.2013.1308

Maxwell, J. (2007). *Failing forward: Turning mistakes into stepping stones for success.* Thomas Nelson Publishers.

McDaniel, C. O. (1984). The role of leisure in career development. *Journal of Career Development, 11*(2), 64–70.

McDougall, C. (2009). *Born to run: A hidden tribe, super athletes, and the greatest race the world has never seen.* Random House.

McGonigal, K. (2019). *The joy of movement: How exercise helps us find happiness, hope, connection, and courage.* Penguin.

Merton, T. (2007). *New seeds of contemplation* (reprint ed.). New Directions.

Milburn, J. F., & Nicodemus, R. (2011). *Minimalism: Live a meaningful life.* Asymmetrical Press.

Miller, W. M., & Tonigan, J. S. (1996). Assessing drinkers' motivation for change: The Stages of Change Readiness and Treatment Eagerness Scale (SOCRATES). *Psychology of Addictive Behaviors, 10*, 81–89. http://doi.org/10.1037/T00536-000

Miriam-Webster (nd). *Miriam-webster dictionary.* www.merriam-webster.com/dictionary/happiness

Moreno, J. A. (2013). *Psychodrama-third volume.* Null Publishers.

Mueller, P. A., & Oppenheimer, D. M. (2014). The pen is mightier than the keyboard: Advantages of longhand over laptop note taking. *Association for Psychological Science, 25*(6), 1159–1168. http://doi.org/10.1177/0956797614524581

Navarra, R. (2015). 3 research-based tips for a happy and healthy relationship. *The Gottman Institute.* www.gottman.com/blog/3-research-based-tips-for-a-happy-and-healthy-relationship/

Newberg, A. B., Wintering, N., Waldman, M. R., Amen, D., Khalsa, D. S., & Alavi, A. (2010). Cerebral blood flow differences between long-term meditators and non-meditators. *Conscious Cognition, 19*(4), 899–905.

Niagara University Men's Basketball (2020, March 23). *Paulus named Joe B. Hall coach of the year.* https://purpleeagles.com/news/2020/3/23/mens-basketball-paulus-named-joe-b-hall-national-coach-of-the-year.aspx

O'Hanlon, B. (2013). *Do one thing different: Ten simple ways to change your life* (20th anniversary ed.). HarperCollins.

Oxford University Press (1973). 1 Corinthians. In H. May & B. Metzger (Eds., 1977), *The new Oxford annotated bible with the apocrypha.* Oxford University Press.

Palmer, P. (2000). *Let your life speak: Listening for the voice of vocation.* Jossey-Bass.

Palmer, P. (2007). *The courage to teach: Exploring the inner landscape of a teacher's life.* Jossey-Bass.

Parker-Pope, T. (2015, January 19). Writing your way to happiness. The Well Column. *New York Times.* https://mindingmatters.com/writing-way-happiness-nyt/

Peale, N. V. (2003). *The power of positive thinking: A practical guide to mastering the problems of everyday living.* Touchstone.

Pennebaker, J. D. (2004). *Writing to heal: A guided journal for recovering from trauma and emotional upheaval.* New Harbinger.

Perls, F. (1969). *Gestalt therapy verbatim.* Real People Press.

Peters, T. J., & Waterman, R. H., Jr. (2007). *In search of excellence: Lessons from America's best-run companies.* Harper Business (Re-print).

Pressman, S. (2021, March). American Counseling Association. *Counseling Today, 63*(9), 5.

Prochaska, J. O., DiClemente, C. C., & Norcross, J. O. (1992). In search of how people change: Applications to addictive behaviors. *American Psychologist, 47*, 1102–1114. http://doi.org/10.1037/0003-066X.47.9.1102

Robin, V., & Dominguez, J. (2018). *Your money of your life: 9 steps to transforming your relationship with money and achieving financial independence.* Penguin Books.

Rogers, C. R. (1961). *On becoming a person.* Houghton-Mifflin.

Rogers, C. R. (1965). *Client-centered therapy.* Houghton Mifflin.

Seligman, M. E. P. (2002). *Authentic happiness: Using the new positive psychology to realize your potential for lasting fulfillment.* Simon & Schuster.

Seligman, M. E. P. (2006). *Learned optimism: How to change your mind and your life.* Vintage.

Seligman, M. E. P. (nd). *The authentic happiness test.* Authentic Happiness. Com. www.authentic-happiness.com/home/Discover-Your-Strengths

Seligman, M. E. P., Steen, T. A., Park, N., & Peterson, C. (2005). Positive psychology progress. *American Psychologist, 60*(5), 410–421. http://doi.org/10.1037/0003-066X.60.5.410

Sheehan, G. A. (1978). *Running and being: The total experience.* Penguin-Random House.

Snyder, D. K. (1997). *Marital satisfaction inventory manual.* Western Psychological Services.

Society of Clinical Psychology (nd). *Research-supported psychological treatments.* Society of Clinical Psychology. https://div12.org/psychological-treatments/

Steger, M. F., Frazier, P., Oishi, S., & Kaler, M. (2006). The meaning in life questionnaire: Assessing the presence of and search for meaning in life. *Journal of Counseling Psychology, 53*, 80–93. http://doi.org/10.1037/0022-0167.53.180

Sternberg, R. J. (1998). *Cupid's arrow: The course of love through time.* Cambridge University Press.

Stuart, R. B., & Jacobson, B. (1987). *Couple's precounseling inventory* (rev. ed.). Research Press.

Suedfeld, P. (Eds.). (2001). *Light from the ashes: Social science careers of young holocaust survivors.* University of Michigan Press.

Thittila, B. U. (1958, February). The meaning of Buddhism: Fundamental principles of the Theravada doctrine. *The Atlantic.*

Tomer, A., Eliason, G. T., & Wong, P. T. P. (2008). *Existential and spiritual issues in death attitudes.* Francis & Taylor.

United States Senate (nd). *Sputnik spurs passage of the National Defense Education Act.* Washington, DC: Author. www.senate.gov

Van der Kolk, B. (2014). *The body keeps the score: Brain, mind, and body in the healing of Trauma*. Penguin.

Wang, D. J., Rao, H., Korczykowski, M., Wintering, N., Pluta, J., Khalsa, D. S., & Newberg, A. B. (2011). Cerebral blood flow changes associated with different meditation practices and perceived depth of meditation. *Psychiatry Resources*, *191*(1), 60–67.

Wang, W. (2020, November). The U.S. divorce rate has hit a 50-year low. *Institute for Family Studies*. https://ifstudies.org/blog/the-us-divorce-rate-has-hit-a-50-year-low

Weir, P. (1977). *The last wave*. McElroy & McElroy: South Australian Film Corporation.

Wilder, T. (1927). *The bridge of San Luis Rey*. Albert & Charles Boni.

Wong, P. T. (2009, February 25). Positive existential psychotherapy and pathways to death acceptance. Review of the book, *Staring at the Sun*. *PsycCRITIQUES*, *54*(8). http://doi.org/10.1037/a0014829

World English Bible. (2000). Gospel of Matthew. *World English Bible*. www.ebible.org/

Yalom, I. D. (2009). *Staring at the sun: Overcoming the terror of death*. Jossey-Bass.

Zhang, Q., & Kim, H. (2019). American young adults' debt and psychological distress. *Journal of Family and Economic Issues*, *40*(1), 22–35. http://doi.org/10.1007/s10834-018-9605-4

Zhang, Q., Zheng, W., Wang, X., Liu, L., Zhang, J., & Zhou, R. (2019). The effects of different stages of mindfulness meditation training on emotion regulation. *Frontiers in Human Neuroscience*, *13*, 208. http://doi.org/10.3389/fnhum.2019.00208

Index

For Product Safety Concerns and Information please contact our EU
representative GPSR@taylorandfrancis.com
Taylor & Francis Verlag GmbH, Kaufingerstraße 24, 80331 München, Germany

www.ingramcontent.com/pod-product-compliance
Ingram Content Group UK Ltd.
Pitfield, Milton Keynes, MK11 3LW, UK
UKHW022018180926
475701UK00005B/898
9780367764357